The Black Penguin

Living Out

Gay and Lesbian Autobiographies

David Bergman, Joan Larkin, and Raphael Kadushin
FOUNDING EDITORS

THE BLACK PENGUIN

Andrew Evans

The University of Wisconsin Press

Publication of this volume has been made possible, in part, through support from the **Brittingham Fund**.

The University of Wisconsin Press
1930 Monroe Street, 3rd Floor
Madison, Wisconsin 53711-2059
uwpress.wisc.edu

3 Henrietta Street, Covent Garden
London WC2E 8LU, United Kingdom
eurospanbookstore.com

Printed in the United States of America

This book may be available in a digital edition.

Library of Congress Cataloging-in-Publication Data

Names: Evans, Andrew, 1975– author.
Title: The black penguin / Andrew Evans.
Other titles: Living out.
Description: Madison, Wisconsin: The University of Wisconsin Press, [2017]
    | Series: Living out: gay and lesbian autobiographies.
Identifiers: LCCN 2016041573 | ISBN 9780299311407 (cloth: alk. paper)
Subjects: LCSH: Evans, Andrew, 1975– —Travel. | Voyages and travels.
    | LCGFT: Travel writing.
Classification: LCC G465 .E835 2017 | DDC 910.4092 [B]—dc23
LC record available at https://lccn.loc.gov/2016041573

ISBN 9780299311445 (pbk.: alk. paper)

"Soul Meets Body," words and music by Benjamin Gibbard, copyright © 2005 EMI Blackwood Music Inc. and Where I'm Calling From Music. All rights administered by Sony/ATV Music Publishing LLC, 424 Church Street, Suite 1200, Nashville, TN 37219. International Copyright Secured. All Rights Reserved. Reprinted by Permission of Hal Leonard Corporation.

"Bus to Baton Rouge," words and music by Lucinda Williams, copyright © 2001 Warner-Tamerlane Publishing Corp. All Rights Reserved. Used by permission of Alfred Music.

For
MY FAMILY,
near and far

'Cause in my head there's a Greyhound station
Where I send my thoughts to far off destinations
So they may have a chance of finding a place
Where they're far more suited than here.

BEN GIBBARD (Death Cab for Cutie),

"Soul Meets Body"

Contents

Preface

On the sunny morning of January 1, 2010, I stepped onto a city bus in Washington, DC, and set off for the end of the world.

Up until then, all my grown-up attempts to reach Antarctica had failed—the formal grants and scientific missions, every expedition I hoped to join, and the exotic support jobs I applied for over and over in vain. I thought it totally unfair that such a glaring and prominent section of the globe would prove so elusive to someone like me.

Discovering that one is merely average is troubling, but I responded in kind, with my own average measures. If fate had refused me the chance to reach Antarctica, then I would invent my own opportunity, getting as close as possible to my dream with the everyday means available to me.

I had no car, nor did I have any money, but I had the bus. I had been riding buses since kindergarten—it is the simplest and most accessible form of public transportation that exists. If I could just keep connecting from one bus to the next, then eventually I would reach the bottom of the world.

My rules were simple: take the nearest bus to the farthest point south, then hop on the next one, and another after that. I traveled this way for over ten thousand miles—without any planned route and without any advance tickets. When I felt too tired to go on, I took a break. Sometimes I checked into hotels—to sleep, to wash, and to write. Sometimes I rode the bus all night long and all the next day. Occasionally I cheated: a taxi to the border post, a lift with the milkman, a boat through the Panama Canal, and a twenty-minute plane ride over the impassable jungle.

For me, the gift of overland travel was the joy of gradual transition: from swamp to desert, from mountain to prairie. Taking the bus allowed me to feel the latitudes of Earth in a way that is lost by those who merely jet set from A to B.

Social media let me share my observations from the road in real time. At the time, Twitter was enough of a novelty that my editor assigned me a feature for *National Geographic Traveler* magazine. The formal assignment helped secure my final passage to Antarctica on the Lindblad Expedition ship, the *National Geographic Explorer.*

My original "Bus2Antarctica" story was told from the road in the form of sixty-four blog posts, a dozen videos, and over five thousand tweets—but even the culminating magazine feature felt inadequate and limited. How do you squeeze a life-changing adventure into a few colored pages? What about the ups and downs of travel, the many hours spent staring out the window, and this odd compulsion to ride buses to the bottom of the world? Some stories cannot fit into a tweet, and others get only half-told, but for those who cared and asked, this book details my epic bus ride across the world, and the even longer story as to why.

The Black Penguin

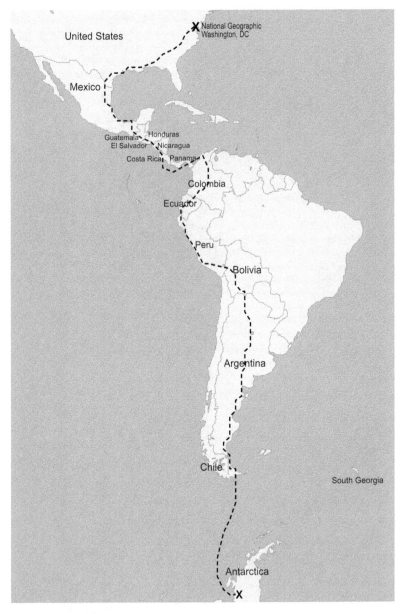

Route from Washington, DC, to Antarctica, January 1 to February 14, 2010

1 COLD PITCH

Fall 2009

"Nice office!"

The words left my mouth too soon—I was just a desperate boy, giddy and overflowing, screaming for attention. Mine was a miscalculated attempt to seem cool and familiar in front of a man I respected, but instead I sounded lousy and pedestrian, like a redneck reality star wooed by fancy drinks. My first five seconds with Keith Bellows and he was already frowning back at me.

Though I had meant what I said—Keith's office *was* nice. It was the type of corner office I had dreamed I would end up in someday. Glass walls framed the scene of M Street below with the editor in chief posed behind his desk, commanding the editorial spaceship from his fourth-floor cockpit. Travel flotsam cluttered the inside walls and floor, hiding the sleek and minimalist architecture with dyed Berber rugs shipped back from Morocco, rough-hewn ebony stools from Africa, dainty parasols of painted Chinese silk, and a coffee table fashioned from a lightning-split log. A well-used globe, just like the one in my childhood bedroom, sat next to a laden set of stained wooden bookshelves stacked with leathered volumes.

Keith caught me gawking and locked eyes with me, leaning forward. He looked exactly like his head shot in the front of the magazine, except that he was taller and more imposing with a deep tan and an unbuttoned collar that showed he really didn't give a damn. There was paper everywhere—finished stories and story ideas; colored proofs needing to be signed off; and outdated foreign-language issues, destined never to be read.

"What can we do for you?" he asked, straight to the point. No. This would not be a thirty-minute meeting or even a fifteen-minute meeting. It was a five-minute meeting tops, and if I blew it now, there would be no meeting. There was no time for my detailed synopsis of my lifelong obsession with National Geographic and how I was more deserving than the rest.

"I want to write for you," I announced point-blank. If Keith could be direct then so could I, though I guessed he had heard that line before. Alas, my direct approach failed to impress and by the look on his face, I imagined he was searching for a small red button to push that would open a hatch and shoot me down into some undisclosed basement where I would be added to the society's secret collection of shrunken heads.

"What experience do you have?" he asked.

"I've written four books," I answered, pulling out my two biggest volumes from my backpack. My own name stood out below the titles: *Iceland, Ukraine.* Keith flipped through the hundreds and hundreds of pages I had written—whole years of my life condensed into tiny print.

"You wrote all this yourself?" he asked.

"Yes," I answered shyly. "You can keep those."

"That's a helluva lot of work." He laughed, adding my books to the piles on his desk. Now he was listening—I had waited my whole life for this one meeting—and I was not going to bungle it. I breathed in deeply, channeling the courage of the original National Geographic explorers and then laid out my plan.

"So I want to do this expedition," I began. "I want to go to Antarctica."

"Sure," Keith interrupted. "So do I. So does everyone." I swallowed and kept talking without hesitation.

"Yes, but what matters is the journey itself. I want to go overland—I want to take the bus." Keith cocked his head, surprised, and I kept talking, afraid to give him even a moment to respond.

"I want to take an old-fashioned expedition to the bottom of the world—but I want to use the Internet and recount the adventure as it's happening. I want to tell the story in real time, online."

"*Hmmm*," said Keith, but I still kept on talking rapidly, busy with my one idea. I pulled out my grandfather's old 1972 National Geographic map of South America and unfolded it hurriedly on his desk.

"I would start right here, at National Geographic headquarters." I stabbed my finger outside the map, right below Keith's face. "Just like the original National Geographic explorers who launched their expeditions from these very offices." Keith smiled a little, amused at the idea, or by my own small theatrics.

"I'll take the city bus that runs outside down to the Greyhound station, and then I'll just keep heading south, farther and farther south until I get to Mexico. Then on to Central America and beyond through the entire length of South America." I traced my finger along an imaginary route.

Keith listened intently, his eyes lost in thought. Either I had bored him into a coma or he was thinking—I did not ask him which, only kept on talking: "I don't want to buy any tickets ahead of my trip or plan too much in advance. The whole point is to be spontaneous, to let the road lead the way."

"I admit it's a cool idea," he began, "but first you have to determine if it's even possible."

"It is possible," I argued. "I already know. I've researched every bus company from here to Argentina—I'll have enough options to hop on and off and cover the distance." Keith seemed to believe me. I had only checked out a few of the bus stations online and I had studied a high-resolution road map that showed a web of roads that might make it possible. And I had traveled enough in Central America to know that I could always grab a chicken bus moving south. I was convinced I could cover the entire distance overland no problem—what I needed from Keith was his blessing and support. I needed the editor in chief to wave his magic wizard wand and make things happen. I needed Lindblad

Expeditions to give me a berth on their ship, the *National Geographic Explorer*, and I needed Keith's magazine, *National Geographic Traveler*, to tell my story.

"Can you even get phone reception in the Amazon?" asked Keith, wondering aloud if it was even possible to tweet from such remote places.

"I don't know," I said. "But I'll find out."

Keith rolled his eyes to the ceiling and tapped his fingertips together before inhaling. For twenty silent seconds he waited contemplatively, holding his breath, then exhaling long and slow.

"Yes," he spoke. His chair squeaked as he leaned back. Keith looked right into my face and said it again. "Yes. We're gonna do this."

I heard his yes; I heard him say it out loud, but even then, my brain failed to accept the news. For so long—for my whole life it seemed—the answer had always been no. No, Andrew, you can't do that. You can't go there. You can't win. You can't succeed. You can't love that man. For so long, my life had been a ferris wheel of false hopes, spinning so close to the ground but never allowing me a moment to hop on. I did not know how to respond to yes, so I kept talking to Keith.

"Well, it's ironic-like, because this will be an old-fashioned expedition except in the Internet age, get it?"

"I already said yes," Keith said. "You can stop pitching me."

Now he was smiling—his sour face was gone and he was watching my own reaction.

"Yes? Really?" I triple-checked.

"Yes." Keith had already moved on to the next steps, shouting out names and offices to contact. He would take care of getting me on the ship, but I had to do the rest. When I looked up from scribbling down his commands in my notebook, I saw that Keith was pacing his office, his mind already racing.

"You'll take pictures. And shoot some videos. Videos are good. We'll have a big send-off for you out front, check in with you along the way. Hey—I might even come down there with you, ride down the Pan-American on a motorcycle!" He gripped an imaginary handle-bar and revved the engine, rolling both his hands back. Now the spark of adventure burned in his eyes, and while I had never mentioned a motorcycle—*it's a bus, Keith*—I could see that my own burning dream had caught up with his; and now we shared that in common.

"It's a good idea," said Keith, talking to me now like an ally—as if I belonged.

"When do we leave?" he asked.

"New Year's Day." I picked a day on the spot.

"Then we better get busy," said Keith.

2   SANDY CAY

Summer 2002

The island was perfect—the kind you see on calendars in the winter months, on luminous screensavers in the windowless cubicles of sullen accountants: crisscrossed coconut palms sprouting from a ring of silver sand, a dream of paradise dropped like a smooth pebble into the great turquoise puddle of everlasting ocean.

Except my island was real—the heat of the sun was real, and the boom of the waves, too. I was really there, standing alone, my toes curled in the sand. I tossed my bag on the beach and squinted at Brian's boat on the horizon. The fine white wake dissolved like smoke on the water, and the motor's high nasal hum softened to a distant whir, outsung by the sweeping surf and papery palm leaves in the Caribbean breeze.

Each new wave swelled to a hopeful crest before it shrugged against gravity, then collapsed, slapping the shore and sending a rush of shapeless saltwater back into the sea. Over and over, the rolling rhythm of the sea continued—eternity in motion—the whole world spinning around me while I stood motionless on the beach, squinting at the sun, aware of the oppressive heat as well as my own solitude.

At twenty-six years old, I was tired of hearing life-weary adults talk about things they would never do. My greatest fear was turning into the man who was all talk and no walk. Everyone has their desert island fantasy but mine had to come true, and now it was—I was alone on an uninhabited island, with no one to save me.

You can do this.

8

Except I only *thought* I could do this. I had never actually survived alone in the wild before. Yes, I was an Eagle Scout with a merit badge in wilderness survival. I had built shelters in the forest and camped rough on the coldest winter nights in Ohio. I could build a fire without matches, I could find true north both day and night, and if I really needed to, I could eat caterpillars, ants, or grasshoppers.

I thought I knew how to survive. As a kid, I had read *Robinson Crusoe* and watched *Swiss Family Robinson*, and in case I forgot anything, I could look up the answer in my official *SAS Survival Guide*. *Who Dares, Wins* was the motto of the Special Air Services, the most fearless regiment of the British Army. I had discovered the bent copy of the guide in a used bookshop in England, back when I was avoiding my own thesis on Russian foreign policy. The piles of UN documents in my damp student room at Oxford seemed a lot less compelling than learning what to do if your parachute drops you in the Arctic, or how to braid a strong rope from nettles and animal tendon, or how to avoid getting bitten by vampire bats (always keep your toes covered).

Now, in the summer, this tiny island was my self-imposed test, a way to force my casual book learning into action. Could I survive alone, unaided, stranded on a desert island? I had to try it for myself—one week alone on this sandy speck in the sea.

I left the shore and hiked into a cool grove of crooked palms; then I opened my canvas bag to sort through my gear: a loop of fishing twine and a single fishhook, a mask and snorkel, a box of matches, and a shaggy straw hat. A bar of chocolate poked out from the side pocket. Brian must have slipped it in—just in case. He was only being thoughtful, but I was determined not to eat the contraband. I had resolved not to cheat on my quest—I wanted to survive by my own wits and knowledge, to cut myself off from every convenience of civilization and rely solely on the nature around me.

Regardless, Brian had forced me to bring two gallons of emergency drinking water—just in case.

"You don't have to use it, but should you ever need it, you'll have it there," he had told me.

"The whole point is that I have to find my own water," I had argued back. "Otherwise I'm just camping!" I had shown him the pages of my guidebook dedicated to finding water on desert islands, but the vague diagrams left him unconvinced. He simply filled two plastic jugs with fresh water and left them on the beach—then I buried the jugs beneath a pile of cool sand.

My Caribbean island was the size of seven city blocks in midtown Manhattan—small enough to walk its shores barefoot in twenty minutes. I had chosen Sandy Cay from a half-dozen eligible spots in the British Virgin Islands: Sandy Spit was too small; Great Tobago was too steep and had too many sharks; and Dead Man's Chest was plain unsafe, as the local police used it for a shooting range.

Sandy Cay had plenty of solid coconut palms for food and shelter. It was far enough from the main island to keep me isolated, but close enough that I could flag down a passing yacht to get away. The island belonged to the private estate of Laurance Rockefeller, so my little survival stint may have counted as trespassing, but I could not imagine that old Laurance would mind so much; the man was well into his nineties.

The sun grew even warmer, and I prodded myself into action, gathering up the fallen palm fronds to build a roof, shuffling them into a pile of green and brown leaves. As I worked, I thought back to my social studies class in the seventh grade, and that repeated question from our teacher, "What are the three basic needs?"

"Food—water—shelter," we sang back mechanically, though all of us were middle-class midwesterners who lived in four-bedroom houses with gas heat, ample refrigerators, and at least a half-dozen sinks from which fluoride-enhanced water flowed freely.

"And love!" she added. "You can have all the food, water, and shelter in the world," she counted off with her hot-pink fingernails, "but without love, we'd all just die!" Our teacher's version of social studies resembled a medieval morality play delivered with Bible verses and an Appalachian accent.

She ended each class with some horrendous true tale, pulled from her own life—like how just the other week during that big ice storm, a motorcyclist crashed at fifty miles an hour and how the guy was lying on the pavement in front of her car, his torso ripped open with his guts all spilled out and freezing fast to the subzero asphalt. But she had saved his life by calming him with gentle conversation and prayer, warming his intestines with her bare hands before stuffing them back into his body one foot a time. She acted the story out with hand motions, as if she was moving a rope of pork link sausage down the line. That's pretty much all I remember from seventh grade—the three or four basic needs and being called "faggot" about a hundred times a day.

As the day grew hotter, my need for shelter grew more pressing, but I could not find any straight sticks to build my little house. *Gilligan's Island* was a lie: shrubs and trees that dance in the breeze do not grow in conveniently aligned, ready-made six-foot-high poles. Instead, I battled with the ropey trunks of banyan trees and the locked arms of overgrown sea grape shrubs. Jungle vines laced back and forth, with spritely green anoles that jumped up and down the silvery limbs. I found more success with the driftwood from the beach, lashing end to end in a firm framework that held up against my own weight. Weaving palm leaves into a thick roof took several more hours but in the end, my hut looked waterproof and legit. I expected it to rain—I needed the runoff for drinking.

By noon I felt quite weak, so I napped in the shade I had built, conserving my energy until the lingering sun dropped low with the afternoon. When the air began to move, I ventured out for a short tour. A sketch of a trail looped around to the highest point of the island, some sixty feet above sea level, with gulls and pelicans darting at the cliffs. Spongey cacti grew near the rocks, and on my way back to the beach, I stopped to pick the needled spines from my callused feet.

I had lived the whole summer without shoes, a dive bum in nearby Tortola, and now I looked like some storybook castaway, my drab linen shirt faded like a dishrag, open and flapping in the breeze. My hair was sun-streaked and shaggy, and my stringy shorts were cut from a pair of charcoal dress slacks, the remnants of the conservative costume I had worn in my former life of church meetings and toner-scented offices. Now they were stained with boat engine fuel and frayed with so many holes that the black Speedo beneath was no longer a secret.

Every gay man owns a Speedo—whether he ever wears it in public is another matter. My lanky, lumpy body never did merit such a sporty swimsuit, but as the shy and self-conscious member of a succession of competitive swim teams, I swam from kindergarten to college in Lycra briefs. In school, the other boys had mocked my athletic failures—how I threw like a girl—but nobody could tell me that I was a bad swimmer. Perhaps I was tall and clumsy on land, but in the water, I felt strong and powerful—even manly. I felt so confident as a swimmer that I had stranded myself on Sandy Cay with the sure knowledge that should I ever need to get off the island, I could easily swim the mile of open sea to the nearby island of Jost Van Dyke, home to around three hundred easygoing islanders.

For now, I simply swam to cool off, dropping my clothes on the beach and stepping out into the clear and rippled glass of the calming sea. Schools of invisible fish shot away from my legs and I dropped into the forgiving water and kicked away a good distance. My head bobbed alone in the waves, and I gazed back on my little island and felt revived and content.

Perhaps I did not know where I might find my next meal, and I would probably need to drink my emergency water, but the dull mechanics of living vanished against the tremendous beauty that enveloped me. No postcard can ever capture the feeling of being the only human on your very own island with its scene of coconut palms under a blue sky etched with inoffensive clouds.

That night for dinner, I picked at a dried-up coconut I found, then lit the bristly husk to start a fire, feeding the flames with sun-bleached driftwood. When the coals began to glow, I roasted periwinkles gathered from the sea rocks. The roasting shellfish smelled wonderful and I sucked the salty mess from my fingers. Slimy and gray, they barely resembled the *bigorneaux* I ate in France, but for now, it was a safe and nourishing meal that would get me through to the next day.

That evening, I gaped at the sunset like a child in the TV aisle of a department store. First the west turned orange, then lavender and indigo, before a thousand stars emerged into night. I had no camera—no way of capturing the spectacle of dusk as the wooly air brushed away the sand on my skin one grain at a time. I watched the stars, enveloped by utter silence and the calm feeling that I was now part of some great secret—that while the rest of the world sat indoors watching TV or listening to their car radios with engines running beneath yellow streetlights, I was the lone witness to the immensity of the heavens.

Like a live ember in the solid black sea, the orange glow of Saint Thomas lifted the night. I took comfort in the presence of all those people over there, in America. Only twelve miles separated that little piece of the United States from my own feathery shore, but the deep-blue distance felt eternal—as if I was standing on the dwarf planet of Pluto, some four billion miles from the lost light of the smoldering sun.

I had been to Saint Thomas the year before, to meet up with Brian over the Labor Day weekend. After months apart, we had come together, lying side by side on the beach and hiking through the jungled mountains of the Virgin Islands. We went diving on coral reefs until our fingertips turned shriveled and white, and after our final swim, we scrambled onto an old wooden boat dock and let the sea drip from our heads. Together, we watched the sky turn pink, and then Brian asked me to marry him.

The drying salt made my back itch as I considered the perilous notion—I knew that I loved him, and I also knew that the news would shatter my family. They would never accept me as a gay man, nor would they ever accept Brian as my husband. Back then, marriage was an

impossible fiction. But that is what I wanted with Brian, and so I said
yes. We traded silver rings, and though no one in the world knew it, we
were now engaged.

A week after that island tryst, I was back in Washington, DC. I was
running late that September morning and when I walked into the office,
the news hit me like a wave. After the second plane came the shrieks and
tears from my colleagues, and then moments later, a chorus of mournful
sirens echoed through the streets below. The capital was under attack,
too.

I remember standing silently by the tinted windows and watching
gray-and-white smoke blow across the Potomac. I smelled it, too—the
evil burning scent of manmade things that grew stronger as we ran from
the building. Outside there was only hopeless confusion. It seemed as if
the entire city had collectively lost their minds. After the smoke and
sobbing strangers came the horrific knowledge that in this very moment,
people were dying—in Manhattan and here in Washington, DC, human
lives were going out like birthday candles.

Like Pompeii, the pavement captured a sudden still life of random
objects dropped by the white-collared Washingtonians who ran dazed
and shouting into the gridlock. The city felt frozen with uncertainty.
Cell phones stopped working and rumors seeped across the square: the
Capitol was on fire! No, it must be the World Bank. More planes were
on the way. Was the White House next? *No, not the White House. It's
too beautiful—too irreparable.* I was standing just a block away from the
president's home—unsure if it was going to blow up like the other
buildings on TV.

I broke away from the chaotic exodus and walked north and into the
bank, where I withdrew my entire savings account in cash. The teller
worked calmly, counting out my money while the TV in the lobby
showed gray smoke billowing up from the two towers in New York.
Already my own city was shutting down—the bridges were closed, the
police were blocking streets, and the stoplights stopped working
downtown.

I was less afraid of the supposed terrorists overhead and far more terrified by the irrational people all around me. There was no sense in trying to get back to my home in Virginia—all the bridges were blocked and the traffic had stopped. Instead I jogged a mile in dress shoes to my friend's empty apartment and let myself in with a set of spare keys. As if locking out all the evil in the world, I set the deadbolt, filled the bathtub and sink with fresh water, closed all the shades and fell back onto the couch. Then I dipped into a tub of chocolate pudding, flipped on the television, and watched the world fall apart.

A year had passed since that awful day—a year that took me far away from the capital and its madness and rumors of war. Now I was alone on my very own island, safe from the impending catastrophe of the world, comfy in the house I had built myself, blinking up at my leafy roof, stretched out on a queen-size pile of soft sand, my shirt for a blanket and my backpack for a pillow.

Sleep was short and intermittent—the sand crawled with termites, and when I shifted my body, I disturbed the nocturnal highway of commuting crabs and anxious lizards. Something furry and brown kept scampering up to my bare feet and as I dozed, I kicked at the thing, shooing it away before falling back into dreams that came and went like the waves outside.

It was still dark when I left my hut and stumbled down to the beach. Bioluminescent plankton washed up with each wave and the wet sand glowed with green glitter. I watched the dawn rise up from Africa in the east, spreading its clean and timid light, the stained clouds turning paler until the yellow ball of summer sun punched through the sky and the new day began.

I bathed in the sea, then set to work finding food and drink, knowing I only had a few hours before the heat would force me back into my shelter. I drank the rain collected in my traps overnight, then headed off into the middle of the island in search of fresh green coconuts. Alas, I quickly discovered that all the easy-access coconuts had already been hacked down by day-trippers and yachties for their beachside piña coladas. I resented their careless greed and cursed the stupidity of whoever it was that used sun-bleached coral stones to knock down the loose nuts. Now dozens of lumpy rocks remained lodged in the treetops, which swayed dangerously and threatened to bombard me with the next fluid breeze.

The closest coconuts I could find hung some thirty feet off the ground, so I braided a mess of vines into a loop, then bundled it all up with some fibrous bark that I had pulled from the base of the coconut tree. I stepped inside the loop, clasped my feet around the trunk, and scooted right up like a chimpanzee. With each upward leap, I bent my knees and closed my feet back on the trunk, then pulled the rest of my body up with my arms. I made it to the top of the tree in less than a minute and knocked down six young coconuts with a long cheer of triumph. I felt victorious, as if some imaginary audience was cheering my achievement with whistles and applause—I had climbed a tree and snagged breakfast.

That's when the vines snapped. Suddenly I was dangling from the treetop, thirty feet off the ground. There I swayed, hanging on with just my two hands, knuckles burning. I looked down at the ground, littered with broken coconut shells and the brittle combs of dried-out palms. Such an ignominious death, I thought—to fall from a tree and break my neck, then perish alone atop a pile of uneaten coconuts.

With aching muscles, I swung myself inward, over and over until I could wrap my legs around the trunk. I hugged the tree, then slid down, bump after bump, all the way to the ground. I yelled from the pain, as if I had been punched repeatedly in the groin. My forearms were scraped raw.

I returned to the beach and soaked my flayed arms in stinging saltwater, then spent the next hour trying to open a single coconut. I tore at the rough brown husk, then punctured a hole in the eye of the shell and drank about a half cup of the sweet clear liquid inside. I had worked all morning for that drink.

The sun was high now, baking the island with white heat, and so I returned to the shade and spent another hour working out the gloopy flesh of my coconut. Then I moved onto my second course, picking off the spines on the prickly pear cactus and peeling back the skin to chew on the green slime inside. For the next days I lived off of coconuts, cactus, and sea snails, and my stomach curled up into a tight ball of muscle that groaned and gurgled in strange ways.

Not eating was not new for me. As a Mormon, I had been skipping meals since I was eight years old—it was such a normal part of my life— the first Sunday of every month. Abstaining from all food and drink helps the soul transcend the body, and in this heightened spiritual state, we are closer to God and more able to commune with the world we cannot see. Yet here, on my island of one, I was not fasting—I was simply hungry.

Only on my fourth day did I catch a fish. I crushed up a few sea snails as bait and stuck them on my one precious hook, then dropped the line inside a hollow of coral. Each time the little fish pecked at the bait until it was gone, and then I would add more bait and drop it back down into the hole, again and again. With mask and snorkel, I watched closely underwater. Only after one hour did a tiny orange fish actually latch onto the hook, and before I could pull on the line, a spotted rock hind jumped in and swallowed the smaller fish whole, taking my hook with him. I yanked up my line and with it came a jumpy grouper that I snatched with a splash.

He was brown with red spots and his jaws gaped wider and wider, searching for breath on the beach. I felt guilty for destroying such a beautiful creature, but after four days, I needed this meal. I thanked God for the food and I thanked the fish for its life. Then I killed it, quickly, with a rock to the head. I looked down at my shaking hands, shocked by the violent act I had just committed. Then I cleaned the fish with the twisted edge of a sun-bleached Coke can I had found washed up on the rocks.

I built a small fire on the beach, and soon the scent of grilled fish hit my nose and wet my mouth. I gobbled it up with a broken piece of coconut shell for a spoon until only the bones and head remained, and I kept those for later—just in case.

On the fifth night, I discovered that the furry brown things rumbling around my feet were rats—big brown rats all clamoring for my stash of coconuts. I kicked them away and threw stones at them, but they kept coming back, sniveling and obsessive, munching at my food supply like greedy robbers.

By the next morning, all my coconuts had vanished and a cluster of busy hermit crabs were having a fiesta with the melted bar of chocolate from my pack. If I didn't die of thirst or some clumsy accident, then surely the wildlife of Sandy Cay would kill me by stealing all my food.

I had grown so hungry and weak that I began to plot exactly how I would spend my energy. Like a kid at the county fair with a ten-dollar bill in his pocket, I carefully economized each moment, knowing that every activity would burn precious energy. I took small sips from my emergency water, then napped for hours in the shade, waiting for the sun to fall. In just a few short days, my schedule had dwindled to sleeping and swimming.

I could not even remember the day of the week, but somehow, on that particular day, I remembered. It was my sister's wedding day—far away in California—and my whole family was there, except me.

Months prior, my parents had disowned me by e-mail. "Don't come home," said the message from my father. My mother cried to me on the phone, begging me to change, but each conversation became more awkward and strained until we stopped speaking altogether. I had crossed the inevitable impasse of my life and now I was no longer welcome in their world. They claimed that I was no longer part of the family—not in this life, or the life to come. What wasn't spelled out in furious letters and scripture quotes was clearly explained by the silence and separation that followed. They could not cope with me as their gay brother and son, and I could not cope with their judgment.

They don't even know where I am right now, I thought. The entire world moved around me while I sat alone in the sand. Solitude, silence, and nature—these are the only real luxuries left on Earth, and all three are elusive to most humans. Apart from monks and prisoners, few men ever know true solitude, but on that island, I did. I heard the hollow echo of my own footsteps and the odd sound of my own voice. I was hyperaware of every living intricacy—I could stare into the deep black holes of barnacles that hung halfway between air and water or sit silently and watch the vines grow around me. My own breath followed the rhythm of the waves and I sensed every break in the silence.

When the motor hummed across the sea, I did not recognize the stranger in the dinghy. Only in the falling sun did I realize that Brian had returned a day early. "I was getting worried about you, honestly," he said, then opened up his pack, loaded with good things to cook over the fire: pork chops and roasted plantain, baked potatoes with sour cream, hunks of banana rum cake, and cold bottles of ginger beer. Beautiful places are always better shared, and the two of us slept curled together in my little lean-to on that island of sand and palms, warm with body heat and wrapped in the sleeping bag and feather pillows Brian had carried over from the main island. That night, another squall passed over our little island, but we stayed dry, and in the blue light of the seventh day, I woke up to his calm, sleeping face.

3   SIXTEENTH AND M

January 1, 2010

The same bus passed my apartment every day—every
twenty minutes on weekdays and every hour on weekends and holidays.
Today was a holiday—the first day of the year, yet there was not a single
flake of snow on the ground or in the sky. There was only the snappy
breath of winter, and except for the bare trees and small crowd dressed
in coats on the curb, it could have been a summer morning.

"Go, Andrew! *Wooooooo!*" my editor Janelle screamed with great
enthusiasm. My friends cheered and whistled as I climbed the salt-crusted
steps of the bus. A few held their fists high in the air, victorious—others
blew on cardboard horns from their all-night New Year's Eve parties,
honking like a chorus of tortured geese. The rest waved cardboard cut-
out penguins and screamed my name like proud parents at a high school
football game. All the attention forced a self-conscious smirk onto my
face.

I dug into my pocket for the money I had counted out that morning:
a wrinkle-free dollar bill, one quarter, and a shiny silver dime. With shaky
hands, I dropped the buck thirty-five into the meter. Brian slipped in behind me as two camera crews crouched in close to catch my final farewell.
Then the door flew shut and the bus moved south down Sixteenth Street.

After all the hoopla and celebration outside National Geographic, I
was suddenly alone with Brian on a city bus, riding down an empty
street. From my jacket, I pulled out my iPhone and tapped out my first
message to Twitter.

"I'm off!"

Then I heard my name.

"Drew?" A woman called to me from the back of the bus. I blinked through my glasses at this person sitting next to her loaded suitcase—an old friend who had moved away to the west coast and whom I had not seen for years.

"What are *you* doing here?" we asked each other at the exact same time. She was headed back to California. "Are you flying to Africa?" she wondered out loud and nodded at my backpack and traveler's clothes: khaki nylon pants, cotton safari shirt, and sensible leather walking shoes.

"I'm going to Antarctica," I blurted out. The words still felt strange to me—like a lame joke, though I had never been more serious. I was relieved she had no more questions because I had no real answers. I did not know how or when I would get there, if I ever did, or where I would go or what I would do. All I knew is that I was going *to try* to get all the way to Antarctica—by bus.

The S2 metro bus turned left at the White House, still decorated for Christmas. The lights were out on the second floor and I imagined the first family was still asleep after the long party the night before. My own short party was over, too, and though I had only traveled six blocks, I felt a tad morose. No matter my nifty National Geographic Explorer backpack and the brazen logo on my jacket, no matter my exuberant send-off from National Geographic, or even my last-minute contract with *National Geographic Traveler* magazine—I was not a *real* explorer and I knew it. I was not climbing the Matterhorn or backstroking the English Channel. I was not crossing the Sahara with camels or skiing to the North Pole—I was just a dude who had clocked a mile on the bus while chatting with a friend.

We bid farewell at the terminus and Brian and I made our way to Union Station, where a five-story Christmas tree twinkled beneath the golden arched ceiling—this was my favorite building in all of Washington, DC. No other place inspires more wanderlust for me than that railway station—a portal to endless destinations across the world.

In the 1930s, my grandmother rode the train over two thousand miles from Arizona to Washington, DC, to marry my grandfather. It was her first time ever traveling east of the Rockies, and when she finally stopped at Union Station, she was overwhelmed by the grandeur of the massive colonnades and gilded ceilings. She stepped outside and into the glorious scene of marble fountains and the glistening white dome of the Capitol, then turned toward my grandfather and exclaimed, "I am going to live here for the rest of my life." And she did. She stayed and lived and died in Washington, DC—although in between, she also roamed the world with my grandfather, who worked as a diplomat for the Department of Agriculture. They lived for years in Bombay and traveled by steamship back and forth across the oceans. They wandered around Europe, and if there was ever an excuse to get to Paris, they went to Paris. My grandparents traveled for work and for fun and their love of travel trickled down through our entire family. Forever after, I saw Union Station as the place where they began their lifelong voyage together.

Now my own journey passed through this same hallway, minus the bride from Arizona. Instead, there was Brian, with brown hair and clear eyes, pushing through the holiday crowds and plodding two blocks north to the Greyhound station. Cracked orange tile covered the floor, wet with chemical streaks of Lysol. Centipede lines of passengers dragged oversize duffels like dead pets on a leash.

"Richmond—Richmond, *Vah-jinya!*" shouted a tinny speaker voice. This was not the place for two men to kiss farewell, so I simply hugged Brian good-bye and whispered, "Thank you, honey. I'll see you in Panama." He smiled back and wished me a safe journey. After almost a decade together, I knew the kind of good-bye that Brian preferred— quick, deemphasized, and British. "I'll be following you online!" he said, stepping away and barely kissing the air.

"Now, just where is your final destination, sir?" demanded the petite bus driver, sifting through the many pages of my ticket that I had printed off the Internet. His name tag said "Frazier," he had cropped salt-and-pepper hair and a trim mustache, and he wore a Greyhound-issued cardigan. He did not seem happy to be working the early shift on New Year's Day. "Where are you going?" he repeated.

"Antarctica," I offered, amused by the truth.

"*Whassat?*" Frazier sounded slightly annoyed and he leaned in closer to hear me better.

"I'm going to Antarctica," I repeated, worried that if I did not keep saying it out loud, my lofty dream might evaporate, and I would be left there, aimless, just another bombed-out character riding Greyhound.

"Naw man, you're going to *Atlanta*. Looky here," Frazier corrected me, then stapled the pages of my ticket together before sending me onto the bus with a shove disguised as a kindly back pat.

The front seat of the shiny silver Greyhound was empty, and I slid in sideways, wedging my backpack below the seat. I pulled out a cold bottle of Evian, found my iPod and untangled the headphones, then unwrapped the cellophane cover of one of my fresh new notebooks, smelled the pages, clicked open a pen, and scribbled down the two city buses I had boarded so far. We had not even left the station and already I was suffering from that basic urge of all travelers—to fit in.

Frazier stood at the front of the bus and counted us two by two, checking his list. When he sat down, the throne of the driver's seat made him look even smaller, but his voice bellowed large.

"This bus is now departing for Richmond, Virginia—our next stop is Richmond . . ." Frazier guided us through a long list of no-no's—no smoking, no alcohol, no drugs, no talking loudly on cell phones, no loud music, no leaving trash on the seat, no talking to the bus driver—and then finished with a sassy postscript: "I ain't kiddin' folks! If you break the rules, don't think I won't pull over and throw you off my bus, 'cuz I will!" Frazier finished with the sweet voice of a funeral director, "We thank you for choosing Greyhound," then backed the bus out of the lot like it was a cement mixer.

As we bumped our way toward the Capitol building, I switched on Sally and stuck her to the window with a suction cup. Sally was my GPS tracker, and she addressed me in a refined and uppity British accent, not unlike the librarians I knew back at Oxford University. "Repositioning!" she blurted out, my GPS blinking red as we rolled down Constitution Avenue. That was Sally's favorite word, her only vocabulary, and she said it often. Around the Jefferson Memorial, Sally's blinking red light switched to green and she politely confirmed: "Position fixed!" Then our big Greyhound bus crossed the brown Potomac. My heart jumped from the small thrill of departure—I felt like a captain unfurling the sails and hitting the open sea.

"Virginia Welcomes You!" exclaimed the billboard. The Pentagon loomed behind, and for the next hour we passed the silent Virginia suburbs and the outlet malls and open fields. I felt the overture of empty time that lay ahead—not hours or days but entire *weeks* on a bus.

I was crossing the world at sixty miles an hour and my watch, phone, laptop, and GPS were quietly counting every mile of dry Virginia winter. We whooshed past peeling red barns and RV sales—fields of thoroughbred horses in felt coats that nibbled patches of dead, brown grass beneath circles of old snow. The low afternoon sun emerged from the patterned clouds and behind a line of naked toothpick trees, the sky beamed a little brighter.

4 Ohio

If I were giving a young man advice as to how he might succeed in life, I would say to him, pick out a good father and mother, and begin life in Ohio.

WILBUR WRIGHT

Mom, I missed the bus" was perhaps the most hurtful thing I ever said to her, unless you count the time I asked her if I was adopted, or some years later when I told her I was gay.

To miss the bus was to upset the order of things in a house that hummed with daily attempts at order. As the middle child of nine, I knew what the world expected from me, and in case I forgot, the instructions were cross-stitched, framed, and hung at eye level over the toilet, so that I was forced to read them every time I peed: "Wash Your Hands, Brush Your Teeth, Say Your Prayers."

"Don't Miss the Bus" never made it on the wall, but it was cross-stitched on my brain. From the moment I crawled down from my bunk bed, I was chasing the bus that passed at 8:05 a.m.

"The bus is coming!" lulled me down to the kitchen and got me pouring cereal into a bowl. "The bus is coming!" got me back upstairs and out of my Star Wars pajamas. "The bus is coming!" got me dressed with hair combed and shoes tied and teeth brushed and prayers said—it got me making lunches for my younger brothers and sisters, and it got me out the door and sprinting to the corner, my backpack jiggling with pencils and library books.

Some days we made it, others not. To miss by a minute was to miss by a mile—the bus came and went, and afterward the world fell silent, like a cold spot of ocean where the Titanic had just sunk. Sometimes I could still see it flashing through the oak trees, a bus more yellow than macaroni and cheese, but a bus long gone, far beyond my reach. As children, our sense of failure was immediate, and we walked back home in the slow motion of shame, knowing full well that we had flunked out on the singular duty that our young lives demanded of us—to catch the school bus.

I remember the disappointment in my mother's eyes and how she resigned herself to the job at hand—to change out of her pink cotton nightgown, to put on lipstick and drive us to school, encouraging us to try harder tomorrow. The school was only a mile away, so we passed the bus along the way, but driving with my mother was better—there were no stops along the way, and there were no kids making fun of me from the back of the bus.

They began calling me faggot in the fourth grade. I had to look up the word in my parents' dictionary, but "Noun. Bundle of sticks; England, origin 13th Century" offered me little to work with. Whatever it meant, *faggot* was not a desirable status for any boy, especially a ten-year-old with an aptitude for sewing quilts and skipping rope.

"Are you a girl?" the other boys shouted, lunging at me in the aisle of the bus. My clothes were wrong, my hair was wrong. I held my books like a girl, they said—I walked and talked like a girl, I threw the ball like a girl, and when I flinched at their punches, I was scared like a girl.

Every morning I trudged up the steps and sat near the front of the bus, waiting for the insults to begin, and every morning they came, like a shower of flint-tipped arrows shot from the back of the bus. My only shield of defense was the magazine that I pulled from my backpack—a worn copy of *National Geographic*. My Grandpa Bob owned every issue going back a century and before I reached the seventh grade, I had read every single one—meaning, I had flipped through all the pictures and read the captions. *National Geographic*s were my great escape on the bus and from the battle of each school day. Like some ancient magic spell, those shiny pages plucked me out of the Midwest with its bleak days and mean kids and dropped me atop the daunting peaks of Tibet, or drinking cow's blood with the Maasai, or crouched inside a blue-lit submarine with my imaginary French friend, Jacques Cousteau. I craved the adventure depicted on those pages, and I sought them as my own in flat, boring Findlay, Ohio.

Why did I keep taking the bus when I hated it so much? Why did I let myself be a punching bag day after day? Why did the bus take such a roundabout way to get home, more than tripling the actual distance from school? It made no sense, and so when the bell rang at 3:15, I went my own way.

With all the coolness of an escaped convict, I jumped behind a bush and stole through the leafy backyards of town, running in a straight line, far from the road, jumping streams and crunching acorns underfoot as I made my way home.

Suddenly I felt like an explorer, guessing at the direction of my house and following my intuition, carefully pushing down the rusty barbed wire as I crossed between farmers' fields. The sky was boundless and I had never felt so free. I had entered the great limbo of travel—away from the cramped sphere of school and the safety of home. At that moment, nobody in the world knew where I was—walking alone felt blissful.

"Where were you?" My mother tried not to shout, but she was shouting. "Did you miss the bus?"

"I decided to walk," I said.

"You walked all the way home?" My younger siblings circled around my mother, unsure if I was in trouble or not. I nodded yes.

"I went the back way, through the woods," I said. "But it's OK, Mom. I looked both ways before crossing the street."

"Andrew, you can't just walk home alone," she explained. The world was dangerous, and I should never go anywhere without telling an adult. Normally, my mother let us roam freely, to ride our bikes to the swimming pool or library by ourselves, but she insisted on open communication. But there were things I could never tell my mother—not about the kids at school and what they did to me, how I had no real friends to play with, or that I always spent recess alone, walking the perimeter of the playground, daydreaming of the places I saw in magazines. I never told her the word they called me—it was a bad word and we never said bad words in our house. Calling someone "dumb" earned us five minutes of time out—I figured that "faggot" would get me locked in the bathroom for weeks.

I preferred my own time-out, locking myself away, surrounded by the books and maps that I loved. On my globe, I traced the coastline of every continent and memorized the intricate contours of the oceans. I studied how each country fit together and felt the bumpy mountain chains that rose up between India and China, France and Spain. Then I slapped the globe with all the vicious force of a child, spinning all the colored countries into a melting, whirling rainbow. I saw the whole world wobbling on its squeaky metal axis, a blur of possibility, then froze it still with a single jab of my fingertip.

"*Zaire!*" I whispered the name beneath my finger and promised myself that someday, I would go there. Spinning the globe was my own fortune-telling game that transcended me beyond the state of Ohio. Stuck in the most uneventful corner of America, I invented elaborate escape plans with maps.

I scribbled a blueprint for my life inside the 1975 *National Geographic Atlas*, a table-size book that offered two Germanys, East and West, and an intact Yugoslavia, along with the forgotten nations of Dahomey and Rhodesia. This was my favorite book in the world, and I filled its pages with penciled lines of the journeys I would make someday.

"Day 45: Lake Baikal," I wrote in the margins. "Day 60: Sail across Baffin Bay." My imaginary itineraries lasted for months and took me all the way around the world. Long before I ever left my own country, I had traveled everywhere in my mind. *National Geographic* fed my fetish in monthly installments, with free maps that tumbled out from each issue.

My bedroom was a kid's art gallery of wishing and dreaming, bedazzled with maps and photos cut from *National Geographic*. Mine was an endless cycle of yearning, in which maps kindled my wanderlust, and wanderlust pushed me back to maps and their whispered promise of another world beyond the one I knew. Maps made life seem infinite and hopeful; maps held the keys to my escape—far from Ohio, far away from the hell that was seventh grade.

There were days when I spent study hall wondering how much dynamite I would need to bring down Central Junior High School. A lot, I guessed—tons and tons of gunpowder planted strategically around the cafeteria and the gym. I sketched the scene in my notebook with red pen explosions and a heap of smoking rubble, but in the end, I was too scared of not making honor roll to ever blow up the school.

Instead, I kept riding the bus, day after day—now a much longer trip into town, granting the older kids an extra twenty minutes to torture me. The bus was a one-way ticket into the prison yard of junior high, where long hallways loomed with adolescent cruelty. I remember the ringing thud as my own head smashed against the metal lockers and carefully wiping up my own blood off the gritty tiled floor with recycled brown paper towels.

Before they had only called me faggot, but now I was *the fag*—the school's unofficial homosexual mascot and walking punching bag. I heard it more than my own name. "Hey fag!" preceded a quick shove, a wad of spit, or a knuckle to my head. Perhaps if I had been bigger or stronger, or even known how to fight, then maybe I could have gotten the other kids to shut up—but I only knew the capitals of sub-Saharan Africa and how to play the flute, and neither of those talents helped me very much.

I had always known I was different, but seventh grade taught me that different was dangerous. Being different got you hurt, it got you picked last in gym, and it got you laughed at every day. There was no chance for me to try to fit in: I read the encyclopedia for fun, I sang alto in choir, and at lunch, I was the only boy at the girls' table. Over time, I learned how to survive by becoming invisible, speaking less, dressing average, and walking at the edge of the hall with my shoulders slumped and head bowed.

※

"OK. So where is . . . Ouagadougou?" my father asked, smiling. He wanted to trick me.

"Burkina Faso!" I shouted back, pushing against the seat belt and drumming my hands on the sunny dashboard. It was summer, the world was warm, and out of all the kids in the family, my dad had asked me to sit in the front seat.

"All right," he said, contemplatively. "Lima?"

"Too easy—Peru! Gimme harder ones, Dad."

"OK," he said, steering with one hand while he adjusted his sunglasses. "Bern."

"Dad!" I rolled my eyes sarcastically. I wanted him to give me the really crazy capitals—Nouakchott and Bamako; Kigali, Jakarta, and Montevideo. Anywhere in Europe was just too easy.

"Then what is it?" he asked, still watching the road.

"Bern is the capital of Switzerland," I replied.

"That's right," he said, still smiling while guiding the car forever west on I-80. The road was gray and unbending and I wondered why my dad even had to steer. We drove this way every summer—there wasn't a single turn for at least eight hundred miles. Couldn't he just set the wheel straight and then put the car in cruise control? Like in *Knight Rider* where KITT just drove himself wherever David Hasselhoff wanted. I wished that I was sitting shotgun in a shiny black Trans Am, but our family van looked more like a bus—a converted airport limousine with fifteen seatbelts and an extra-long back end for luggage. My sisters joked that it was a BMW—a Big Mormon Wagon—but it was in fact a Dodge that my father had named "Boudreau."

I was happy to be chosen out of all my brothers and sisters to sit up front with my dad. My job was to keep my father awake through the

mind-numbing landscape of the Midwest. From the moment we turned
onto the highway, the corn stretched on forever. There were no gently
rolling hills, only flat fields of leafy green stalks, the kind that grew
"knee-high by the fourth of July."

By the time my dad announced "Indiana!" most of the family was in
a coma, their sleepy heads lolling back on the long van seats. Indiana
meant nothing—only that we had another twelve hours of cornfields to
go. By the time I was twelve, I had ridden back and forth to Utah at least
five times—I knew the road well. Soon came Illinois, and then Iowa.
Only in Nebraska did the corn disappear, giving way to nine endless
hours of green wheat fields, and then came Wyoming—brown like a
peanut butter smudge on the map of America.

My own ancestors had treaded this same path across America, one
hundred fifty years before. As Mormon pioneers, they had walked these
Great Plains, pulling covered wagons or handcarts, crisscrossing the
rippled waters of the Platte River, marching onward to Zion. Nowadays,
the road to Utah was just a three-day drive on I-80, a road that roughly
follows the original Mormon Trail.

"Your great-great-great-grandmother walked this entire way—
barefoot," my mother reminded us. "Imagine doing this same trip but
pulling a cart filled with all your belongings!"

While my father drove and I copiloted, my mother played stewardess,
preparing and serving us multicourse lunches over a span of fifty or sixty
miles. First came chopped apples, sun-warmed carrots, and celery sticks
that smelled of Tupperware, then cold-cut sandwiches cut into little
triangles. Each of us had colored plastic cups with our names written on
them, and these were passed back and forth with refills of ice water from
a five-gallon Coleman jug.

Meanwhile, I kept my father awake by having him test me on all
fifty states, and then all the countries of the world. He knew how much
I loved to play—this was our special game, and while he always tried
stumping me with some obscure capital, I never missed a question
twice.

"Next up," said my father. "What is the capital of Burundi?"

"Bujumbura," I shot back. My father shook his head, feigning surprise.

"How do you know these, Drew?" he asked, and I grinned. I liked being smart, and I liked better that my dad thought I was smart. I liked that he recognized me for something I was good at. If he ever tried taking me out in the yard to play catch, it would have been a disaster—but instead, he played the game I loved best, pitching me the fast curved balls of strange countries, as I batted back with the correct capitals again and again.

Rumbling across Indiana was nowhere close to my globe-spinning dreams, but I was thrilled to be traveling nonetheless. Every family vacation was an amazing expedition where we explored America, from rest stop to national park to relatives' homes. Even the trip to Utah was captivating for me, when places I knew from the atlas, like Cheyenne and Ogallala, turned into real places where people wore cowboy boots and went to rodeos for fun.

Travel made me happy—this much I knew. I counted the mile markers like exclamation points, ticking us closer and closer to somewhere new. I loved reading the license plates from faraway states and I loved crossing borders and reading the signs aloud, "Welcome to Illinois! Land of Lincoln!" I loved popping open a side window and catching a blast of road air in my face, and I loved snapping it shut and feeling my eardrums pop with the change in pressure.

When my turn was up, I gave up my seat as copilot and climbed to the back of the van, where l lay down on the carpeted floor, fixing my right eye to an empty screw hole that let me peer down to road below. I watched the hot asphalt rushing below me, a mere twenty-four inches from my face. The whole van rattled on spinning wheels, sending a rhythmic rumbling through my whole body, shaking my forehead, knees, and chest—mile after mile of travel spelled out in the Morse code of white dashes painted upon the road.

This is where I wanted to be and where I wanted to stay—forever traveling, going west or north, south or east, just driving and driving on the longest road in America and never going back to Ohio.

🔅

My geography skills never helped my social status at school, but they did get me into the first ever National Geography Bee. Sponsored by the National Geographic Society, this was a contest I could win. I beat out my social studies class in a single period, then won first place at a school assembly. By the time I made it to the contest in Columbus, I already felt more comfortable standing beneath the bright lights and talking into a microphone. The state competition had opened with the top one hundred students in Ohio. One by one, they left the stage— one by one, the questions became more difficult, and one by one, I answered them correctly.

I was dressed in my Sunday best—dark blue slacks, white button-down shirt with a clip-on tie, and leather shoes that shone from the stage. My father had polished them the night before, and that morning, we had kneeled down together and said a family prayer that my mind would be clear and that I would remember everything I had studied. My mother fed me oatmeal sprinkled with raisins, then drove me the two hours to Columbus. She had sat patiently in the audience of parents, but after two hours, I could tell that even she was a little surprised by my success.

If I won, I would take her with me to Washington, DC. That was the state prize—an all-expenses-paid trip to the capital to compete for the national title of Geography Bee Champion, with its $50,000 scholarship and a lifetime membership in the National Geographic Society.

"Pictured in this slide is a rare feature found only in certain 'hotspots' around the globe," said the state judge, reading each word carefully. "Name this feature and list the three different countries where it can be found." The man looked up at me and blinked from behind his glasses.

I already knew the answer, but I waited, counting five Mississippi in my mind. Rushing an answer was the surest way to screw up. The picture on the screen showed Old Faithful—we had seen it on a family vacation just two years before. I remembered the heat that rose up from the ground and the stinky sulfur smell of the air.

"It's a geyser," I answered. "You can find them in Yellowstone National Park, which is in Wyoming, in the United States—also they are in Iceland, and . . ." I paused, making absolutely sure of the words in my mouth. "New Zealand."

"That is correct," said the man, double-checking his answer sheet. The audience clapped, and parents turned and asked one another, surprised, "Did you know that?"

Only three of us remained on stage, and with every round, the judges increased the level of questions. Eventually, I was the only kid on stage, staring at the panel of judges with my toes crossed. I was the last man standing—the smartest geography student in the entire state of Ohio. It felt wonderful and nauseating.

"Congratulations, Andrew!" said the judge, tapping his pencil on the table. "But we're not done yet. The regulations say that you must answer one more question correctly to confirm you as winner."

Bring it on. I was two seconds from becoming state champion and I loved how it felt—up here on stage I wasn't the loser fag that hugged the walls and turned away from every other kid in the hall. Up there, I mattered. I was good at something, and an entire audience of grown-ups was sitting and waiting, hoping to applaud my victory.

"Dinosaurs once roamed the area that is now called La Brea, California, known for its tar pits," read the judge. "What natural resource today is derived from prehistoric tar pits?"

Tar was dark, black, and sticky, just like oil. My father worked for an oil company—he had taught me this. There was the Sinclair dinosaur at the gas station. But wasn't that too obvious—oil? It had to be a trick question—my future, my college education, and my entire life depended on out-tricking this most tricky trick question. I waited, silent, shifting my weight from one leg to the next on the scuffed stage, feeling the sweat on my face and prolonging that moment of almost-glory.

"Can you repeat the question?" I asked. The judge repeated the question, and then I answered.

"Tar?" I said bashfully—hopefully, but the moment I said it, I knew it was wrong.

"The correct answer is petroleum," he echoed from the panel, and the audience of a hundred parents moaned with a collective "*Awwwwww.*" It felt like a public execution. I remained standing, stunned, until I was asked to step down from the stage. My legs trembled, but I walked slowly away from the spotlight and into the darkness. The two runners-up came rushing back up on stage for a second chance, and after knocking out answers to softball questions, they were given first and second place.

I took third, which felt like a punch to the gut. The photographer said, "Smile!" but I stood frozen, third place certificate in one hand, my prize in the other—a savings bond for less than I earned in a day of babysitting. As I struggled to reach my mother at the back of the hall, strangers stopped to shake my hand and pat my back. At first I flinched, afraid of getting hurt—afraid of all the pity in the room. They called me "super smart" and "whiz kid"—I tried to be polite and repeated "thank you" like a sad robot, but I just wanted to vanish away.

The next day I was back at school, stewing away in a pot of self-doom. Despite my note from home, my English teacher gave me an F for missing class to attend the geography bee. In gym class we wrestled, giving every eighth-grade boy a chance to slam my head into the floor. The taste of the foam rubber mat lingered in my mouth until I got home, where I quickly retreated to my room of maps and about eight hundred back issues of *National Geographic*.

That is where I felt safe, and these were my friends—the adventurous men and women inside the magazine—explorers who traveled overland by boat, horse, dogsled, camel, bicycle, or donkey cart. Guys like Joseph Rock, who hiked the Himalayas with a canvas bathtub and dodged bandits in the Hindu Kush, or Maynard Owen Williams, who drove a Renault halfway around the world from Lebanon to Shanghai and who was among the first to stare into King Tut's newly opened tomb. Or women like Ida Treat, who dressed up like a sailor to infiltrate Djibouti's slave trade, and Eliza Scidmore, who preached the virtue of packing light and wrote about everything from Alaska's blue foxes to the tea-scented streets of Yokohama.

I wanted to be like them—bold and undaunted. I wanted to travel uncharted paths and send back the never-before-seen image of a Fijian warrior chief, or the endless summer sunset at the North Pole. National Geographic promised me a world so different from the one I knew, so far from the dull pain of eighth grade, that it became my obsession. I would work there someday, I told myself. *I will travel.* That is all I wanted, and I clung to that dream like a life ring.

5   VIRGINIA

Day 1

My phone rang and "DAD" flashed on the screen.

"*Hey!*" I whispered too loudly, huddled against the window and cupping my mouth to the phone with one hand, pretending to be quiet. "Well, we left DC an hour ago."

Sixty minutes into my epic bus trip and my dad was already checking up on me. Was the weather nice? How was riding Greyhound? I was thirty-four years old but felt more like twelve, reporting on my first day at school.

"Well, I'm still in Virginia," I said, staring out at the dull winter fields that spread across the middle of the state.

"*Sic semper tyrannis!*" My father quoted the state motto: Thus Always to Tyrants. He was raised in Virginia—all I had to do was read the road signs aloud and he would turn each place into a story of tragic Civil War battles. Even on the phone, his description was so detailed, I could imagine rows of Union soldiers marching on the lonely horizon.

We were OK now, my dad and I. There had been a time when we had stopped speaking altogether; too many awkward conversations were followed by years of silence without any visits, but now he was calling me in his most enthusiastic tone, thrilled by my own real-life adventure.

"You know, back in the sixties, your uncle and I broke down way out in North Dakota . . ." My father began his story and I settled back into my seat, watching the dirty fields of snow outside my window.

". . . So we finally hitch a ride to the Greyhound station and ask the guy if we can get a bus ticket to Chicago—and he says, 'Where's that?'"

My dad laughed. "You know you're in the middle of nowhere when they've never heard of Chicago."

This is how my dad and I talk. We swap stories—sometimes he gives advice. We dissect the state of the world in the form of an essay: "How will China adapt to the Internet age?" We can open with a discussion on our favorite tube stations in London and finish with reflections on the U.S. Constitution. We can talk for two minutes or two hours. At some point he will probably bring up the church and I will listen politely and try to say something agreeable. Then, to lighten the mood, he will catch me up on the latest developments in his quest to capture the armadillo that's destroying their backyard. Finally, we say good-bye and "I love you," and we both mean it.

"Good-bye, Dad."

"See you in Texas," he said, and then my dad hung up. Speeding through Virginia reminded me of him. This was a land of military schools and good ol' boys—such a male state, really, with its whisky, corn, and tobacco.

I turned away from the window and glanced at the lady behind me. She wore a fancy feathered hat and rose-colored spectacles that teetered on the bridge of her nose, secured with a zirconium chain around the back of her neck. White lace gloves masked her small hands that clutched a pink leather handbag in her lap. I imagined her sitting the same way in a pew at some Baptist church.

"I'm Miss Carolyn." She blinked behind her glasses. Miss Carolyn was going to a funeral—her elderly aunt had died right after Christmas.

"I'm really sorry to hear that," I said.

"Oh, it's all right, sir." She folded her lacy hands. "But thank you for your kindness." Miss Carolyn had good Southern manners, and she did not seem horribly upset—even cheerful.

"And where might you be traveling to?" she inquired.

"All the way to Atlanta." I smiled.

"Oooh, Atlanta's nice," she offered, though we talked mostly about Baltimore since I know that city and its weather patterns better than

those of Atlanta. We chatted all the way to Richmond, where I escorted
Miss Carolyn to a posse of younger family members, who smothered
her with hugs and laughter, then pulled out embroidered handkerchiefs
from purses and began wiping their eyes. I watched from afar, touched
by their bittersweet reunion in Sunday dress, trying to imagine where
all those different people fit on some huge sprawling family tree.

The Richmond bus station was a far more impressive place than the
Greyhound depot back in Washington, DC. Even the floors looked
new and in every corner, flat-screen TVs flashed with closed-captioned
scenes from *True Blood*. While I recharged my phone in the corner, a
buxom vampire launched fireballs from her fingertips. I kept my eyes
fixed on the screen with pretend interest, trying to ignore the kooky
lady standing next to me. She seemed anorexic with twice-dyed hair
that lifted from her shoulders with too much static, and she spoke to
everybody in the station in a projected voice, as if she was workshopping
her one-woman show, titled "Reasons I Ride the Bus."

"It's a hundred bucks cheaper to fly," she scoffed, then gave a re-
hearsed shrug to the void, before spinning and pacing in the opposite
direction of the station.

"But I'm just way too scared and that's why I take the bus," the lady
said to herself. She threw back her frazzled mess of hair and cackled
nervously, then honed in on me, circling me while retelling the last two
days of her life in bullet points. She was coming back from Albany and
on her way to Key West, where she lived. This was the eleventh time she
had made the trip, a journey of 1,400 miles and forty-eight hours.

"Still better than flying," she cried out, squinting her wild eyes and
throwing her hands upward. So she was a little bit crazy. Who isn't? I
empathized with her fear of flying things. Nature never intended human
bodies to browse magazines at thirty thousand feet, and yet we fly—that
year alone I had flown over a quarter-million miles to more than thirty
countries, while this woman had not stepped on a plane in twenty years.

"Nineteen eighty-nine! That's the last time I flew," she proclaimed
with an echo that rang through the station. Then she started an open

survey, comparing the distances each of us was traveling by bus, asking around until she got to me.

"Actually, I'm headed to Mexico," I said, trying the answer on for size. If all went well, I hoped to be in Mexico in a few days.

"GAWD!" She cackled and then raised her knee high enough to slap it. Her face flushed red and she exploded with insane laughter. As she laughed, she ran backward, pointing both hands at me like two pistols, screaming out to the world, "He's goin' to Mexico! THIS GUY'S GOING TO MEXICO!"

Security guards appeared out of nowhere and stared at me strangely. The crazy lady disappeared into the restroom, but everyone in the station could still hear her shrieks that matched up with the fighting vampires happening on multiple TVs.

Back on the bus, my backpack appeared unmolested—my first test of the social experiment a silent success. I had noticed other passengers marking their seats with jackets or bags of food. I imitated their behavior, but I was still certain some lousy hoodlum would steal everything. That Frazier closed the door during the bus stop did not help my peace of mind. When I tallied up the contents of my pack—computer, cameras, lenses, and gear—I was carting over $10,000 worth of equipment on a Greyhound bus. I had refused to check the bag because I did not trust it out of my sight, which, it turned out, was exactly how it would be every time we stopped for a break.

I stuffed my pack beneath my legs and tried to relax as we rolled through Richmond. We passed brick warehouses and vacant lots until we came to the giant sprawl of Philip Morris headquarters. Steamy smokestacks and massive concrete boxes comprised the factory where they make some four hundred million cigarettes per day.

Minutes later we were zooming through Virginia's tobacco fields, littered with brown tobacco leaves from the last harvest. At the far edge of the field, a group of bearded duck hunters hiked through the undergrowth dressed in camouflage jackets and resting rifles on their shoulders. Already the daylight was thinning into shadow—the first day of the year seemed so short.

Two new riders joined me near the front of the bus. Across the aisle sat an Arab student with a Duke sweatshirt. In his left hand, he steadied a laptop that flickered with some Bruce Willis action movie, while in his right hand, he gripped an open copy of the Koran, flipping the pages with his thumb as he read. Clearly a multitasker, he mumbled Arabic into the glowing Bluetooth in his left ear—a rabid conversation that lasted all the way to the North Carolina state line.

Behind me sat an even younger man sporting a bushy goatee and a backward baseball cap, along with an oversize Red Sox shirt. He slumped in his seat with his eyes half-shut. Given the volume of rap pumping from his headphones, I surmised that he was not looking for friendly conversation. The digital age lets us all travel together in solitude, and so I finally switched on my own music, clicking through my Bus2Antarctica playlist that I had compiled especially for the trip.

Song after song, we moved down the road, the tires keeping time with Van Morrison's "Into the Mystic." Now the Arab student was praying to Allah, bobbing his head over the Koran, while behind me, Red Sox bobbed to his furious rap. I dozed lazily, waking every few minutes to send text messages to my growing band of Twitter followers.

Sunset. Beautiful streaks of hot pink behind black silhouette forest. Airplane tracks in the sky. Half-frozen roadside ponds.

North Carolina felt so scenic—the winter so much softer than just a few hours north. Sitting there half-asleep, my playlist arrived at James Taylor's "Goin' to Carolina" just as the evening sky burst into bright pink-orange sunset. As if on cue, a flock of Canada geese seemed to chase us overhead.

Any anxiety I had carried from the city simply evaporated in North Carolina. Suddenly the long road felt dreamy and poetic. Night fell, a first star appeared, and then suddenly, a five-story fiberglass statue of Paul Bunyan popped up, followed by a parade of random glowing signs that emerged from the dark roadside, one after another: "Real BBQ," "Waffle House," and a burned-out Applebee's that simply read "__bee's."

After a nap, I woke up to the stoplights around Duke University. The Arab guy hopped off on campus and Frazier repeated all the rules for any new riders, ending with his singsong jingle, "We thank you for riding Greyhound." But when we got to Greensboro, his tone changed.

"There is absolutely NO smoking on the bus—no cigarettes, no pipes, no nothing. Not on the bus and NOT in or around the bus station. Everybody got that?" He shot me a glare with a nod.

"I don't smoke," I said defensively, but Frazier still frowned. The man had something against me—perhaps he knew that I was riding Greyhound ironically?

Greensboro's bus station turned out to be a funky old-time Southern train depot with painted red benches and smoked glass walls etched with historic buses. An antique fortune-telling machine stood in one corner, offering character readings for just a quarter. I dropped a coin in the slot and waited—hoping for some poetic insight into my journey— but nothing emerged. It was busted. Back on the bus, a beefy policeman began interrogating me.

"You traveling with anybody?" he asked.

"Nope—I'm solo," I said coolly.

"That white dude with the Red Sox shirt—where's he sitting?" he asked, and I pointed to the empty seat behind me. Then the cop reached back and began picking through all of the guy's bags, pulling everything out and then stuffing it all back in again. Then he bundled everything under his arm and stepped off the bus.

Sliding over, I pressed my face against the cold glass window and watched the red-and-blue lights spinning in the night. Hunched over in the backseat was my fellow passenger of five minutes ago, handcuffed and head bowed.

A minute later, Frazier stomped back onto the bus and began ranting, "See now? I wasn't kidding, folks! You wanna smoke, you go to jail. That's the way it works around here. I say it to you out loud and what do you do? You get out and smoke!" His voice was high-pitched, his jaw shaking. Thoroughly pissed off, he flipped on the rumbling engine and began backing out the bus, ever so cautiously.

Red Sox had smoked a joint inside a public building—apparently right in front of a security camera. A little stupid—and a little illegal in

North Carolina. Instead of traveling on our midnight bus to Georgia, he was getting booked for possession at the nearby county jail.

At least he'll have a bed for the night, I reasoned, wondering if I would get any sleep in my hard vertical seat. Honestly, I felt a little sorry for Red Sox—to get sideswiped like that, shunted off to a very different kind of adventure. On the plus side, now the bus was blissfully silent—the crappy rap music was gone, and the only sound was that of the trembling wheels on the road.

A small *beep* shot up from my pack.

"Repositioning!" Sally the GPS cried out with her shrill one-liner. She must have got disconnected from her satellite when we started driving through all these underpasses. I grappled in the dark to muffle the noise and hide the flashing red light, but all the while, Sally whined in her sassy electronic voice:

"Repositioning! Repositioning!"

6 | TWO LETTERS

National Geographic Society
1145 17th St. NW
Washington, DC 20036

Dear Sir or Madam:

My name is Andrew Evans and I live in Findlay, Ohio. I am fourteen years old. I own every issue of your magazine and I have read them all, too. I like the pictures and the captions. I was in your first geography bee and I won third place for the state of Ohio. For Christmas, I got the National Geography Bee board game. I like it.

When I grow up, I want to work for National Geographic Magazine. I am writing you to find out what I should study in college so that I can get a job with you? I am thinking about taking geography because I like maps, but I also like art, too, and taking pictures. I hope you will write me back and let me know.

Thank you for reading my letter.

Sincerely Yours,
Andrew

Two months passed before the reply arrived in our mailbox, with my name hand-typed on the envelope. The embossed stationary proclaimed

"National Geographic" in heavy Old English print. Simply touching the letter was a thrill.

> Dear Mr. Evans,
>
> Thank you for your correspondence and inquiry regarding careers at National Geographic. Please understand that we receive far more requests than we have available positions. Some examples of the regular openings we have at the Society include cartographer, photographer, editor, researcher, and administrator.
>
> The National Geographic Society is an esteemed organization and we take pride in the professional achievements of experts and explorers. As such, we tend to employ individuals with proven expertise in their respective fields, such as anthropology, archaeology, astronomy, botany, history, oceanography, and paleontology.
>
> Rather than fixate on a specific career with National Geographic, we encourage anyone with interest to pursue academic excellence in one of the aforementioned fields.
>
> We thank you for your interest and wish you good luck with your studies.
>
> Sincerely—

The letter was signed by somebody's secretary, someone whose job it was to type dozens and dozens of letters like this every day. Still, I had a real letter from National Geographic, and while it was not the early job offer I had secretly hoped for, it was not a definitive rejection, either—more like a "Don't call us, we'll call you" kind of letter.

I could live with that—I was patient and I still had four years of high school to finish.

7 ATLANTA

Day 2

Humans are damned territorial creatures—even on Greyhound. As I walked down the aisle, my fellow passengers lowered their eyes, their blank faces pleading, "Not here. Don't sit next to me." A posse of male youths had spread across the back two rows of the bus. They looked up from their tipped baseball caps, then kicked their Timberlands across the aisle, forming a barricade of baggy jeans and rubber tread.

I looked back to the front of the bus, but Frazier's eyes met mine in the rearview mirror.

"The front seats are for disabled people!" he reminded me. "And I've got a pair of folks getting on here who are actually *disabled*," he said. "You gotta find somewhere else to sit!"

"I'm sorry—I didn't know," I whimpered to the whole bus. A couple of new passengers huddled in the cold outside, wrapped together in a fluffy pink blanket, their faces struck with the awed gaze of Down syndrome. Once they occupied my former seat, I hauled my backpack over my head and tramped up and down the aisle, dancing and tripping over people's legs, searching for a single seat. The other passengers had carefully colonized the space next to them with bags of food, thermoses, sweatshirts, scarves, and jackets—every object sending me the same clear message, "Not you, not now."

A familiar fear filled my chest—the same dreadful thing I felt every day in Ohio—how nobody wanted to sit next to me on the bus, how I ate lunch alone in the school cafeteria, how I was always picked last in gym. Even now, in my thirties, I sat up front because it felt safe and free from humiliation, while the back of the bus reminded me of the truth—that nobody really wanted me around. Deflated, I flicked away the crushed Doritos from the fuzzy blue seat cushion and slid myself into a middle row, hiding my face from my new seatmate. I busied myself on Twitter, telling the world that I had changed seats.

"Now you know how Rosa Parks felt!" one of my followers tweeted back from California, except that as a tall white male who was riding the bus for fun, I had absolutely no idea how Rosa Parks felt. I imagine that she was pretty fed up, and as my own bus barreled on through the night, I was reminded how the greatest advance of civil rights all boiled down to one lady refusing to change seats.

Back in Washington, DC, the Greyhound carried a pretty mixed bag of riders, but the farther south we drove, the paler I felt among the crowd of mostly African Americans. The only other white passengers were military, all dressed in camouflage and heading back after Christmas at home. At every station, parents and kids and young wives cried tears and embraced their soldiers before sending them back to base and back to war.

As we bounced along in the dark, the soldier in front of me rolled up his olive-green shirt, exposing a tattoo on his muscled shoulder. In the hour it took to drive to Charlotte, he rubbed half a tub of Vaseline into the new ink: a provocative pinup girl, naked and kneeling with piles of blonde hair floating down over a prominent bosom, but with a shocking stump for an arm—some kind of strange and sexy amputee. A date was scrawled out beneath the design, rudimentary numbers that pointed to just a few months back. Who was the real girl behind the one inscribed in this man's skin? How oddly had her life crossed into mine, this sorrowful image of a woman carried home from Iraq, breasts bouncing merrily with the rhythm of the road, missing an arm and reminding me that even here, deep in the heart of North Carolina, my country was still at war.

The Rose Bowl played like gunfire in the Charlotte station. At the neon-lit "Nite Café," a bleary-eyed server in a paper hat dished up plates of hot southern biscuits drowned in pasty white gravy. Lynyrd Skynyrd jammed from the jukebox and off in the corner, a refrigerator case buzzed with electricity, displaying wobbly chocolate pudding cups like museum pieces behind the glass door. In the opposite corner, a group of soldiers coached a young recruit through a roll of quarters as he failed again and again to win a stuffed animal toy with a flimsy mechanical hook.

Electrical outlets were scarce, so I plugged in my splitter and offered up the spare plug to another traveler who was playing a DVD on his laptop. His fuzzy screen moved with music—pixelated dancers floating beneath stage lights. I saw legs spin around, then a pair of quivering hands that shot up into the air.

"Michael Jackson?" I asked, and the guy smiled and nodded back. A few other passengers moved in for a closer look and soon our cozy little corner swelled from five to fifteen. Whispers shot through the station that Michael was "on the TV" and bored travelers walked over to see the fuss.

It was Michael's last movie, *This Is It!*, released after his death—a movie so insanely popular that fans had waited days and days in lines for tickets at theaters around the country. The DVD that played from the laptop would not be released for another month, and the bootleg copy had the sound quality of a car radio with water damage. Michael Jackson had only been dead seven months, and the crowd was totally transfixed by the small and grainy images of the Ghost of Pop. The subtitles were barely legible, yet the words looked familiar to me—as I strained to read, I recognized the Cyrillic letters.

"That's Ukrainian!" I cried out, a bit too excitedly. Michael's muffled monologue was spelled out in a foreign language that I knew how to read. I translated a few words for the guy with the laptop.

"Wait, you know what he's saying?" he asked, happily. "Tell us, man, tell us! What's he saying?" By now the crowd had grown to some forty people, all hooked on these shaky images from a movie that did not yet exist in the public domain. I quoted another line of subtitles and waited.

"The white guy knows what they sayin'!" The group tightened around me, straining to hear my rather rough translation of a movie with very limited dialogue. I struggled to keep up with the pace on-screen. I mean, I only *kinda* know Ukrainian. Yes, I lived there and studied the language—and I know Russian, which is somewhat similar—but in a bus station at ten thirty at night, surrounded by Michael fans in mourning, that was enough. Line for line, I translated the movie, louder and louder, answering the call from the back of the station. The crowd grew larger, responding to my spoken word with shouted declarations, like congregants overcome by the Holy Spirit at a Baptist church, waving hands in the air and screaming, "Hallelujah!" over and over again.

The mood turned rapturous, and one man began dancing in the back of the station, mimicking Michael's steps.

"They the old Jackson 5 moves!" he said.

"He had so much left to give!" cried another, woefully.

"Michael looks so healthy right there." A large lady with a red wool coat dabbed the tears from her eyes. "You know he was fine—he was just fine!"

Life had granted me just enough Ukrainian—perhaps not enough to quote Shevchenko in the original, or to work out the nuances of dialect in Gogol's short stories—but enough to give voice to a bootleg DVD for grieving Michael fans huddled in this bus station. As I spoke, the crowd pushed in closer, as if I was some kind of street preacher, breathing words of life from the silent mouth of the deceased.

"Good Sound. Good Sound," I translated another one of Michael's lines from the subtitles as grateful fans came by to give me a squeeze on the shoulder or a light pat on the back. Beyond the sea of affirming nods stood Frazier the bus driver, lingering at the back wall and smiling with approval. Only after I finished interpreting Michael Jackson's posthumous performance did he start herding the passengers back onto the bus.

"Where's that white guy?" Frazier called out. Everyone pointed to my seat, where I was already huddled down with a blanket wrapped around my legs.

"Here," I peeped, raising my hand like a kid at school. So now I was the white guy—no matter that the airman who had just boarded was also white. The kid was in uniform, and he picked the seat next to me, calling me "sir" about every three seconds.

"Sir, yes, sir, I'm on my way to Biloxi, sir," he said, as if I might slap his apple-cheeks should he ever forget the "sir."

"At ease, dude," I joked, and the kid relaxed, shaking my hand. As the bus gunned onto the highway, we began to chat and he explained with pride how he was a mechanic who worked on C-130s—the gargantuan transport planes used to move tanks and people around the world.

"I do all the electronics," he boasted, though he couldn't have been older than twenty. He wasn't really into talking, either, preferring the Nintendo game that his mama had stuck in his stocking for Christmas. He quickly went back to blowing up things on the phone-size screen.

I tried the guy in front of me, but he only spoke Spanish, so I made my best attempt.

"*No más trabajo*," he explained with a shrug. "There's no more work." After failing to find a job in the Carolina tobacco fields, he was heading back to Mexico for winter. I tried to discuss the recession, but my Spanish is pretty lousy and Jorge was not interested in teaching me anything else—he just wanted to sleep.

"*Ahora, voy a dormir*," he whispered, then pulled his cap over his eyes. I leaned my face against the cold window and felt the road tremble through my jaw.

"Welcome to South Carolina!" the sign shouted from the darkness. Sleep was uneasy. I was fighting the adrenalin of my first day on the road. The midnight rumble of bus tires on blacktop offered no hint of exotic world travels, but inside, I felt it coming. Even on that bitter January night in the far corner of South Carolina, the road was hopeful and invigorating. Only in Georgia did I begin to doze, off and on until the blast of the bus horn woke me up to the white lights of downtown Atlanta.

Through frosty windows, I caught a fleeting view of the city as we careened down MLK Drive. In the deep winter night, Atlanta felt postapocalyptic—like a silent black-and-white movie without any actors. Streetlights sapped color from the trees and houses, and the office buildings resembled shiny new toys with dead batteries. Construction cranes lay like crosswords on the skyline, plastic sheeting whipped in the wind, and each passing scene was framed by another concrete overpass.

It was nearly 3:00 a.m. when the bus engine stopped with a delayed sigh. The door swung open and I heaved my pack down onto the fluorescent-lit platform; then I turned and thanked Frazier. He waved his hand like it was no trouble.

"It's all right, man. You have a good trip," he said. This was the end of the line for him, and for me, it was time to change buses. On a globe, I was barely an inch away from home—but after a full day's ride, I felt like I was finally covering some distance. I watched my fellow passengers spill out of the bus, exhausted and half-asleep, and heard them gasp as they sucked in the icy air of the city. Some swore out loud from the cold—I stood in shock, listening to my own chattering teeth. They called it *Hotlanta*, but my body felt paralyzed from the unforgiving freeze. Simply walking to the bus station door felt painful, my ungloved hands gone rigid with cold. The temperature was somewhere in the low teens—absurdly cold—as cold as I had imagined Antarctica to be.

I waddled indoors and was met with slow chaos and the warm blast of bad ventilation. CNN blared from the boxy overhead TVs, clashing with the country music and constant announcements of delayed and arriving buses. Rows of connected plastic chairs were bolted to the floor and tired travelers were encamped around industrial-strength table-and-chair combos, like the ones they have in prison. The immense room reeked of bad food.

Filthier still was the bus station bathroom, which smelled like the back of a pet store. Pools of urine made the floor yellow and slippery and the stench of pink hand soap and human waste hovered in the air, right about nose level. Tired, shirtless men splashed tepid water into their sweaty armpits, then wet their heads, blew their noses, and popped greasy whiteheads onto the mirrors. The tiled room got so crowded, some of the guys gave up waiting for the urinal and just whizzed across the walls. Two of the three stalls were missing doors, and some unseemly person had unfurled an entire industrial-size roll of toilet paper on the floor, leaving a soggy mess of pee-stained papier-mâché that showed a parade of combat boots marching to and from the toilet.

All I wanted was to change my clothes—to put on something a little looser and fresher for the next full day ahead—but that was not a simple task. I held my pack in the air, then stepped out of my hiking boots and balanced delicately on the tops of the leather toes, attempting to dress. Changing one's socks and underwear while deadlifting a pack in a private stall, trying not to breathe in the smell, and holding the door shut because the lock is busted and others are pushing their way in—well, it's not easy. Afterward, still breathing through my mouth, I washed my face and brushed my teeth in the sink, then finally added a fresh coat of deodorant.

The life and lights of Atlanta's 4:00 a.m. bus station were a welcome change to the dark and silent hours I had spent aboard Greyhound. I circled the immense rectangle room, absorbing the moment—a bus was boarding for Fort Leonard Wood with some sixty troops lined against a wall like camouflaged zombies. Sleepy passengers snored while standing up, wrapping blankets around their heads and ignoring the inescapable TV voices. Those of us who were still awake sought out one another's company, reaching anyone and everyone human. As I stood half-alert in the middle of the station, a US Army Ranger walked up to me and asked me where I was headed.

"South," I told him. The man was short, at least a foot shorter than me, with olive skin and cropped black hair. He wore three different jackets, one on top of the other, so that he looked even more muscular than he was. He hated the cold, he said, then pointed out how we looked exactly alike, even though we looked nothing alike.

"Both of us are wandering around this station, and both of us have canvas backpacks!"

"Yeah, that's true," I agreed. He had come all the way from Indiana, he said, but found the people on the bus too antisocial. Nobody wanted to talk to him. Did I think he was Latino? Because he wasn't Mexican or anything like that. Lots of people made that mistake, he confided, but he was definitely not Latino—he was Corsican. Did I know where Corsica was?

Well, actually—I replied in French—I had once walked around the entire island of Corsica—back in my early twenties. When I told the Corsican that I had spent a week in his hometown of Bonifacio, his face lit up like a happy elf.

Sergeant Major Antia was a born-and-bred Corsican but an immigrant to America, a US Army Ranger, and a member of the French Foreign Legion. He had just finished a long combat contract in Africa and then gone back to the Midwest for Christmas. In small-town Indiana his wife greeted him at the door with a new man living in his house and the cheerful holiday news that she had just filed for divorce and wanted full custody of his daughter. As he spoke the words, the sergeant began to choke. His eyes turned wet.

"She's only three," he said, still speaking French, then swallowed hard and blinked tears from his shiny black eyes. The man was suffering, and so I merely listened. I had an hour until my bus left, and this guy was far more interesting than anything playing on CNN.

Realizing that his tearful breakdown had not scared me away, Major Antia opened up some more, hinting at the daily dance with death that was his job. He offered quick and stunning tales of dodging gunfire in foreign streets and the antics of his criminal comrades in the Legion— mercenaries who killed people for a living. He wasn't trying to shock me—he just needed to tell me.

"I've only ever killed bad people," he said, then followed that with "but who can ever really say who is bad?" The sergeant paused his confession and asked me about my own adventures.

"I've never killed anyone," I began, though I had a few stories of my own. I recounted my time back in Corsica, walking on the beach and in the mountains, remembering the beautiful smell of the *maquis*. We stood facing one another, the sergeant and I, heavy backpacks on both of our shoulders—no longer awkward strangers but rather, a strange pair, oddly connected by the faraway village of Bonifacio with its tan stucco walls and sun-baked houses clinging to cliffs above the clear blue Mediterranean. I had been there—I knew this man's home and spoke his language. To travel much is to know a little bit about everyone's home.

The station's anonymous atmosphere offered us a rushed intimacy—at 4:00 a.m., the constant tide of buses could drop two people side by side with the promise that they would most likely never meet again. In just a quarter of an hour, this legionnaire had shared some of the most painful moments of his life with me. He had confessed his failures and fears and exposed his most emotional wounds without fear of judgment, because in the underworld of Greyhound, our names carried no permanent meaning. When his bus was announced, the Corsican shook my hand firmly, then leaned in and thumped his arm around my back.

"*Au revoir*," I said, though I was confident I would never see him again.

"Good luck out there." The sergeant smiled and then disappeared out the door, and an hour later, I left for Alabama.

8 | ETHEL, DORIS, AND MABEL

Do you want croutons?" I asked, touching the soft cotton lace that covered Ethel's frail, bony shoulder. Like lace, white wisps of hair covered her balding head and she stared through me, expressionless. Ethel never wanted croutons, but I had to ask. My boss was watching.

I knew what Ethel wanted: a heaping pile of corn relish in a bowl, with a spoonful of applesauce on the side. It was the same "salad" I made for her every day of the week, and though it seemed repulsive, I loved that she only trusted me to make it for her.

Sweet breakable Ethel had no words left—her voice was like a high-pitched whisper that evaporated with every vowel. Nor could she stand on her own, so that after limping with me to the salad bar, I had to carry her back, my left arm wrapped around her fragile waist and my right hand balancing her white porcelain salad bowl. Despite my nametag, Ethel never really knew my name. I was the young man in the black apron and shiny black shoes who listened patiently to her whistling words.

But Doris knew my name, and she said it after every sentence she spoke. After dinner, she liked six sugar cubes in her cup *before* you poured the coffee in, then she checked to make sure it was decaf.

"It's decaf, I promise," I said every time. "I made it myself."

"It tastes like regular coffee to me, Andrew," she argued, but then she kept sipping and flashing a hidden smile behind her cup. According to the staff nurse, Doris hadn't tasted normal coffee in over fifteen years.

No matter that the residents of Cardinal Retirement Village were all over eighty and I had only just turned fourteen—these creaky old widows were my friends. I laughed more with them than anyone I knew at my high school—the kids there were only preoccupied with making out in the cafeteria, on the steps of the library, backstage in the auditorium, in the chemistry lab, or behind the bleachers at the gym. I'm fairly certain I was the only kid in the tenth grade who didn't catch mono. Even in high school I was still the faggot, and in case I ever forgot, the older classmen would stop me in the hall and shout it, sending an echo through the school.

"Are you a fag?" they asked, repeating it louder and louder. I tried explaining to them that no, I was not that way—it's just that my girl-friend did not go to our school. I didn't count it as a lie, because eighty-seven-year-old Mabel in fact did not go to our school. She sat alone in the corner of the dining room at the retirement home, painted with elaborate eye shadow and rouge, dressed in lavender silks and high heels with a gold earring clipped to each ear. Long necklaces hung from around her wattled neck—fantastic costume jewelry from the 1930s. Every time she held my hand, I felt the coldness of gold and silver rings on her thin, translucent fingers. Mabel liked to hold my hand, and she kept holding it for as long as it took me to dig out an extra-large scoop of vanilla ice cream from the five-gallon tub on my dessert cart.

"Is Mabel your girlfriend?" Doris asked me more than once.

"She's my friend," I replied. "And she's a girl, so yeah!"

"I see how she holds your hand, and you give her more ice cream than anybody else!"

"Mabel really likes ice cream," I said, and from that point forward, according to the geriatric gossip girls, I was Mabel's boyfriend. Aside from our brief hand-holding at dessert time, our relationship remained chaste, though in the end, our love was short-lived. It turned out that Cardinal Retirement Village was violating child labor laws by employing me—and so I was let go from my $3.25-an-hour job. On my last day, I wheeled the dessert cart over to Mabel's table and gave her two scoops of ice cream. She smiled at me, but she had sparkly tears in her eyes. She squeezed my hand one last time, then pulled it beneath the table and wrapped my fingers around an envelope.

I waited until I got home before opening the lilac-colored thank-you card, filled with long and looping script. Mabel thanked me for taking such good care of her and wished for me to go far in life. Inside the card was a velvety, wrinkle-free fifty-dollar bill—my very first tip.

Every week, I checked to make sure the money was still in my used cigar box—I would stare at Ulysses S. Grant with his bushy beard and beady eyes, then carefully turn the bill on my fingertips to see the Capitol sprawled across the back. For months, I was in awe of this money and what it could do for me. Then I spent it.

On a cold and snowy February morning, my mother drove me to the Hancock County Courthouse, where I handed over my signed application with two smiley school pictures, my pale-green birth certificate from Texas, and Mabel's money. Fifty dollars was the exact cost for a United States passport, and six weeks later, the small blue booklet arrived in my mailbox. I flipped through the empty pages of this unwritten book, as if it were a master key to the rest of my life. Now I was free—I could go anywhere in the world.

It took some time, but within a year I had left Ohio, thrilled to be four thousand miles away from a school and town that hurt me so much. I was happy now, so far away, going to a new school in a new country. I had escaped my life for a time, though I never forgot my home. I even sent postcards to Ethel, Doris, and Mabel, licking the stamps before pressing them onto the envelope and underlining my new address: FRANCE.

9 | DIXIE

Day 2

I woke up with the morning sunburst outside Columbus, Georgia. A red-gold flash flickered through the windows of the moving bus, warming my face with moments of light. It was the second of January, my second day on the gray road—a racing strip of stone between the bare ash trees all around. As the bald sky took shape, the sun lit up the inside of the bus, revealing a dozen huddled bodies jostling in sync.

We crossed the Chattahoochee River—flooded, brown, and flowing fast—where Georgia ends and Alabama begins. The top corner of the welcome sign glinted as we rushed past, and I counted out the states on my fingers—Alabama made six. I wanted to jump from my seat and shout "Alabama!" with hands raised in victory, then cue a Dixieland jug band to strike up a perky ragtime overture, welcoming us all to the Deep South. But I did not cheer—not like I used to on family vacations every time we crossed a state border. Today, everybody else was asleep. The only sound came from the tires rolling on the asphalt interstate, and so I laid my head against the window and watched the fleeting scenery.

Alabama is beautiful—an exotic country where mint-green moss drapes every scene like stage curtains of flowing chiffon. Toothpick trees poked up from rippled swamps and hawks circled overhead. Chocolate milk rivers curved through the sun-bleached grass of winter. The khaki landscape reminded me of parts of Africa. This was a foreign place for me—a land of whitewashed churches and unfenced lawns that spread a vast green blanket around every house. Our bus passed the Winn-Dixie, drove down Hank Williams Drive, and then stopped at a traffic light right outside the First White House of the Confederacy. By some kind of cinematic coincidence, our bus paused just long enough for us to witness a dutiful employee raising the rebel colors up the flagpole. We got a fifteen-minute stop in Montgomery, where I stretched my legs and left my phone charging under the watchful care of some gamer wearing a coffee-stained wifebeater. Then I sprinted across the four-lane highway to grab breakfast.

Like any other American, I love McDonald's but I kind of hate it, too. As a child, McDonald's was a rare treat that meant road trips and summer vacation. I remember when my own father leaned out the driver's seat window and over-annunciated the lunch orders for nine children. Certain hamburgers were allowed to have pickles or onions or mustard, others better not, or else there would be no peace in the family van. In high school, McDonald's was fast fuel for my big teenage body. After two hundred laps in the pool, I could devour a Big Mac in less than a minute. But then I got older and stopped loving it because fifteen minutes after swallowing the stuff, I wanted to kill myself.

No matter—I still ate it; drifting through a world of airports and highway rest stops, the special McDonald's *parfum* of burgers, buns, and french fries was a universal travel balm broadcasting familiar comforts to my nose. Whether in Paris, Moscow, or Wellington, a traveler can depend on a static McDonald's experience—a predictable menu and clean bathrooms, approved and civilized.

In America, you cannot avoid McDonald's because they've planned it that way. Thus I found myself crammed against the red counter of an Alabama McDonald's with a platoon of hungry military—one young marine with a freshly buzzed head and a hard-boiled drawl complained to his comrades: "I just can't believe we're gonna spend two whole days on a bus!" Another older soldier laughed, then punched him hard, right between the shoulder blades.

"*Ow!*" The kid doubled over the counter, wincing. An older soldier yelled at him, "Suck it up, man—you're a fucking marine!"

Most of these guys were tested veterans, just back from Iraq with its car bombs and flying grenades. Now they were moaning about a two-day bus ride but laughing and joking, too, relieved by the low stress of American life. Staring at the backlit menu of sausage and egg sandwiches, I questioned my own ability to cope with the distance ahead. I had only been riding for twenty-four hours, and I wasn't just crossing the state or the country—I was crossing the world. I had barely slept on the bus the night before. My face was stubbly, my hair oily, my legs felt numb, my back was killing me—and this was only day 2. *Suck it up, man.*

I downed my warmish sack of morning McDonald's as we motored out of Montgomery and down I-65. Despite the legacy of freedom riders and bus boycotts, the passengers underwent a kind of voluntary segregation. I had been the first to board, but not one of the African American travelers sat next to me. I was still *the* white guy riding alone in the middle of the bus, until one young rider climbed on, scanned up and down the aisle with his eyes, and then sat down next to me.

He was a soft-spoken, skinny sixteen-year-old with sandy blond bangs that fell down his face, hiding his vacant cheeks and a freckled pink nose. I introduced myself with a handshake and he answered back with a cell phone picture of a cherry red 1969 Pontiac Firebird. "Thas m'car," he said, with a kind of cocky pride. I nodded with approval and that got him going with his story.

"I was born in Mississippi," he said. "I'm one-half Cherokee Indian and the other half German," he explained. His dark narrow eyes and golden hair looked about right. His parents split when he was four. "I grew up playing out in the woods, shootin' stuff and workin' on cars. I was smokin' and swearin', and so when I was thirteen, my mamma kicked me out of the house," he continued.

"Every Christmas I take the Greyhound up north to be with my dad. He tells me if I want, I can come up and live with him in Pittsburgh. I don't wanna leave the South," said Cole.

"Yeah," I agreed. "It's nice down here. Warm, too."

His Mississippi twang was so thick that I began to think he was putting me on, but his story was sincere and spun on and on like some redneck docudrama. He liked to fish, and he offered me detailed instructions on how to catch a giant catfish in a muddy pond. "Hell, I just caught a fifteen-pounder two weeks ago!" he boasted. He had been driving cars since he was twelve, and every weekend, around midnight, he drag raced his Firebird on barren country roads. "Oh, the police never nab us," he said. "Their cars are too slow." I was riding the bus next to a bona fide good old boy, straight out of the *Dukes of Hazzard*, and the longer I listened, the taller his tales grew.

"Here's my girlfriend," he said, flipping to a cell phone picture of a bleach-blonde Alabama babe whose balloon-shaped breasts looked so heavy, I was certain they would explode through her pink T-shirt and tumble right off the screen.

"She's goin' to college," Cole said, boasting that she was two years older than he, though it was hard for me to feign interest in his so-called girlfriend. I wondered if the woman in the picture even knew that some scrawny teenager was showing her photo to strangers on the bus.

"So where do you want to travel to?" I asked him out of the blue.

"Berlin," Cole shot back at me, staring into my eyes. "I want to see the new Holocaust Memorial." Was he serious, or was he being sarcastic? Did he really dream of paying his respects to the victims of hatred and intolerance, or was Cole one of these neo-Nazi youth with a highlighted copy of *The Turner Diaries* in his backpack?

"Where you headed, sir?" Cole asked me politely.

"Texas—to visit my folks," I said, which was technically true. Something about the closed confines of a bus breeds a strange intimacy where people wear their souls on their sleeves. Ultimately, it all comes down to "Why are you on the bus?" Answer that single question and you've tapped into a person's existential reasoning: *where are you from, where are you going, why are you taking the bus?* Young Cole was traveling back from a distant piece of his broken home.

"Why you riding the bus?" he asked. "You don't like to fly?"

"Oh, I don't mind flying. I just wanted to take the bus this time," I said. For a half mile or so, we both sat silently, lurching along on the potholed highway.

"You know what?" I broke it to him. "I'm actually going all the way to Antarctica—to the very bottom of the world." I chuckled a little. "And I'm taking the bus the whole way!" It was the first time I had told a fellow passenger about my true mission. For months I had been telling friends and family about my upcoming journey, but now I was telling strangers. Cole just stared at me blankly, unimpressed, and I kept talking, like a nervous lunatic.

"See, I'm taking buses the whole way. I'm just going to keep riding all the way to the end of the world," I said with gusto, shaping an imaginary globe with my hand and pointing to the invisible white swirl of Antarctica down below.

"Yeah?" Cole mumbled incredulously, and I nodded back at him like a busy cartoon chipmunk. He grew silent, then turned and stared straight ahead, no longer speaking or moving. Only when the bus turned off the highway and slowed at an intersection did he move. The second the light turned red, Cole popped up from his seat, snatched his backpack from the shelf overhead, and leapt forward five rows.

That hurt. I was more than twice his age, but getting rejected felt the same as it did back in high school. I turned toward the window and stared at my tired reflection. My eyes were red and bleary, my face all grizzled like a hobo with a shine of grease on my forehead. Two days on Greyhound and I already looked like a drug-addled maniac. It would only get worse. Pretty soon I would look like one of *them*—bus people.

Bus people are drifters, alcoholics, unwashed, homeless, meth addicts, emotionally unstable, fugitives, escaped convicts, and the criminally insane. At best, riders of Greyhound have a dubious reputation—at worst, they're just crazy. Yet two days on the bus had shown me the truth—that people who ride Greyhound represent the disenfranchised members of America's car culture. In a country where cars are king, anybody without a driver's license is an outsider. That means the homeless, but also the physically and mentally handicapped, the blind, the very young, the impoverished, the military, and everyone who is terrified of airplanes, which is a much larger group than one might imagine.

Now I was a bus person, feared by Cole in his faraway seat. No matter my college degrees and decades of going to church, my volunteer service and annual filings with the IRS—all he knew was that I was the weird scruffy guy talking about riding the bus to the bottom of the world. Given my disheveled state, I would probably never sit next to me either, except that I *like* crazy people—some of my best friends are crazy.

When a tight-lipped security guard waved an electronic wand over each of us, I wondered who on my next bus was actually crazy.

I sized up the others in line: teenagers in hoodies waddling like ducks with droopy pants on the verge of collapse, a few smelly homeless types with ZZ Top beards, and a dozen freshly shorn soldiers who looked like delinquent newborns. I was surrounded by bus people and it scared me a little. Anyone who reads the news knows just how dangerous riding Greyhound can be. A year and a half before my own trip, way up in Manitoba, a crazy man stabbed his twenty-two-year-old seatmate before decapitating him with a hunting knife and then devouring some of the victim's flesh. Two months later, a twenty-year-old Japanese exchange student was stabbed in the chest while riding Greyhound in Ontario—he survived, miraculously. In 2007 six teenagers forced a Greyhound bus to stop near the Alberta–Saskatchewan border before beating up the bus driver in the street. The same year in California, a man attacked his bus driver, rolling the bus off the road and killing two passengers. Less than a month after the September 11 attacks, a mentally disturbed passenger in Tennessee got up from his seat, slashed the bus driver's throat with a box cutter, then crashed the bus, killing himself and five other passengers. A quick scan of the headlines shows that Greyhound keeps a regular schedule of assault, hijacking, and murder, not to mention that a startling number of serious criminals are apprehended aboard Greyhound buses every year. Knowing that Greyhound is the public transportation equivalent of a getaway car, I couldn't help but assess my fellow passengers to guess which of them was a psychotic killer.

We stopped for ten minutes in Biloxi, where half the bus emptied off to report for duty at Keesler Air Force Base. As they spilled out with their green canvas bags, a single airman boarded with a violin case, followed by a fresh batch of military, all of them surrounded by weeping women. A young mother held a baby on her hip with one arm, clutching her husband with the other. Her face glowed red from her endless crying, her eyes squinting in pain. Then her husband let go and boarded the bus, hiding his face in his hands before hitting his seat. The young woman rushed over, reached as high as she could, and slapped her tiny hand repeatedly against the pane of the bus window. Then the dutiful soldier reached out his own hand, clicking the glass with his gold wedding ring. He gulped with pain, refusing to cry, while his wife sobbed alone in the parking lot. The bus backed away slowly, and I watched as she shook with sadness, clutching her tiny baby over one shoulder.

Now the bus was silent. We drove onward, past the flat white sand beaches of the Gulf Coast, past the forest of fluttering confederate flags at the Jefferson Davis plantation in Beauvoir, and past the countless concrete slabs in Gulfport, the ghostly foundations of houses blown away by Hurricane Katrina.

The low land melted away into brown water. Puddles turned into ponds and shoreless lakes, dead trees bleached white in the sun poked up from the bayou, and then Louisiana welcomed me in French. Our bus began the long, elevated journey across the strange and watery world of Lake Pontchartrain. This was the longest bridge in America— twenty-four miles from end to end. I counted the concrete pilings like the ticking seconds on a clock. Minute after minute, we zoomed down the single strip of interstate, a fragile thread strung across a silver mirror of water. For twenty minutes, we were out at sea, with no land to be seen on either side, and then, there was New Orleans, like the Emerald City of Oz, rising up from the swamps. In the faded light of evening, the shadowy skyscrapers felt huge and hopeful. Our sleek silver Greyhound bus slowed and snaked with the traffic, up and around the tangled pretzel of overpasses, before rolling down a single-lane ramp and dumping us into the dark, blind streets below.

10 LIGHT BLUE

"Maybe in America sixteen-year-old kids can *voyager partout sans adulte*, but in France, well-raised children *ne font pas ça.*"

My French host parents agreed that I could take the bus to London, as long as I brought a friend. And so I asked Joe, a fellow American exchange student living in a nearby town. He was seventeen, a senior, and he looked good in a Speedo. I knew this because the year prior, my high school swim team in Ohio had lost against his swim team in Michigan, and I had spent more time watching their team than cheering for my own.

Checking into my first hotel room without any grown-ups felt so sophisticated. I led Joe up five flights of creaky spiral steps, then fiddled with the bulky iron key to open the oak door covered in a century of paint. The room smelled like moldy flowers and hairspray, and the afternoon sunlight revealed a snowstorm of swirling dust particles. Joe and I walked up to the French windows overlooking Rue de Rivoli, busy with mopeds and black taxis, then we turned around and confronted the iron-framed double bed that looked like a prop from a stage play.

"They didn't have two beds," I explained, but Joe only shrugged and tossed his bag onto the chenille bedspread and suggested we go find dinner. I had never been on a date before, but we spent Saturday night walking up and down the Right Bank, discussing all the things we liked versus all the things we did not like. Every time Joe liked something I liked—swimming, Rodin, the Fourth of July, or Perrier with raspberry syrup—I was glad and felt like I had finally made a true friend. But when he disagreed with my dislikes—backstroke, the German language, and Esprit shirts—then I felt inferior and sad.

Back at the hotel, I tried not to look when Joe unbuckled his belt and undressed before crawling into bed (how was he already tan in April?). I felt embarrassed by my tighty-whities and my soft and sunken chest, and I was terrified at the prospect of sharing a bed with someone who was neither my brother nor any other kind of family relation.

Joe and I talked a bit more in the darkness, but my voice felt as stiff as my body. All the fears of my life had balled up into the greatest fear of that night—touching Joe, accidentally or otherwise. I knew that if I touched Joe, then everyone who had ever screamed "faggot" would be right. Except that I was a fag—I knew that. I knew that I liked having Joe next to me. I could feel his warmth and hear his slow breathing in the dark. Yet in that one-foot-wide chasm of empty bed between us, there was a line I knew I could never cross. If I did, I would break the trust of my parents and God, who would punish me forever. My life would take a left turn down the inevitable path of evil, public failure, and shattered dreams. No, nothing would happen in Paris that night. I was a good Mormon, and Joe was a good Catholic, and we both remained that way for many years to come.

My greatest sin that weekend was breaking the Sabbath, or at least bending it. Up until that morning, I had never spent a dime on Sunday, or done anything else that would cause a soul to labor on the Sabbath. But now it was 7:00 a.m. at Porte de la Chapelle and I was hungry. I had forgotten to buy food the night before, and though the bus would surely stop en route to London, I could not let myself spend money on Sunday. I thought about asking Joe to run into one of the bakeries and buy me a bag of croissants, but then I would be forcing him to break the Sabbath.

So I prayed and told God that I was sorry for traveling on this Sabbath Day. I promised him that I would not break any more commandments, and that I would be happy to fast that Sunday if that is what he wanted. My prayer was interrupted by the loud bang of a rolling metal door, and I looked up at the épicerie across the street. A bearded man with a long black coat was opening his shop for the day. His wide-brimmed hat reminded me of the Amish back in Ohio, and over the door hung a blue-and-white sign with large Hebrew letters. So the man was Jewish, and this was a Jewish store! It was a miracle and I dashed across the street, leaving Joe at the bus, which had already begun boarding.

"*Allez-y*," said the Orthodox grocer, letting me in and pointing at the shelves. "Everything is kosher." I grabbed a bottle of grape juice, a few red apples, and some cheese and crackers, then paid the man with the francs in my pocket. Yes, I was handling money on Sunday, but technically, it was not *his* Sabbath. And if I wasn't forcing the shopkeeper to break his Sabbath, then I wasn't breaking my Sabbath either, right?

Such was my logic as I ran back to the bus and showed the driver my ticket. Although I had missed church that morning and was clearly violating the spirit of the law, I had followed the letter of the law, right? God was on my side—I belonged to his only true church and he had provided me with a Jewish grocer on a Sunday morning—yet I still felt God judging me every minute of the day and night, waiting for me to slip up. As the bus sailed through the budding fields of springtime Picardie, I considered the greatness of God compared to all the small print of his laws. An hour later, I was biting into my very first matzo while crossing the English Channel on a ferry.

After my year in France, Ohio seemed even duller and bleaker than when I had left. The land was too flat, my school seemed too bland, and now I was too cool. The bullies I had once feared seemed pitiful and oafish now, and if any of them shouted something derisive in the hall, I simply shouted back, "*Va te faire foutre, espèce de connard.*" It didn't sound like swearing when I said it in French.

Knowing another language made me feel powerful, and the travels I'd made granted me a newfound confidence in my abilities as a functioning human. There was not a single teenager in Findlay, Ohio, who had ridden the bus across an international border or skied in the French Alps or marched in a strike at his school. None of them had been to the places in the pages of *National Geographic*, but I had.

The Louvre, the beaches of Normandy, the fairy-tale towns of Alsace, and the prehistoric Caves of Lascaux—my family grew tired of me stabbing a page in the magazine with my finger and declaring, "I've been there!" Out of all my cardboard boxes packed with *National Geographics*, my favorite issue was July 1989, *France Celebrates Its Bicentennial!* Not only was the entire issue dedicated to my favorite country, France, but two of those particular pages contained blatant images of explicit, nonsexual male nudity. After so many decades of gratuitous African bosoms and Amazonian bottoms, *National Geographic* had published something just for me. I kept that issue separate from the rest, hidden away in my closet, which seemed rather empty all of a sudden.

"Where are all my *National Geographics*?" I asked my mom.

"Oh!" she remembered. "I donated them to the school library. You're off to college next year, so I thought maybe the school could use them."

"But they're MINE," I said, feeling dizzy with anger. "Grandpa gave them to me. You don't have the right to just give my things away!" Passionate tears followed. I felt betrayed by my own mother and felt that the only thing I had ever really loved had been stolen away and handed over to uncultured kids who would cut it up for thoughtless collages and school projects that would never earn above a C+. I felt as if my own mother had sent my favorite pet to the pound.

"Oh, I'm sorry, Andrew," my mother offered. "If I had known you still wanted them—they were just piled up in the closet and you were gone, so I cleaned them out."

The next day I stormed into the school librarian's office like a one-man SWAT team. The gray-haired lady in spectacles looked up at me with alarm, but before she could speak, I was pacing the back shelves of her office and panting crazily, "Mine! Mine!" There sat my prized collection, stacked into my mother's cardboard boxes and labeled with her neat handwriting on the side.

"Those were just donated—we haven't had time to get them all on the shelves yet," said the librarian, but I was already down on my knees, counting through the collection one issue at a time.

"They've just been un-donated," I said, before panicking a little. "You're missing everything after 1987!"

"Already on the shelves." She nodded back toward the library, eager to get me out her office. I ran to the periodicals, where about fifty issues of my own collection were now in circulation. Then I started yanking yellow magazines off the shelf, twelve at a time. At a nearby table, a bored freshman was flipping through a single back issue, and I pulled the magazine right out of his hands.

"This is mine," I explained and walked away. For the next week, I rode the school bus, carting home box after box of *National Geographic* magazines, which I restacked like gold bricks in my closet.

A year later, I left home for good. With my permission, my mother re-donated my entire collection to the same library—everything except the July 1989 issue. That one she mailed to me at college, where I kept it out in the open, on my shelf, next to a window that faced the snowy peaks of the Wasatch Range.

"It's here," I told my sister over the phone.

"Come over at five!" she said. "I'll tell the others. Congratulations, Drew." I thanked her and hung up, then hid the letter under my pillow and locked the door to my college dorm.

Twenty minutes later I was hiking alone in the mountains, knee-deep in purple larkspur, white columbine, and red Indian paintbrush. Over a hundred years before, my ancestors had walked these same flowered foothills. Most had come from Scotland and Wales—Mormon pioneers who had given up everything to enter the great American wilderness plains. They had come to build Zion, a city for the saints, far from the hatred and violence they had suffered back east. Now Zion had a ten-lane highway, where drivers gauged their location by the nearest temple spire, and where giant billboards advertised cheap suits and family-friendly video stores.

Seven generations later, it was my turn to build Zion—to go out in the world and grow the Church of Jesus Christ of Latter-day Saints one convert at a time. I was almost nineteen, my wisdom teeth were gone, and I had been found worthy. I obeyed the commandments, I paid my tithing, and I attended all my church meetings. I prayed and fasted, too, and I taught Sunday school every week.

"Brother Evans, have you ever engaged in any homosexual activity?" the bishop had asked me in a private interview in the basement of my dorm. Every pause was filled with the rumble of the washing machine outside his makeshift office.

"No," I said and looked him straight in the eye, with hands to my side and both feet on the ground. I had been practicing my answer for months, if not years. It was an uncomfortable question—the bishop was uncomfortable asking it—but I was telling him the truth. You could not be a missionary if you were gay, and though my heart knew that I was very gay, my head knew that I had to show a clean slate.

"Have you ever committed any kind of immorality at all? If you have, now is the time to confess." The bishop stared into my eyes once more.

I shook my head and repeated, "No." All those talks about not kissing with the tongue and keeping girls out of our rooms never made sense to me, but I heard stories about guys who had crossed the line. They were racked with guilt and had to go home in disgrace. Not me. I was good—I had answered all the questions honestly and correctly, and then answered all the same questions again for my stake president. I was worthy, and they signed my application for missionary service.

Three weeks had passed before the letter arrived, and now there it was, locked away in my room with my future inside. I had three more hours to wait, so I hiked higher into the mountains, stopping now and again to gaze across Utah Valley, gauzy in the afternoon haze. Where in the world would I go? God could send me anywhere—Argentina, Cameroon, Japan, or France. The family had placed bets—most guessed I would be sent to France or Belgium because I already spoke French. But that's not the way the Lord works, I reminded them. He knew the right place for me, and that could be anywhere on Earth.

I knew all the countries in the world—and their capitals—and I wanted to go somewhere really strange. I desired the truly exotic: Tahiti or Thailand, the Greek Isles or Ghana. I kneeled on the mountain and prayed once more—prayed that I would get sent to the right place for me, prayed that I would have a cool mission president without too many rules and that none of my companions would be too attractive. Then I walked back down the mountain, carefully picked up the sacred white letter, and pedaled over to my sister's house on the west side of Provo.

"Open it! Open it!" my brother shouted, but I took my time, holding the large white envelope with my fingertips before carefully ripping the top flap. Some of my family surrounded me on the couch, while the rest were back in Ohio, crammed around the speakerphone, hushing one another in order to hear me better.

"Dear Elder Evans," I read slowly. "You are hereby called to serve as a missionary of the Church of Jesus Christ of Latter-day Saints . . ." My mother began to cry on the phone.

"You are assigned to labor in the Ukraine Donetsk Mission," I read aloud, and the room erupted into loud cheers. I felt arms around me, and then an onslaught of high fives and big hugs. For one staggering moment, I was smothered with the love of an amazing family.

"What, where?" said my older brother. "That's fantastic!" said my dad. "Oh, how wonderful," said my mother. "Where is that, Drew?" my sister asked.

"Ukraine," I said. "It's next to Russia—it used to be part of the Soviet Union." The family all cheered once more, and then my mother hushed them once more and asked me to read the entire letter.

I continued, "It is anticipated that you will serve for a period of twenty-four months. . . . You will prepare to teach the gospel in the Russian language."

"Awesome!" said another brother. "So cool," said my dad, and the whole family cheered once more. I would be learning Russian, and for the next two years, I would live in the far eastern fringe of Ukraine.

"Tell us where it is on the map!" my mother said over the phone. I heard them flipping through the immense pages of my National Geographic atlas, trying to find Ukraine.

"It's a new country," I said. I had read all about the breakup of the Soviet Union in *National Geographic* and had already memorized the fifteen new countries and their capitals.

"But it's not on the world map!" said my mother—and she was right. Ukraine was not on their map of the world, and that made me happy. God was sending me to a place that was not yet on the map—a true *terra incognita*.

✹

Summer in Ukraine is a strip of sunflowers beneath a cyan sky. It's digging potatoes in the black earth and sipping cold *kvas* from a peddler's reusable glass. It's the trolleybus smells of body odor, garlic, and unfiltered tobacco. The hot water disappears, so I washed my shirts in a pail of water boiled on the stove. After hours of scrubbing and rinsing, I hung them in a row on the balcony, like a ghostly legion of missionaries flapping in the wind.

Summer meant turning so tan that when I stood naked in front of the mirror, it still looked like I was wearing a white shirt. It meant warm nights beneath a single sheet, shifting left to right, sleepless under the dark ceiling. Summer meant my twenty-first birthday was coming soon, and after that, I would be leaving the starkness of Ukraine and going back to America, where my life was laid out like a blueprint—temple marriage to a good wife, a steady parade of obedient children, a secure corporate job to pay for the four-bedroom house and orthodontist and viola lessons and dance class, and every spare hour spent in glad service to the church.

I had always known this—I had always accepted it—but now that I was just a few months away from the rest of my life, I was panicked. I had always done everything the church had ever asked of me—I was an Eagle Scout, I had been through the temple, and I had read the Book of Mormon over twenty times in English, and five times in Russian. But what the church wanted next, that I marry a woman and make babies— that was impossible.

My anxiety swelled like the heat outside, and for a few weeks I stopped sleeping altogether. Each night, after my companion fell asleep in his bed, I slipped into the other room and read books. Some nights it was the Bible, others it was Chekhov or Akhmatova, lifted from the shelves of the apartment we rented. I read until I could no longer read, and I prayed until I could fall back to sleep.

One night, Elder Shypovnik walked into the room with a pair of shorts pulled halfway over his garments, rubbing his eyes in the light.

"What is it?" he whispered in Russian. Shypovnik was a recent convert from Kiev and he spoke no English. "Come back to bed," he urged, but I only stared at the peeling pink wallpaper. If I looked him in the eye, I might cry—and if I cried, I would tell him—and if I told him, then I could never go back to the way things were before.

"You've been up every night. Something is going on, and you need to tell me what it is." Shypovnik was several years older than me, but he was also a newbie—new to the mission and new to the church.

"I just can't tell you," I said. It seemed unfair to burden him with my biggest secret. Besides, Shypovnik was straight—before he became a Mormon, he had been quite the active heterosexual.

I waited silently, staring blankly at my Ukrainian friend, hoping it would all just go away. There was no way out of this one, and when I realized that, a trembling tear spilled out one eye, then another. Elder Shypovnik place his hand on my shoulder—a kind touch.

"Just tell me," he whispered. The silence continued. We were two friends in a standoff, though I wanted him to win. I was so afraid of telling him the truth, but in the end I was more afraid of never telling anyone at all.

"I think I'm *light blue*," I spoke, using the Russian slang for "gay." For the first time in my life, I said the words out loud, and though my heart jumped inside me and I felt my face go red, there were no crashing cymbals or secret police barging through the door.

Elder Shypovnik sat silent across from me, his arms folded in his lap. This was not what he had expected, but his face seemed calm and his eyes clear.

"God knows how you feel," he said. "God understands what you are feeling, Elder Evans." It was such a simple idea, one that I had shared before, when church members came to me with their problems—that their son was in jail or they had no more food for their children—but now, this new convert was speaking those same words back to me. God knew that I was gay. Of course he did.

"Now. Come to sleep," said Elder Shypovnik, as if nothing had happened at all. He showed no fear of me and acted no differently than before. That I was gay remained our secret—he never told the other missionaries, and he never turned me in. He could have—most missionaries would have felt it their duty to report me to the mission president—but Elder Shypovnik worked next to me until the very last day of my mission, when we walked the August streets of Kharkov, stopping total strangers to let them know all about Jesus Christ and his universal understanding.

11 | GOING HOME

Day 2

> Ghosts in the wind, that blow through my life
> Follow me where I go
> I'll never be free from these chains inside
> Hidden deep down in my soul
>
> LUCINDA WILLIAMS, "Bus to Baton Rouge"

They were sad lyrics, but I listened to Lucinda Williams's "Bus to Baton Rouge" on repeat until the bright lights of Tiger Stadium lit up the view. My own bus to Baton Rouge had arrived.

"Excuse me—Andrew?" a girl said to me in the station. "Are you @Bus2Antarctica?" Spoken out loud, my Twitter handle sounded remarkably awkward.

"That's me," I admitted to the stranger before me, who was wrapped up inside a shiny purple LSU jacket.

She grinned and reached toward me to shake hands. Then she gushed, "Oh my gosh! What you are doing is so cool!"

I smiled back, flattered and self-conscious. I had been riding the bus nonstop for thirty hours. I worried that my breath stank, and as we chatted, I kept licking my teeth with my tongue, hoping there were no stray bits of turkey sub hanging around. Hundreds of bus passengers swarmed around us but Sarah only wanted to chat.

"I only started following you yesterday afternoon—I found you on the National Geographic website and I love all of your tweets and pictures. They're amazing!"

"Thank you," I offered, shocked that she had tracked me down by Twitter alone. The Internet makes us famous one person at a time, and here I was, the end of day 2 on my journey, with my fan club of one.

"I want to go to Antarctica, too!" she explained. "But I gotta finish college first. I'm not sure when or how, but *I will* go someday. What you're doing is just so inspiring."

"Thanks—that means a lot." The digital age may grant us the accelerated intimacy with an avatar, but nothing beats two humans speaking face to face. I was touched that she was reading what I was putting online, and that she had figured out my bus schedule and driven twenty miles to come see me.

We were strangers from two very different places, different genders, and nearly ten years apart in age, yet we had already shared a strange closeness—she had been reading my thoughts all day long, we shared a dream of a faraway place, and now we were sudden friends chatting in a bus station. We sat in the waiting room and talked about travel and food and Antarctica. She told me her dreams, and I shared mine, then she watched my bag while I dashed to the men's room.

"I got you a present!" she said, handing me two foil bags: spicy cajun corn nuts and Zapp's Crawtator crawfish-flavored chips. "You gotta have a taste of Louisiana—I hope you like hot stuff."

"I do. Thanks," I said and hugged Sarah good-bye. "Thanks for coming out to see me—I hope you make it to Antarctica someday."

"I will. One day," she said, wistful yet determined. "If you can do it, then I have hope I can, too." Like an old friend, I waved to the girl in the purple coat from the bus as we pulled out of the station. If I had felt any loneliness that day, it disappeared after Sarah's short visit. She reminded me that the names and comments on my phone were real people from around the world. In one day, another three hundred had joined me on Twitter, following every word that I sent them from the road. I felt honored and overwhelmed, too. Even online, I had stage fright.

The bus moved through the darkness, riding the bend back to I-10 and heading up across the Horace Wilkinson Bridge. I gazed out at the black void beneath—the Mississippi River at night, cutting through Baton Rouge and the whole of America. At the edge of the darkness stood the Louisiana state capitol, glowing like a tall, square lamp. I had crossed the Mississippi on so many family vacations, but this time felt different—I was on a bus and I'd come halfway across the country in just two days. I had crossed a real line on the map—a thick wet line that separates east from west.

Soon the bus was racing across the hollow highway over the Atchafalaya Basin. The rubber wheels echoed on the road as we rolled for mile after mile through the starlit swamp. I regretted not seeing America's biggest bayou by day, but it was equally beautiful at night. A full, clear moon shone upon a million white trees that poked up from the black water, and as I gazed out at the sunken forest, I considered how all my favorite maps had lied to me. There was no such land as Louisiana— there was nothing but water down here, and perhaps a hundred thousand alligators squirming in the mossy soup below. I saw their eyeshine in our headlights, like tiny golden stars blinking at me from the black.

"All the way to San Antonio!" Jessica told me when I asked her destination. My new seatmate was a perky girl with a bundle of braids who seemed to float in her own cloud of brassy perfume. I had never met a black cowgirl before, but Jessica sported purple boots, a white cowboy hat, and a suede jacket with dangling fringe. Delightfully Texan, she sounded like honey on a hot day. She was a sophomore at the University of Texas–San Antonio, "still undecided," and she had run off to New Orleans for New Year's.

"I rode a mechanical bull in the French Quarter. I was better than most of the boys, but I still got thrown. Flamin' Hot Cheetos?" she offered, tilting the extralarge bag of chips at me.

"Thanks," I said, grabbing a handful of squiggly corn curls powdered with fluorescent red dust.

"Zapp's Cajun Crawtator?" I offered back, and she cupped her hand politely while I spilled out a few of my chips.

"Where do you want to travel in the world?"

"Anywhere, really," she answered right away. "I've been to Mexico—
you know, Cancún for spring break—but I think I'd like to go to
Hawaii and maybe somewhere in the Caribbean." Jessica wanted all the
places in the vacation brochures. She wanted sunshine and umbrella
drinks and white sand beaches.

"I used to live in the Caribbean," I boasted. "On an island shorter
than this bridge we're on now."

"Really?" she said.

"Yep. It was wonderful—always sunny. Except for hurricane season."
A strip mall sign glowed with gigantic red letters: "Dan's Homemade
Boudin & Crackling!" Then we passed the Piggly Wiggly.

I dozed on and off to Lake Charles, where I caught the blur of
twinkling lights from the oil refineries we passed. Clouds of smoke and
steam glowed orange, and flames hovered over the tangle of pipes and
towers that stood like giant tiki torches. The Texas flag unfurled across
an oversize green road sign: "El Paso—875 miles." Oh, Texas. I felt that
surge of pride in my chest. I was born in Texas, which makes me a lot
more Texan than most. Crossing the Texas border felt like coming home.

And I was heading home—to my parents' home. Years ago, they
had moved back to Texas, into a lofty house with enough bedrooms to
accommodate the tide of children and grandchildren that flowed in and
out their front door. It took them five years to invite me back, and even
now, I was only welcomed alone, without any of my brothers or sisters
or nieces and nephews around. Even now, I always asked permission
before making the rare visit to Houston. Once you've been told never
to come home, it's kind of hard to go back.

Food and hotel chains lit the highway beyond Beaumont. From the
back of the bus, a lady shouted, "We're freezing—turn up the heat!"
Our driver stayed silent, but a few minutes later, engine-warm air wafted
up from the floor, cooking my feet in their boots while my head remained
chilled. I rubbed my eyes through the downtown lights of Houston. At
the station, I heaved my backpack upon my shoulders, then switched
off Sally the GPS and her blinking green light. I would pick up my

journey from this exact spot—I wanted digital proof that I had never skipped a step along the way.

The time was 2:00 a.m. and I was totally, completely, and utterly exhausted. I felt delirious, stumbling through late-night traffic, scanning the sidewalk for my dad. And there he was, across the street, leaning against the family van and reading a book in the dark. I felt like a child again, waiting outside school for my dad to pick me up, and when I came up to him, he hugged me tightly.

"You made it!" he said, pulling me against his chest. My dad's embrace felt wonderful, calm, and strong.

"Sorry I'm late," I apologized, though given the slow speed of Greyhound, I was amazed we had reached Houston at all. What took me three hours to fly took thirty-eight hours by bus. The real distance to Texas is two days and two nights. My dad drove us back home, across the empty freeways and into the sprinkler-system suburbs of Houston. I cracked the window and breathed in the warm Texas air. This is where winter ended. From now until the equator it would just be getting warmer. I sat shotgun, just like on family vacations when my father quizzed me on all the states, countries, and capitals of the world.

"I was in five states today," I told him, loopy with lack of sleep. "Georgia, Alabama, Mississippi, Louisiana, and Texas—nine hundred miles in a single day." I rambled deliriously, glad for an audience upon which to unload all that I'd seen and done in the last two days. I was drunk with fatigue and overstimulation.

In the kitchen, I pulled off my boots and my dad poured me a glass of lemonade. We chatted some more, whispering so as not wake the family that was asleep. All the bedrooms were taken, did I mind taking the couch? Not at all—after two days and two nights sitting upright on a bus, lying down felt simply remarkable. In the morning, I would get to see at least one brother and sister, and I was glad. I undressed on my back, then pulled the blanket up to my neck, stretching my body and blinking at the ceiling with bloodshot eyes. My heart was still pumping with excitement, my fingers fluttering with movement, wanting to tweet everything I felt—the joy of arrival and the peace of coming home.

Instead, I turned off my phone and held my palms against my closed eyes, trying desperately to quiet my mind from the racing memories of Greyhound. I breathed in and out, happy in the stillness of my parents' home—happy to be back. Maybe I was older now, and maybe I was on a business trip, but after so much effort and so many miles, I was back at home and sleeping on my parents' couch.

12 THE SHAPE
OF THE EARTH

Two years after my first missionary interview, I was back in that same shoebox of a room in the basement of my college dorm, listening to the cranky washing machine banging against the wall while my new bishop carefully explained to me how not to be a homosexual.

"You can start by lowering your voice." His voice got deeper. "And change the way you walk. Men walk tall and proud, head up, shoulders out." He puffed up his chest in demonstration. "You need a different haircut, too," he said. "That's part of the repentance process."

I wasn't sure from which sin I needed to repent, since I was still very much a virgin and I had the same missionary haircut I had when I departed Ukraine two weeks prior. Still, I believed that my bishop was inspired to guide me in my life. He had the gift of discernment and leadership, and I listened closely to his instructions.

"If you start acting like a real man, then you'll become a real man," he explained lightheartedly. "Don't you worry about a thing—I'm going to help you, and the Lord is going to help, and we're going to find you a wife . . . this semester, even! How does that sound?" It sounded like my greatest fear had just been given a deadline, and I regretted opening up my soul to this man who smelled like hair tonic and mothballs. I masked my dread with an embarrassed smile.

"Now don't go telling anybody else what you just told me," he continued with his Utah twang. "You are NOT a homosexual and nobody else will ever have to know about this. It will be our little secret, and once you're married, your wife will never ever have to know. Got it?"

The bishop was true to his word and set me up on a blind date with the oldest old maid in our ward, a twenty-three-year-old returned missionary from Alaska with a fondness for sewing quilts and wearing ankle-length skirts. We spent the evening discussing quilts before I went back to her apartment to un-euphemistically examine her quilt squares. The date ended at nine thirty with a brief handshake and a wave good-bye.

"You're home early," said my roommate. Ben was from Michigan and was snuggled up with his fiancé on our thrift store couch. "How was your date?" he wanted to know. At BYU, engaged couples want everyone around them to be engaged, too—as if it's a race.

"Well, I am seriously considering entering a quilt at the next county fair." Ben laughed, and I left him alone in the dark, cuddling with his companion. In a few months, the two of them would be married in the temple—sealed forever as husband and wife—beyond this life and for all of eternity. I was happy for them—glad they had found one another in the act-fast cattle auction that is marriage-crazy BYU. I envied how openly they held one another, without any sense of shame, here on the couch or at church, nestled in the pew like two enchanted lovers basking in divine approval. Would I ever know such closeness with another person? I wondered.

"How was your date?" asked my bishop the following Sunday. We met weekly now, in the private room in the basement, where I could report my progress toward heterosexuality.

"It was fun," I answered.

"Did you schedule a second date?" he asked. No, I had not, but I had designed a quilt for one of my art classes. It would be a map of the world, but all the countries would be different pieces of cut fabric. My date said she would help me.

"Are you sure that art is the best major for someone like you?" asked the bishop. "A lot of homosexuals do art and theater—so you might be surrounding yourself with the wrong kind of influence." He tapped his hand on my knee. "I think you should pray about changing your major."

In the alphabetical list of wrist-slitting majors offered at Brigham Young University (accounting, actuarial science, bioinformatics . . .), only two held any appeal for me. After art, there was geography, and while I was ill-informed about what it was that geographers did after college, it was the closest thing I could find to pursue my dream of working for National Geographic. Besides, doing art at BYU was problematic. For her senior project, a friend of mine had crafted twenty-five enormous ceramic spheres, each with a single opening sculpted in the unmistakable form of a vulva. After two weeks and lots of young Mormon children crawling in and out of the vagina sculptures at the art show, some scandalized mother complained to the administration. Until then, no man wanted to admit that he recognized the abstract display of female genitalia, which (I think) was the whole point of the installation.

Then there was the time when the art museum opened their exhibit of authentic bronze casts from the original sculptures by Auguste Rodin. I was ecstatic—but four days later, after shrill complaints from students, parents, faculty, and the administration, the university closed the exhibit and nailed all those cold, naked statues back into the crates from whence they came. Aside from the overt sensuality of *The Kiss*, BYU president Merrill Bateman claimed that Rodin's John the Baptist made it seem like the ancient prophet was masturbating—unarguable proof that BYU's president knew nothing about art or masturbation. When they banned Rodin, I officially changed my major to geography.

In my first geography class, we spent two hours learning the shape of the Earth. "The Earth is not merely 'round,'" explained my professor, miming a big invisible ball in the air, rotating on its axis. "The Earth is not a globe . . . or even a sphere!" he continued. "No. Earth is a *geoid*." He pronounced the word again, "*Geoid!* Which means?" He did not wait for any response. "That's right—it means 'earth-shaped'—Earth is earth-shaped! Remember that—it *will* be on the exam!" He dropped his hands from the air, and the imaginary planet vanished. I wrote it down: *Geoid. The Earth is earth-shaped.*

Then he began writing out the mathematical description of the true shape of our home planet, factoring gravitational pull and Earth's rotation toward a hypothetical equipotential surface based on mean average ocean levels—"*if* atmospheric conditions are constant," the professor snickered, "which they are not."

In fact, the shape of the Earth is forever changing, so that despite the mathematicians' best efforts to numerically describe its "true shape," the actual surface of the earth is alive, forever changing and pulsing, like a beating heart in space.

These were heady notions, not at all the kind of geography I wanted—the stained maps and raw adventure, the exotic-sounding place names and awesome exploration in *National Geographic*. I wanted to dive into the sepia memories of the past—to wander the world with reindeer-gut snowshoes and steamer trunks, woolen cloaks and pilot's goggles. I wanted to paddle Henry Stanley's canoe down the Congo and follow Lawrence through Arabia on the back of a camel. I wanted to stack tea tins below deck on the *Endurance* and pose in the snow for Frank Hurley's cumbersome camera.

Clearly I was born in the wrong century. I mourned the spirit of true adventure from the past era—a spirit lost in the wake of today's technology, rendered empty by the need to always know where one is headed and when one might arrive. I envied the open globe of the early explorers—theirs was a world white with blank spaces for scribbling—they were the true geographers who discovered new miles of earth, while my atlas was filled with place names and borders, a world where every *terra* was *cognita*.

Now geography meant taking statistics and geographical information systems (GIS). Luckily, my major was filled with ROTC members who excelled in math while harboring only remedial knowledge of Earth itself. Not a single soldier among them could find Bulgaria on a map or remember the capital of Guinea-Bissau. And so I survived college by trading secrets with the military—when blank maps needed labeling, I was there to get them their A, and in return, the men in light-blue shirts carried me through the painful mathematics of GIS and remote sensing. I was grateful for their left-brained ways but found it strange to be the lone and disheveled civilian among so many spit-polished officers. I was obsessed with old paper maps, while they were obsessed with modern warfare. For me, geography was discovering the Earth, over and over again—for them, geography was the art of hitting their intended target. That we found ourselves in the same classroom amazed me—I wanted to dogsled the Antarctic, and they dreamed of dropping bombs on people's heads with technical precision.

That year, America's global satellite network had opened up to civilian use and my ROTC pals made it sound so cool and space age: "Wherever you go in the world, you'll know exactly where you are!"

"It's called GPS—Global Positioning System," explained our professor. This was long before smartphones and Google Earth and talking cars that tell you to veer left in a half mile.

"Someday in the future, people like you and me might use GPS every day," he said, and with military uniformity, the ROTC crew began clapping like overjoyed monkeys. It was an exciting concept, albeit sinister knowing that a thousand eyes would be tracking our every action. I had enough to worry about with the watchful eyes of every tattletale at BYU. The world was watching and waiting for me to slip, and then I did.

There were no rules about having *boys* in our dorm after curfew, and if a boy and a girl could kiss freely on campus, why couldn't we? The first time, it was late at night, long after my roommates were asleep, and we found ourselves sitting on the same couch where Ben and Marci loved to snuggle. Doug was blond, a ballet dancer, and two years older than me. When we kissed, my chest grew warm and I felt the incredible urge to hold onto him forever. So this is what everybody has been talking about, I thought. At twenty-one years old, I had never felt that way before. All the guys I knew had known this warmth and power since their teens, but for me, I had to wait until now, halfway through college, hiding away from the world after midnight, whispering in the dark with my coconspirator.

In the days that followed, I became more brazen—even kissing Doug good-bye right as Ben walked into the kitchen. My roommate said nothing—only looked at me and then left through the back door on the way to his job at the campus theater, where he cut out sex scenes and bleeped out swear words, turning "bad movies" into "good movies."

When I returned from class the next day, I thought we'd been robbed—a bare mattress sat on the flimsy metal frame, the bookshelves were bare, as were the desk, walls, and closet on the right side of the room. Ben had moved out. A yellow Post-it note was stuck to my desk: *Dear Drew, I know you can't be happy like this. I'm sorry, but I just can't be around you anymore. Ben.*

My fingers shook and I dropped the note, watching it float to the floor. Then I fell to my knees and crumpled into a ball on the brown carpet. The sobs came slowly, in loud gulps, followed by tears and goopy strings of snot that poured from my face like buttery slime. Ben was my only regular guy friend—straight, butch, and cool—and he had dropped me from his life because I was gay. I pressed my face in my hands and my knees to my chest, muffling my cries in the musty carpet, but the tears kept flowing. I cried for losing Ben, and I cried for all the friends I never had growing up. I cried for that little kid on the bus in Ohio, for every time I had been called a faggot, for my clueless bishop trying to marry me off, and for my family that would never forgive me for being gay. I cried because God had made me like this—a defective male who liked kissing guys and not girls, who liked art instead of football—a misfit who would never belong to anyone . . . or anywhere.

13 TELMEX

Day 3

Hot water fell on my neck and the shampoo foam slid down my naked back. I breathed in the steam from the shower and lingered under the water for several long minutes, leaning on one foot, then another. Never had any shower felt so luxurious—the grease and grime of the past two days melted off my body, and with soap and scrubbing, I smelled new. As I toweled off, I stared at my own reflection in the steamy mirror, feeling happy and refreshed.

I had slept until nine and awoke in a silent house. The family had gone to church without me, though I never expected to be invited. The church would ask questions—"Are you married? Do you have any children?"—and I knew my parents would be embarrassed by my answers. Besides, I had no church clothes to wear. I dumped every bit of clothing from my backpack into the washing machine—everything except for the shorts I was wearing. The secret to packing light is doing lots of laundry, so I added an extra cup of detergent to the wadded stench and then swung the dial to Heavy Duty.

My older sister had left a pot of oatmeal on the stove, so I dished up a big bowl for breakfast and read through the latest tweets from my readers. *When will you get to Antarctica? Are you going through Brazil? Take me with you!*

By the time I finished breakfast, I had reached seven hundred followers on Twitter. That's more friends than I've ever had, I thought. It was a good feeling, even if I did not really know any of them. Is this how it feels to be popular?

I downloaded Sally's waypoints and saw my trip spelled out with a single squiggly blue line that stretched from Washington, DC, to Texas. I was making my own map now, but when I expanded Google Earth, my thousand miles of blue seemed like a hyphen on the globe. This was just the beginning—a Sunday pause before the real road ahead. Was I ready to repeat the last two days again and again and again, on and on until the road ran out?

My parents' family room was lined with gratuitous power outlets, and I filled them with all my plug-in devices—computer, phone, cameras, battery packs, and Sally the GPS. Then I got to work writing my first blog post, hunched over the coffee table and tapping away, describing my time on Greyhound. It took me hours to finish, but I e-mailed the file to my editor Janelle right as my family walked in from church.

We had lunch together, and after so many strangers on the bus, I was glad for the familiarity of home. Without any discussion, a truce had been called—no reprimands for my "lifestyle," no exasperating sermons, and no stubborn rebuttals from me. Instead, we had sandwiches, and they listened—my mom, dad, and sister. They had followed my journey online, and now I indulged them with tales from the road.

My family was used to my crazy escapades—the Ohio winter when I used a garden hose to transform our backyard into an ice skating rink; the summer I bred several hundred mice in the garage; that time I hatched three duck eggs in my closet with a light bulb; or when I was thirteen and showed up at a church carnival in gypsy drag, offering complimentary palm readings and home-brewed love potions. Riding the bus to Antarctica was just another one of those things.

"Now—where is it you're going this time?" asked my grandfather when he came over that evening. Grandpa Bob was ninety-seven years old and partially deaf, so I had to project every answer like I was on stage in a school play.

"Antarctica!" I cried.

"Oh my!" he exclaimed, shaking his head. "Which way will you go?" he asked.

"I don't really know!" I shouted. "I'll just keep going 'til I get there."
I pulled out my map of South America and together we traced possible
routes to the bottom of the world. Whenever I pointed to a place on the
map, my grandfather had a tale to tell. He had been to Rio, Lima, and
Buenos Aires—he had floated on the Amazon and seen the Andes.

If anyone inspired me to wander the world, it was my Grandpa Bob.
Born in 1912, his life spanned the first air travel to the first e-mail. It was
my Grandpa Bob who gave me my collection of *National Geographic*,
and described the world to me with his own stories of Khartoum and
Cairo, Rome and Bombay. Before I could read, he held me on his lap
and read to me from the *Wall Street Journal*. He taught me the names of
all the different foreign currencies, taught me which languages they
spoke where, and showed me stamps from countries that no longer
existed. And after my parents told me never to come home, it was my
Grandpa Bob who intervened, confessed he had always known that
I was gay, and told them that no matter who I was or what I did, I
should always be welcomed home—that I should always be part of the
family.

My grandpa was proud of me, and I felt so proud sitting next to
him, showing him my official explorer's flag of green, brown, and blue
with NATIONAL GEOGRAPHIC spelled out in white block letters. He
smiled at me and said, "My, my . . ." and shook his head.

"Tell me, is it winter or summer down in Antarctica right now?" he
asked.

"It's summer, Grandpa!" I said, though he already knew that.

"Yeah, I guess it is. But oh my, it'll be cold down there, won't it?"

"Yes, it will be very cold, Grandpa."

"You be careful in Mexico, you hear?" he said before leaving.

"I will, Grandpa," I promised, though I wondered if anything was
less careful than riding solo, one public bus after another, across some
of the most violent parts of the country. It was not a particularly cheerful time in Mexico—all along the border, drug gangs were at war, and
every day, civilians got murdered in hideous ways.

Though I planned on leaving the next morning, I did not have a ticket for Mexico yet. I felt too uncertain about where to go and which border town to pass through. From Houston, Greyhound sold bus tickets into Mexico via Matamoros, Reynosa, and Laredo. I nixed Matamoros right away—a simple Google search turned up a high school yearbook of severed heads. Laredo was equally marred by the intense drug violence and was too far west. That left small-town Reynosa, in Tamaulipas—a state so notorious for kidnappings, carjackings, and armed robbery, the US Government had banned personnel from the region. Official warnings specified that criminals were targeting public and private passenger buses.

I dressed carefully, stashing fifty dollars in the bottom of one shoe, then a hundred dollars folded tightly into a removable waistband under my pants, and then another fifty in my shirt pocket. Then I packed an old wallet with canceled credit cards, old student IDs, and a wad of five-rupee notes from India sandwiched between two twenty-dollar bills. If anyone did steal my wallet, they would truly steal trash. I had been mugged once before—in Kiev—and the thieves walked away with about a million dollars of defunct Zimbabwean currency.

"Take some granola bars," my dad insisted, pulling out a monstrous Costco box and stuffing bars into all the pockets in my backpack.

"I don't have room for those, Dad," I said, kneeling over my bag on the kitchen floor. My bus was leaving Houston in an hour. Granola bars were the least of my concerns.

"Take something to eat, Drew," said my mom. "Do you want some oranges? These are the best oranges ever!" She pulled an entire bag of oranges from the fridge, but I declined. Then came the apples, the string cheese, bottles of vitamin water, and almond packets.

"No, thank you," I said. "I don't have space for all this. They have food in Mexico—good food—and I probably have enough granola bars to get me to Guatemala."

"I don't know, Drew. With all that sitting on the bus, I'm worried you'll get constipated!" My father revealed the nature of his concern. I stared back at him from the floor. "Constipation has never been a problem for me in Mexico, Dad."

My plan for Mexico was this: don't eat. If I didn't eat, I wouldn't get diarrhea. When I did get hungry, I would tap into my stash of FDA-approved granola bars. I disliked my overcautious behavior, but I was on a mission and that mission did not include getting waylaid in some bus station *baño*.

My dad called from the doorway, then walked out to the car with my bag. We had already said our family prayer, kneeling in a circle in the living room, lit up with the gray winter light of a Texas morning, silent and listening while my mother pleaded with God to keep me safe. Meanwhile I prayed for God to let me send tweets from Mexico. If my international data plan failed to activate at the border, then this project was a bust and a major embarrassment for both National Geographic and myself. Three days before, I had announced on public television that I would be live-tweeting a journey across the world, even though I had no actual proof that this was possible.

I hugged my mother good-bye.

"Be safe," she whispered. I was afraid she might start crying, and then all my guilt would return.

"I will," I promised before hugging my youngest brother, Nathan, and my sister Amy. This was the most family I'd seen in ten years. Amy handed me a packed breakfast for the road, along with a gigantic bag of homemade Chex Mix.

An hour later I was back on the bus, inhaling the noxious fumes of Houston's unmoving traffic. Technically, this was still Greyhound, but the bus was painted with big red letters that spelled AMERICANOS on both sides.

"*¡Rrrrreynosa! ¡Rrrreynosa!*" the bus driver called out on the speaker, rolling his *r*'s and reminding us of our destination, despite the fact that we were still not moving. His announcements were rapid and only in Spanish, as most of the passengers were Latino. They shunned the morning sun, pulling the pink cotton curtains and shutting my view of used car dealerships, stucco strip malls, and geodesic megachurches. The man in the seat ahead of me wore a magnificent cowboy hat, depriving me of any hopeful glimpse out the windshield. And so I talked to José, a white-haired man in his seventies who had lived in Houston for the last forty years.

"I've got family in Reynosa," he said, and though I asked him everything I could about his boyhood home in Mexico, his descriptions remained entirely vague.

"It's a nice place." He smiled.

"What did the driver just say?" I asked, embarrassed by my lack of Spanish.

"He says we're stopping for lunch in Victoria." José pulled down his cowboy hat and fell asleep. I tried to do the same, but I had no cowboy hat, and there were tiny feet kicking me in the back. I turned around and glimpsed a little boy with hair the color of traffic cones. A thousand faded freckles dotted his face like a population map, and his two front teeth were missing. The little redhead blinked at me, then turned to his mother next to him—an obese lady with pallid skin and messy strawberry-blonde hair. She seemed so uncomfortable in her seat, but she smiled back at me and encouraged her son to be polite.

"Tell the nice man your name."

The little boy waited, then said, "I'm Eddy." He bit his lip nervously but answered my barrage of questions. He was ten years old, in the fourth grade, and still believed in Santa Claus, who had gifted him the remote-controlled spider that he held in his lap. After Christmas with his grandparents in Houston, he was headed back with his mother to McAllen, on the Texan edge of the border.

"So what's it like, living right on the Mexican border like that?" I asked Eddy's mother. "Do you just go back and forth all the time?"

"We never go into Mexico—I haven't been to Mexico in over twenty years."

"That's a long time not to visit a place that's right next door," I said. It seemed like such a waste to me—to be a few blocks from another country and then never visit?

"Yeah, but it's just too crazy right now," Eddy's mother explained. "I won't take my kid down there." Even though he lived less than a mile from the border, Eddy had never been to Mexico, and now he was collapsed in a sweaty heap on his mother's lap, fast asleep.

"*¡Quince minutos!*" declared the bus driver before he swung open the door at the rest stop in Victoria. Everybody piled out of the bus and lined up at the McDonald's, then fifteen minutes turned into forty. Time was slower down here, and the air was warmer, too. I traded the old man for his window seat and slid the curtain open just enough to watch the world outside. Texas never ends, and the road unfurled like a thin, gray thread across the brown-green grass that spread knee-high all the way to the Gulf, somewhere beyond the horizon. Like a broken necklace, a row of unlaid concrete sewer pipes lay parallel to the highway—the only feature on the wide-open landscape. The Texas-size cattle seemed utterly bored with life as they stood stationary in the heat of the afternoon. Only telephone poles and barbed-wire fences marked the distance, and in the small town of Refugio (population 2,941) we passed a single, tinny windmill, moving in lazy circles.

I was born in this great state, but it felt like a separate planet from the one I called Earth. Soon the pencil-thin palm trees vanished and in their place came the cacti—top-heavy prickly pear that clung to the weathered fence posts. Then came the tumbleweed, tumbling in the hot wind, across the desert with more shades of brown than a J. Crew catalog.

I slept and sweat my way to McAllen while little Eddy slept on the floor of the bus, his head on my backpack. His orange mop of hair clashed with the green canvas, and soon Eddy's sleeping face was indented with the red imprints of buttons and buckles.

Afternoon became evening—storefronts and high metal signs began to light up, brightening the fading sky with names of fast food brands and mall department stores. Beyond the mass of box stores, streetlights, and tangle of electrical wires stood a single chain-link fence crowned with coils of razor wire that followed the hills and dips of the terrain. Beyond that was the muddy and meaningless river, and on the other side, the bare yellow hills of Mexico.

Eddy and his mother were the only ones to exit the bus in McAllen, waving good-bye to me from the parking lot of the Walmart Super-center. This was the last bus stop in the United States, and several of the Mexican passengers asked to make sure that I really meant to stay on the bus. I squinted through the dusty window at the foreign country before me. Painted shacks clustered around the hillsides, as if everyone was fighting for a view of America to the north. Our bus driver walked down the aisle of the bus, checking every passenger's passport. Half the bus held up their dark blue booklets proving we were American; the rest all held their green-and-gold Mexican passports.

We approached Mexico one stoplight at a time. Tiny raindrops began to spatter the windows, making the bright lights of the two cities twinkle in the impending darkness. We stopped long enough for a lone patrolman to step onto the bus and mumble with the driver. He glanced at the other passengers, made eye contact with me, then hopped off without stamping anybody's passport. The bus moved onto the McAllen-Hidalgo International Bridge, up and over the Rio Grande. For one small moment, we sat still in traffic, suspended halfway between two countries, and I could see the dark line separating one land from the other. Then we descended into the nighttime of Mexico. There were fewer lights down here and the city felt so much darker. Hard rain welcomed me, washing away the view of this new country.

Reynosa is in fact older than my own city of Washington, DC, founded as part of an eighteenth-century Spanish scheme to occupy the empty interior of Mexico. Constant flooding of the Rio Grande forced the town to be moved to higher ground, and like the river, the city's population rises and falls with the sweeping tide of immigrants that pour into the United States. Officially, half a million souls are huddled along this barren fringe of Texas, but at times, the floating population swarms to well over a million. Not so many years before, Reynosa was an attractive city that offered good living and good jobs, mostly in the *maquilas*—American factories built in Mexico for the advantage of cheap and steady labor. Yet in just a few years, Reynosa had become deadly with its daily gun battles and bodies left bleeding in the streets.

I saw no danger from the dark windows on the bus—a pair of uniformed guards swung open the heavy metal gates and led us into Reynosa's central bus station. There was no mariachi band to greet me, no piñatas or twirling dancers waving Mexican flags—only the busy porters who barreled past with lopsided luggage stacked in their wobbly carts. I dodged them like a squirrel on a highway, leaving the bus without ceremony, gripping my backpack and retreating like a scared rodent into a dark corner. My heart was beating wildly and I felt like everybody in the station was staring at me. I felt vulnerable, exposed, and panicked, left with nothing to do but crouch in the shadows and fiddle with my phone. Alas, nothing happened. Even Twitter complained to me: "No Signal. Check your connection."

I switched the phone off and on about six more times. Finally, the top right corner flickered with life and the word "Telmex" appeared, followed by one, two, three, and then four bars of coverage.

Bling! A text message popped onto my screen in Spanish, welcoming me to the Mexican mobile network—¡*Telmex está contigo!* My heart soared—I was tethered to the world once more. I reopened Twitter and scrolled through an hour of tweets, then sent out my own message to the world:

Safely in Mexico at the Reynosa Bus Station: ¡Bienvenido a México!

14 HANNAH

Day 5

The first hundred miles of Mexico offered up a world erased by darkness and wind. Only the solemn parade of stone mileposts marked the midnight nothingness. White beams spilled from the headlights onto the weathered highway—Carratera Federal, number 97. I had traded the welcome warmth of Texas for the coldest, emptiest, blackest place on Earth. There were no revealing road signs, no hopeful promise of some fast food oasis. Nighttime gusts carried pastel paper trash across the asphalt, and tumbleweeds actually tumbled—prickly spheres spinning in the dead wilderness.

We only stopped after midnight, when the *conductor* skidded gently into the roadside gravel and dropped the hydraulics with a tired sigh, then flung open the flimsy door and stepped out into the void to pee behind a bush. I was the only passenger to follow him—the other bodies on the bus all shuffled themselves like sleeping mice in a pile, trying to keep warm beneath their woolen blankets.

I gulped the smoky night air and moved toward the warmth of a lonely fire next to the road. In the flickering orange light, I saw an old Indian woman, crouched over the embers. With busy hands, she slapped out tiny dough circles one by one, her short brown fingers tapping *pat-a-pat-pat*. The cornmeal sizzled, and I smelled the true stony smell of Mexican tortillas. Endless stars shone overhead and the night felt a lot less suffocating. I was no longer alone.

The wrinkled *abuela* paid me no mind but kept patting out tortillas for the fire, like a busy ghost from centuries past. By dawn, she would fade away, just like my own shoe prints in the dust—yet I would never forget her. This was a perfect moment, ruined only by our driver, who was cramming food into his mouth, licking his fingers, and brushing the crumbs from his mustache. He pointed for me to get back on the bus—this was not an official stop. Like me, he wanted to clear out of Tamaulipas.

I had crossed at Reynosa because it sounded less violent than Matamoros, Laredo, or Juárez—but I had been wrong. Reynosa had become the epicenter of a drug war between the Gulf and Zeta cartels, and the violence was getting worse. In the week I crossed, over two hundred people had been killed in that singular border town, mostly in street shootings. Two days after I left, a group of journalists was kidnapped, tortured, and killed, and the United States closed its consulate and advised all Americans to avoid Reynosa altogether.

Security at Reynosa's bus station had been at a maximum with armed guards posted at every entrance and razor wire curled around the high concrete walls. Before I boarded my next bus, a young guard slowly paced along the line of forty-two passengers with a video camera, pausing to film each individual face. I smiled into the hole of the lens, but the whole thing felt rather sinister.

"¿Por qué?" I asked the young man in uniform, but he did not answer me. It was the lady behind me who leaned in to whisper, "They film us to have a record of every person who boards each bus. You know, in case there is a kidnapping, or robbery, or disappearance, or to identify the criminals who might be riding the bus."

A sign flashed in the headlights—México 608 kilómetros—but instead of heading to the capital, we turned left at the fork. By 4:00 a.m., we arrived in Tampico, which made me think of that chemical orange punch we used to drink at school parties, which harbors no connection to Mexico's big oil town by the sea. Once again, the bus turned into a gated, barbed-wire enclosure, and after parking, an armed guard led us single-file into the bus station. Most of us made a beeline for the baños, which I found to be remarkably clean. Synthetic citrus scent overwhelmed me, while the early-morning custodians swirled gigantic mechanical brushes across the faux-marble floor. In the row of shuttered shops, a few hopeful vendors stood next to wheeled stands hung with Jesucristo lipstick holders, *lucha libre* keychains, and cellophane bags of dried plantain chips.

Red-eyed but alert, I sleepwalked through Tampico's fluorescent-lit, tomblike terminal, trailing my fellow passengers like they were my tribe. Most of them looked grumpy, tired, and fed up with the bus, but at that moment, it was the safest place for me to be. I tried talking to some of them, but after hearing my shoddy Spanish, they gave up and walked away. I felt like the most pitiful freshman traveler in the world—exposed, vulnerable, and downright naïve—not to mention that I was obsessively worrying about my backpack, which was hopefully still locked away beneath the bus in the terminal.

As we reboarded for the next long leg of the Mexican highway system, the driver counted quickly through every number of assigned seats, then asked out loud, "*¿Y el gringo?*" Forty-one fingers pointed back at me—like a school class that all knew the right answer. Back in Georgia, I had been the white guy on the bus, and now I was *el gringo* in Mexico. I was still not blending in.

Dawn came in a cooling swell of blue light, just outside Tuxpan. The blank deserts from the night before had given way to the green earth, lush with trees, patches of grass, and square-cut shrubs. Banana plants towered over tin roofs that covered pink, yellow, and orange houses. Chickens darted across side roads packed with dirt, and goats and cows chewed slowly and stared blankly at our passing bus. A burro was tied up to a lemon tree, heavy with sour yellow fruit. White-painted beehives hummed with busy insects and outside most homes, the spray-painted plywood signs offered *miel*, *leche*, and *crema*. We had arrived in Mexico's land of milk and honey.

While the Technicolor dream unfolded outside my window, an artificial laugh track spilled from the dented speakers inside the bus. The mild hysterics of a studio audience seemed to mock the ongoing scene of poverty before me. Every few seconds the television erupted with hair-trigger chortles and guffaws, instructing all to join in the amusing situation on-screen. Meanwhile, out on the street, an old man in a straw hat pushed a wheelbarrow up the hill, and inside it was an old TV set with two antennae that stuck out.

My parents had raised me without television, but now, on the bus, I had no choice but to be sucked into the scratchy screen overhead. My bus had been hijacked by the Disney Channel and there were no survivors. Like lights dimming in the cinema, all the other passengers pulled the cloth curtains closed, ending my view of Mexico. No longer was I the intrepid adventurer rolling south through foreign landscapes— I was just another hapless victim of American television, tortured by the sad acting of Billy Ray Cyrus.

"*¡Es Hannah Montaña!*" whispered one lady to her sleepy daughter, after the fifth or sixth episode played out, but the little girl turned away from the TV and huddled into her seat with eyes shut. If only I could do the same, I thought. The tween reruns were silly and grating, though after two dozen episodes, I had a new arsenal of Spanish words—like *demasiado*.

The rain began to fall outside Poza Rica—a peek through the closed curtains revealed a line of low green hills heavy with January mist. Droopy strings of wet paper streamers, left over from Christmas, hung above the water-slicked road. The lady in the seat next to me awoke suddenly, uncrumpling herself from the seat and pushing long strands of black hair from her face. She broadcast the natural beauty of a Mexican woman underlined by a double dose of eyeliner.

"I am very enchanted to meet you," I offered her in my textbook Spanish. My neighbor's name was Zoraïda, and she was returning from spending Christmas with her family in Monterrey. Under the din of television, we chatted—trading information about ourselves. I told her it was raining outside and she responded that in fact, it was *lloviznando* (drizzling), or better yet, *chispeando* (misting). I scribbled the new words into my notebook. Zoraïda was not content to let me float through her country with some half-assed vocabulary. Right away, she set about tutoring me in Spanish, offering names and synonyms for the new world around me.

As the hours passed, the rain grew stronger, until the tropical torrent filled the streets and shook the coconut palms along the coast. The road skirted the ocean—not the blithe Mexican blue of travel posters, but frothy gray surf that smashed onto the putty-colored beach and rows of crumbling concrete piers. Brown water covered the road, and our bus began to feel like a boat crossing a sea of puddles. Beneath the aluminum sky, thousands of white egrets roosted in emerald cornfields, bordered by bright-red flowers.

Waiting at a stoplight, I spotted a man holding a wire basket with a pair of extraordinary colored parrots sitting inside. The birds preened their vivid red wings and long green tails.

"How much do they cost, *los loros?*" I asked Zoraïda. She leaned over me to get a better look from the window.

"These are illegal birds—he will sell them for less than 2,000 pesos," she said—around $150 each.

"And legal parrots?" I asked.

"As much as 24,000 pesos," she answered—$1,800 for a pair of beautiful birds in a cage. "*Es triste.*"

"*Sí,*" I agreed with Zoraïda, confined by my limited Spanish to express what I truly felt. I kept hearing other birds—loud and free, roosting in the broccoli-shaped trees. Purple grackles yapped for our attention, having fled Texas for the wet warmth of central Mexico.

We made a single, unscheduled rest stop, at an open-air café that seemed to be only half-built, complete with a cement mixer still parked in the dining room. Before the bus had emptied, our pot-bellied driver was already seated at a white plastic table, napkin tucked into the collar of his uniform, flirting with the waitress as she set down a sizzling plate of steak and beans. Rain gushed from the roof, trapping all of us inside the café while the driver folded steak into his mouth and washed down each bite with beer.

"We don't want to stop here!" screamed one woman, holding her purse over her head as she dashed inside. "We're already four hours late!" yelled another. The bus driver ate for free, explained Zoraïda, as long as he came with a busload of hungry passengers, ready to spend. "But it's too expensive here," she said. "We don't like this place." Despite the constant goading from café staff, all passengers refused to purchase any food.

I did not want lunch—I wanted to find the baño. I paid three pesos to enter the whitewashed shack in the back of the yard. There were no stalls or sinks, only an empty cement floor piled high with human excrement, buzzing with chubby flies. I swayed backward from the horrid stench, repulsed and afraid to breathe—this place was literally a shithole.

I ran away from the mess, resolved to hold out for a time and place with plumbing. Meanwhile, back at the restaurant, the passengers were rioting against the bus driver, who was now cutting into his second steak and sipping from his third bottle of beer. The more passengers complained, the more he scowled at us, wiping his greasy hair back with fat fingers. "It's the rain, the rain!" he shouted with his mouth full—blaming our delay on the worsening weather. "We're going to be late anyway!"

We splashed down the miles of flooded highway like a slow turtle. Night fell, and the headlights vanished into the dense black fog before us. There were no streetlights and no more TV—only the radio played with frantic updates on the storm interspersed with gleeful mariachi music.

"Coatzacoalcos is flooded," Zoraïda explained to me as we listened. "The police are closing some of the roads." I began to worry that we would not make it at all—the only road to the city was under water, but our intoxicated driver proved stalwart and got us there by 8:00 p.m.—only five hours behind schedule. As we pulled into the city, everybody's phones began ringing—a discordant symphony of ringtones and robotic beeps. "*Llegamos*," I heard them say to their waiting families.

At the station, Zoraïda offered me her manicured hand to shake, assuring me that Coatzacoalcos was very safe. "The people are nice here," she promised and wished me well. "*¡Buen viaje!*" She waved, exiting through the crowd. In twenty-four hours, I had traveled from the top end of the Gulf of Mexico all the way to the bottom. No great tragedy or crime had befallen me. I had not been kidnapped or robbed or brutally murdered—instead, I had made a new friend and learned more Spanish than I had ever learned in school.

I stared at my face in the bathroom mirror and splashed cold water from the sterile white sink, then combed my hair. I changed my clothes and began repacking my bag, checking to make sure nothing was missing. What I found were another twenty granola bars from my father, secretly stashed in the bottom of my pack: "*Hi-Fiber. Ensures bowel regularity.*"

With every good intention, my father had filled my bag with laxative granola bars. Over the course of the day, I had devoured a whole box of them, with full effect. Tucked away in a side pocket, I found a hidden note from my dad to me:

"*We love you and are praying for you. Have a wonderful and fun trip.—Dad*"

I kept the note and tossed the laxatives. I had to get rid of my paranoia—otherwise I would spend all my time waiting for something terrible to happen. Yes, I was the odd gringo walking around the station, but now when people stared at me, I stared right back at them and smiled.

"Do you need any help?" someone asked me in American English, and I turned to see a young man with slicked-back hair and dressed in the uniform of the bus company. He looked barely twenty years old.

"Yes," I said, because I had no idea where I was going or what I was doing.

"I am Miguel!" he shouted above the noise of the station.

"And I'm Andrew," I said. "Where did you learn English?"

Miguel beamed. "In Baton Rouge. I used to live there with my aunt."

"I was just in Baton Rouge!" Was it one, two, three nights ago? It felt like a year. Miguel and I talked in the midst of the chaotic atmosphere of the station, then he led me to the front of a line at the ticket counter and asked the saleswoman for the next bus to Chiapas. Without even thinking, I bought a ticket, then followed Miguel back down the long corridor and into the next terminal. He had to get back to work and he shook my hand with great force.

"I really hope that you like Mexico," he said and then disappeared into the crush of people. All around me, happy kids ran in circles, fueled by colorful bottles of soda. In one corner, a young woman nursed her baby beneath a frilly red blouse. On a plastic bench, an old woman read a Catholic prayer book and counted through her rosary beads, while another picked out the sleepy crust from her husband's eyes. Three young girls giggled as they shoved a two-peso coin into a large scale and weighed themselves collectively.

I was stopped from taking photos by a sour-faced security guard who held a flat hand up to my lens and pronounced, "No. No photo." She led me into the guard's room for a more thorough search, but when she reached into her locker for a billy club, I saw a fluffy pink baby blanket wadded up inside. On the locker door hung a framed photo of a bald and toothless baby. This petite female guard was somebody's mother, but for that moment, she was searching my bag for weapons.

I had entered Mexico afraid of drug cartels and random violence against innocent American me, but right then, in this guard's eyes, I was the most obvious and imposing threat—an outlier strolling through the norm of her bus station. She poked through my back with her billy club, but after a few minutes, she relaxed and pointed me to the bus labeled Tuxtla Gutiérrez.

I was eager to leave the coast and its flood zone, and to head up into the mountains, away from the rain. No, I feared getting stuck, so I boarded the bus to Chiapas and took my seat next to a smiling grandmother. Across the aisle sat her daughter, who was slapping a fresh diaper on her own gurgling baby. I said hello to three generations of Mexican women, then tucked myself in for the night. First I took off my shoes, then reclined my seat and wrapped myself in my fleece blanket. I twisted two foam earplugs into my ears and waited as the rain and the rumble of the bus engine disappeared. Then I lowered an airplane face-mask over my eyes, blacking out the light of the television above me.

15 UTAH

Technically, we can expel you," he said, tapping a finger on the small print. The academic vice president had read my files and was throwing the book at me, literally. He slid the open handbook across the desk and stabbed the page once more.

"According to this, I *should* expel you," he said, raising his eyebrows over his glasses and pausing for effect. He gazed back down and paraphrased:

"By engaging in homosexual behavior you have violated the honor code of Brigham Young University, which you signed voluntarily. Your actions show you to be an overt threat to the rest of the student body and the integrity of this university."

He sighed gently, then looked back up at me, waiting for a sign of remorse—perhaps a quivering lip—but I said nothing. I only sat calmly, hands beneath my thighs, not blinking but focusing instead on the sounds beyond the closed door—the phones ringing, the click of high heels on laminate floors, middle-aged secretaries tickling computer keyboards. In three years of college I had never been above the first floor of the administration building, but now here I was, one door down from the president's office, awaiting my punishment.

"So the rules are clear—I should expel you and freeze your transcripts." He repeated his threat. "We'll call that Option A."

"And if I go somewhere else?" I ended my silence, wondering if I could still get into Ohio State before next semester.

"Your credits will not transfer," he said very plainly. Could they really do that? I began to panic, my heart beating wildly inside my chest—three years of hard work, erased forever. I would fail to graduate and my life would be ruined, all because I fooled around with a guy on campus.

"However, let's explore Option B." He smiled, flipping through my transcript. "It seems like you're a pretty good student—mostly As." He paused again.

"And this is your first offense—you've never done this sort of thing before?"

"No," I replied.

"You see, Andrew—you are not 'gay,'" he said, forming air quotes with his fingers and kicking back in his swivel chair.

"You don't look gay, and you don't act gay. You are simply confused—you really don't know who you are—but this other boy, he's a ballet dancer and he has a history. He wanted to recruit you into this lifestyle of sin . . . and if that is the case, which I think it is, then my job is to protect you from his influence."

I waited, tense and quiet. The man was dead wrong—I had kissed Doug willingly, out in the open, right on campus. Doug was the discreet one, the guy who kept saying no—I was the one who threw caution to the wind, though I was not about to offer the vice president a more accurate version of events.

"When your parents sent you here, they did not expect you to encounter predators and homosexuals. They sent you here for an education in a spiritual environment. My job is to promote that kind of atmosphere for every student."

He pushed some hair back over his bald spot and continued, "So let me tell you what you're going to do."

I sat forward, attentive, ready to do anything to keep from being thrown out.

"First, you will attend reparative therapy. We have a whole team of professionals who have been quite successful in correcting same-sex attraction. Because you have acted out on your homosexual feelings, you are ineligible for group therapy—you pose too great a risk to the others—but I have already recommended you for one-on-one treatment," he said, as if he'd simply ordered me dinner without asking if I preferred the steak or lasagna.

So he was sending me to a psychologist. I already knew the place—the basement beneath the tower. The nelliest gays had to go there several times a week—some of them were my friends. Most of them told me how they hooked up with other guys they met in group, but they also told me horror stories—how students were shown retro gay porn and made to throw up, or worse, shocked with electrodes attached to their penis or scrotum. I personally knew enrolled students who "by their own choice" had undergone such treatments.

"Next," the vice president continued, "you will stop all contact with homosexual persons. You are forbidden from associating with any of them. We will be watching you closely—including your university e-mail account. Any communication with known homosexuals and we go back to Option A. Got it?"

I nodded obediently. It wasn't like I was e-mailing all the homos at BYU—that's not how we communicated. We just knew one another and talked in passing. Yeah, there was the campus fag hag who passed messages, and we held a secret meeting once, at midnight, inside the Missionary Training Center, but only because there was a gay security guard who booked us the same conference room used by the General Authorities of the Church.

"Finally," he said, "you must write down a list of names of each and every homosexual you know on campus. If there is some kind of gay underground movement, then we need to end it immediately. You will write them down now, and I expect a full list."

He clicked open a black ballpoint pen and handed it to me, along with a blank sheet of paper.

"That is Option B. We expel you, or else you cooperate—you are free to choose."

I tried holding onto the pen, but my hand was sweaty and shaking, so that it kept slipping away. The pen tip vibrated hard against the paper—the tapping grew louder in my ears until it sounded like a line of snare drums on the football field at halftime. He was asking me to betray my friends—to rat out all those guys who had trusted me with their biggest secret. To tell the world something that most of us had never told our own families. I closed my eyes and saw their faces flash before me—the Puerto Rican freshman, the design student from Alaska, some of the guys in my Russian class, the entire folk dancing team, and most of the men's chorus. One page was not enough—there were hundreds, probably thousands, of gay students at Brigham Young University, some closeted and most of them terribly repressed. The vice president had to know that, didn't he?

But no—he didn't. He thought he could weed us out like cockroaches on the kitchen floor. It was like the broken-down Soviet Union that I had just left, only this time I was the dissident, polluting the perfect order of the Lord's kingdom. My options were giving away complete control of my life or getting sent out into the cold and jobless wasteland of spiritual Siberia.

"So, will you cooperate with us?" asked the vice president.

I stared at him with open eyes, terrified by what he could do to me. I was not going to sacrifice my education for this man, nor was I a tattletale. He had forced me into a corner and left me with a single choice—destroy myself or destroy others—and I hated him for it. I wondered how he actually felt inside—an hour from now he would forget me and my icky predilections; he would head home to his wife and six or seven or eight children, then eat his dinner and kick back in his living room and everything in his life would be all right.

I stared down at the blank paper. What did God want me to do? I wondered. I prayed. I waited. God wanted me to survive, I thought. I was just a year away from graduation—and I could do anything for a year. Yes, I was gay. Yes, at some point I was going to have to come out to the world, but I wanted to come out with a college degree and a chance at making it in life. I refused to be a victim—or a martyr. I just wanted to be me.

And so I picked up the piece of paper, set it on the desk, and began to write.

16

CHICKEN BUS

Day 6

The brakes moaned like a woeful Chewbacca as our bus teetered through the gauzy mist of Chiapas, veiling the deep-green slopes of the folded landscape. With the warm flash of dawn came Frank Sinatra, whose vagabond shoes were longing to stray. The driver swayed in his seat to the jaunty beat of "New York, New York" while our bus swayed around every *curva peligrosa* in the rising mountains of southern Mexico. At times I felt the bald tires sliding sideways on the asphalt.

The night before had passed like a dream, staged like a mystery play that spun me through the dark hours of the clock. The bus left me in Tuxtla Gutiérrez long after midnight, and I walked solo through the length of the half-lit station with its stratospheric metal ceiling and everything painted a clean hospital white. Every shop was shuttered and only a single ticket booth remained lit at the far end of the corridor, where a cardboard square had been placed in the window that said "*5 Minutos*" in scratchy handwritten ink.

Now I was wrapped in the silence of the witching hour—a lone ghost in the sick fluorescent glow of the colossal station. I dozed on the rows of red plastic seats that were bolted to the floor, and when I awoke, there were two men sitting across from me, inches from my face.

This is how I get mugged. I felt for my bag—it was still there.

"*Hola,*" said the larger and younger of the two.

"*Hola,*" I answered, unfolding my glasses and putting them back on my face. I looked around to check for a third accomplice in the shadows,

111

but there was no one else. Any second, one of them would pull a knife, or a gun. They would want cash—more cash than I had hidden on my body. They would walk me to an ATM outside the station and force me to drain my account with great fistfuls of pesos. They would take my passport and everything in my back. Give them whatever they ask for— better to go home empty-handed than in a casket.

"*Hola*," said the other man, who was shorter and older, with a full beard and mustache. He wore new leather boots and a cowboy hat, and when he shook my hand, he smiled with silver caps on all his teeth.

"I'm Alejandro," he said.

"And I'm Carlos!" said the other, also shaking my hand. I wondered which would be grabbing a weapon, but neither of them moved.

"What is your name?" they asked, in clear, punctuated Spanish.

"I am Andrew," I replied, trying to act calm.

"You are not Mexican," said Carlos.

"*No. Soy norteamericano*," I said.

"Where from?" asked Alejandro.

"From the city of Washington—the capital," I replied, still gripping my backpack in a chokehold, ready to use it like a shield.

"We are both coming back from the United States," said Carlos, pointing to the other and speaking to me in a slow and easy Spanish. "We work there, but we are returning home."

"What kind of work?"

"Stonemason," he said in English, then pantomimed laying a brick wall between us.

"I work on a dairy farm," said Alejandro. "In Vermont!"

"*Frío*," I said, pretending to shiver.

"*¡Sí! ¡Muy frío!*" Alejandro agreed with a silver smile. "I milk 170 cows every day, twice a day." He began describing his life in Vermont and how it was such good money.

"I make $600 a week," he said. "In Mexico, I can't earn that much in a whole month—so I work in America. When winter comes, I return here to visit my wife." Alejandro winked at me. "But I have a wife back in Vermont, too! So I have to go back and forth." He laughed and then put a finger to his lips and said, "*Shhhh.*"

"Where are you going?" Carlos asked.

"Guatemala," I said.

"Why? Mexico is better," he said, then pulled out a small plastic album filled with photos.

"You want to see?" he asked, and I nodded. One by one I flipped through the pages of his album, but instead of people, each picture showed some shiny new kitchen under construction. There were polished granite countertops and floors, beautiful entryways with freestanding marble staircases.

"My work!" he beamed, pointing at each picture. Carlos measured, cut, and fit the stone, and then laid it in place. He was an artist proudly showing off his portfolio of kitchens, bathrooms, and illustrious hallways far away in the McMansions of Southern California.

"They're beautiful," I said. "How many?"

"Me? I've helped build more than four hundred houses," he claimed.

"Do you have a visa?" I asked, realizing how rude it sounded, though I was curious.

"No, I have no papers to work," he answered truthfully. "But it's not a problem. Anytime I need work, I can go to California and I make a lot of money."

"But how do you cross the border?" I wondered aloud, thinking back to my own crossing in Reynosa—the fences, the barbed wire, the border police and SUVs, and the dogs. Everything I knew from the news made illegal border crossings sound treacherous and deadly.

"It's no problem." He smiled again. "I cross in the desert near Mexicali. I just drink two Red Bulls and then I just walk all night until I get there."

"You go back and forth like that?"

"All the time," he said.

"And border patrol?" I asked, but he waved his hand as if he were shooing a mosquito. "I never see them." His Mexican bravado worked on me—I was impressed. No way did I have the guts to cross illegally into Mexico, at night, in the desert.

"Do you like my country?" I asked.

"Yes, I like America very much," he said. "I like your shopping malls and the girls!"

Alejandro, Carlos, and I chatted for an hour, trading stories about Mexico and America. We were aliens, all of us, meeting at the crossroads between home and faraway. I pulled out my iPhone and showed them the pictures of my trip so far, and then Carlos walked with me to the window at the end of the station to buy my next ticket to San Cristóbal de las Casas.

My third day in Mexico and I was convinced the whole country functioned on a four-hour delay. At 3:00 a.m. the 11:00 p.m. bus from the night before arrived—so technically, I was riding with yesterday's ticket. Carlos and Alejandro shook my hand and waved good-bye from the curb as my bus crawled out of the station and back into the mountains. It was only an hour to San Cristóbal, but it felt like a far colder country than the tropics I had left the day before. Even in the station, my breath came out in small white clouds. There was no heat and no way to leave. Steel bars covered all the windows and doors, and for our own security, the station was locked until morning.

A pile of barefoot children slept on a row of chairs, huddled together like a pack of nursing puppies. Some of them even whimpered like puppies, curling up their cold toes and hugging one another in the fetal position. Suddenly I wished I had a heavier coat to cover them with. A group of four Indian women watched over them, dressed in the most brilliantly colored wool stitched with flowers and designs. These were Tzotzil Maya, and none of them spoke Spanish.

The guard unlocked the station at 6:00 a.m. Outside, a stripe of peach light brightened the edge of the night sky. Across the square, an older woman lifted the lid off a pot of tamales, steaming over a smoky wood fire. I went up to the abuela and held my hands to the flames, warming my fingers. I bought a single tamale, unwrapping the blackened banana leaf and lifting bits of crumbled cornmeal and shredded pork into my mouth. Bunches of black crows hopped along the cobblestone curb, searching for scraps. Buzzing mopeds bumbled past the colored parade of Tzotzil women in the street, all wearing brightly embroidered shirts and clutching happy red-cheeked babies. My last hundred miles of Mexico ticked by in a blur of yellow-brown maize, tin roofs, and clumps of shadowed jungle cached in falling mist. This was Carretera Federal 190, a jagged stretch of the famed Pan-American Highway. Contrary to common belief, the Pan-American is not a single highway from top to bottom with regular rest stops and signage and reliable mileposts reminding you just how far you've come since Alaska. Instead, the Pan-American Highway is like a piece of unraveled lace, draped casually over so many discordant nation-states. Here in Mexico, the road was in fair condition but lousy with sociopathic drivers, axel-snapping *topas* (speed bumps), and frequent army checkpoints with camouflaged jeeps, machine guns, and mustachioed *comandantes*.

Once upon a time, the Pan-American Highway was a kind of utopian dream of international friendship, based on the belief that the motorcar would link North and South America in the stainless steel bond of unity and brotherhood. Of all the signatory nations, Mexico was the first to complete its section of the Pan-American, in 1950. They celebrated by hosting the Carrera Panamaericana along the entire stretch of new road. The "Mexican Road Race" offered the ultimate challenge: drive 2,100 miles for six consecutive days in everyday five-seater sedans.

Out of the 126 cars that entered the race, only forty-seven finished (three entrants died). The winner was Hershel McGriff, a twenty-two-year-old lumberjack from Oregon who drove his "Rocket 88" Oldsmobile the full length of Mexico in just twenty-seven hours, thirty-four minutes, and twenty-five seconds with an average speed of 78.4 mph. Hersh went on to become a NASCAR legend, while the government decided the Carrera Panamericana was too dangerous.

It took me thirty-six hours to journey the length of Mexico, but I crossed the finish line near Ciudad Cuauhtémoc, just like Hersh McGriff back in 1950. The Mexico–Guatemala *frontera* is a place of whirling commerce, where you can purchase everything from life-size plastic clowns and cow brain tacos to king-size mattresses and decommissioned American school buses—should you ever require one.

Borders excite me like nothing else—the way humans draw invisible lines on the ground, splitting the Earth into so many separate categories. A steel archway held a "Welcome to Guatemala!" sign in Spanish, the flagpole flew the white and sea-blue bands of the Guatemalan flag, and on the street, a few orange rubber cones presented the only visible demarcation between the two countries. Both sides of the border spoke Spanish, there were no fences, and all the local shoppers passed back and forth on the street with huge unchecked bundles, as if the border only existed for foreigners.

Moneychangers hung about with wads of cash in their hands, following me around and blocking my path, shouting, "*Quetzales, quetzales,*" or "I give you the best rate, sir!" The Guatemalan currency is named after an amazingly iridescent red-and-green bird, the resplendent quetzal—the ancient Maya valued the tail feathers so much, they used them for money. I had first seen the tropical bird in the pages of *National Geographic*, and it became my inspiration for my first to visit Central America years before.

Just a few blocks from the border, I spotted a rusty Blue Bird school bus in the corner of an empty lot that showed few signs of roadworthiness. A team of young boys was busy roping bundles on the roof of the vehicle. A long time ago, the sides of the vehicle had read "Madison Elementary School District," but now the bus was painted decoratively with vermillion orange and tan stripes, emblazoned with the destination, Aguas Calientes. The windshield was decorated in decaled filigree, with *Guíame Señor* ("Guide Me, Lord") scripted across the top, and the name Jesucristo beneath the windshield wipers.

I boarded without asking where or when the bus was going or how much it cost. Nearly every seat on the bus was already full—entire *familias* crowded into a single seat, buried under bundles and woven bags, bulging cardboard boxes, whole stems of green bananas, and a few baby goats with legs restrained by rope. These were the same brown vinyl bus seats I rode as a child to school—seats that stuck to sweaty skin on hot days. As I wedged my long body into the seat, an angry chicken squawked from below. I peeked down at the bird, tied up in a white mesh bag.

My chicken bus putted uphill so slowly that every truck and moped and donkey cart trotted past my window, as if we were last place in the race across Guatemala's voluptuous landscape. Every time we hit a pothole, the bagged chicken at my feet complained with muffled cackles. The farther we drove, the more the road crumbled away into nothingness. At times, the driver veered sharply into the uphill shoulder to avoid the precarious gap where the outer lane of the road had totally vanished, washed out by recent mudslides. Down below, Mayan women hunched in the streams, scrubbing clothes in the cold water and then slapping the wet wool against the smooth boulders.

Over and over, the bus slowed to a near halt, picking up anyone who waved their arm from the roadside. There were no fixed bus stops—just a narrow highway that moved with people, animals, and trucks that belched toxic clouds of black smoke. Near every market, the school bus veered onto the gravelly shoulder, as the ticket taker hung his entire body out the door and shouted, "*¡Huehue!*"—short for Huehuetenango. We never actually stopped—riders clambered onto the steps just in time and then worked their way down the aisle. The seats were all full, and bewildered passengers packed the aisle, gripping the seats for balance as we swayed around every curve.

Riders only paid when they exited, leaving through the back door, still painted with the cautionary English EMERGENCY ONLY but left unlocked and open. As new riders hopped on in the front, others slowly worked their way down the aisle then passed their money back up to the front before leaping out the back of the slow-moving bus.

Loud Mexican music blasted from the self-installed speakers that hung next to the driver's rearview mirror plastered with Garfield stickers. The repeating CD contained only four tracks, and two of them were the same song: "Y ahora te vas" by the 1970s Mexican band Los Bukis. After one hour, I knew all the words.

The bus grumbled and spat as we pushed higher and higher into the peaks of Guatemala's volcanic highlands. Vendors hopped on and crowded the aisle, selling batteries, polka-dotted hair ribbons, plastic toys, and salty fried snacks. "*¡Jugos, Sabritas!*" they shouted with plastic baskets on their shoulders. It seemed so inefficient—all the pushing and overcrowding—just to sell a single bag of corn chips to a bored bus passenger.

High up in the mountains, one young boy boarded the bus toting clear plastic bags filled with fresh-cut pineapple.

"*¡Piña! ¡Piña!*" he called, shoving his way to the back of the bus before selling a single bag of fruit for just a few centavos. Every other seat was full, so very cautiously, he sat down next to me. His dark Indian skin matched the color of the brown bus seats and his glossy black hair hid his shiny eyes that seemed locked on me. We were two silent strangers, accidentally thrown together in the back of the bouncing bus.

"Hello. What is your name?" I tried to be friendly.

"Lester," he answered, though his voice was barely audible under the Latin dance music that played from the speakers.

"How old are you?" I asked, trawling through the Spanish phrase-book in my head.

"*Siete*," he said, and we continued talking. Seven-year-old Lester worked from sunup until sundown, riding the buses back and forth from Huehuetenango, selling fruit that his mother had picked, peeled, sliced, and bagged.

"Are you in school?" I wondered, and he explained that yes, he was, but it was still Christmas holidays, so he was helping his mother. I thought of myself at that age, riding the bus to and from school, and wondered how many seven-year-olds in the world had to work a twelve-hour day for a pocketful of coins. My own journey felt so frivolous—I was riding a chicken bus for fun, while this little child rode the bus to feed his family. I compared the burden of his young life with my own indulgent woes and came up lacking. To travel is to know the unfairness of the world, time and time again.

I bought three bags of Lester's pineapple and stuffed them away into my own pack. He finally smiled and then broke into his own supply. I watched as he delicately chewed a piece of his mother's packaged fruit, the warm juice dribbling down his chin while he looked outside at the passing world of green.

In Huehuetenango, I followed Lester out the back door and then jogged back to the front door to pay for my ride, which came to just twenty-five quetzales—three dollars. The ticket man smiled and then pointed to another painted school bus that was passing by.

"*Éste*," he yelled, leaving me sprinting across the busy road with my pack jumping up and down on my back. I arrived just in time to scramble onto the moving bus named *Angélica*, where the ticket taker grappled with my monstrous pack, motioning that he wanted to stick it on top of the bus. I kept insisting no and finally forced it under one of the seats, upsetting even more chickens.

"Where are you going?" he asked.

"Guate," I said, referring to the capital.

"No, no," he shouted and called for the bus driver to stop. Then he pulled my backpack out from below the seat and physically dragged me out the back of the bus.

"*Aquí*," he said with a gold-toothed grin, leaving me next to a row of barren shacks on the roadside.

I stood alone and abandoned, feeling the full warmth of the tropical afternoon. Gone was the cooling breeze through an open window. Instead, the sun's heat radiated up from the road until my face was red and dripping with sweat. I felt dizzy and weak, then realized I had eaten nothing at all since that morning. Lester's pineapple had turned to mush in my bag, so I bought some greasy tortillas and a big bottle of water.

I tried sending a tweet into the atmosphere—*Suddenly quite hot. Stranded on a high road, nibbling tortillas*—but each time I hit send,

Twitter shrugged its shoulders with denial. I had a single bar of 3G, but my one-liner to the world kept bouncing back. I had arrived in a dead zone—my first real disconnection since leaving Washington, DC. All I could do was wait in the heat, incommunicado, not knowing when or where I would go, until another souped-up school bus squealed toward me. I waved my arms and began jogging along the road, hoping they would slow down, but they did not. Instead, a man reached his hand out the door and I felt him grab my backpack and pull me up by the straps as I leapt onto the moving bus.

I remained standing all the way to Quetzaltenango, surfing in the aisle as the bus bumped along the road. My parents had raised me to always offer my seat to women, older folks, and young children—but those were the only passengers on this bus. Thus I stayed upright with my back bent and my head cocked to the side for a view of the up-and-down corn and banana countryside.

Enough people got off in Quetzaltenango so that I could sit down on the sloping edge of one school bus seat, which I shared with a mother and her two children, one of whom sat on my lap. My long legs stuck far out into the aisle, disrupting the traffic of vendors that repeated the set course—up through the front door, down the aisle with their racks of corn chips and cellophane-wrapped sun-dried peanuts, their metal pails of tamales, or a wardrobe of lacy pastel dresses for toddlers—and then back out the rear emergency exit.

Though the engine hummed, the bus barely moved beneath the on-slaught of salesmen pleading with us to buy, buy, *buy!* All the while, the music speakers jumped with a plunky Latin tune—"Quizás sí, quizás no"—a kind of cheery wood-block rhythm for the festive parade that shuffled down the aisle of the bus. Among the many characters that passed, a teenage boy stopped and spoke directly at me, pleading for charity. He had a severe cleft palate—his mouth and nostrils merged into a gaping hole in his face, so that he struggled to emit a few spoken words. I handed over a few quetzals, and he thanked me. If I ever imagined I could slum it on public transport and not have the world's misfortunes dropped into my lap, then I was naïve. I was already well acquainted with the cruel poverty of this country—the child labor, illiteracy, malnutrition, preventable illness, and the stray dogs and filth. And yet I loved Guatemala. I loved the Mayan villages hidden away in the highest mountains, the crystalline lakes inside the craters of sleeping volcanoes, the noisy jungle canopy, the smoky, windowless churches, and the ever-benevolent Guatemalans. I even loved this rickety bus, embellished with the red-letter words *Dios Vive* ("God Lives") and *Siempre Juntos* ("Always Together").

It took four more hours on the reconverted school bus to reach the capital. There are no straight roads in Guatemala—at times it felt like we were spinning in circles as we rounded the boundless mountains. Under a pink and failing sun, we descended into the bowl-shaped valley of Guatemala City, which glowed the magnificent orange of ten thousand streetlights. Evening traffic painted the concrete streets with stripes of colored car lights, while macho guys on motorcycles raced against our school bus and won every time. We moved so slowly, I could watch the city intensify with each block. We passed windows stacked high with wedding cakes and open-air storefront churches packed with Pentecostal believers singing hymns on a Wednesday. I could see the Mormon temple in the distance, glowing white with reflected light, and a gold-plated angel Moroni trumpeting from its topmost spire. No matter where I wandered in the world, the church was always there to remind me who I was and what I was no more. I had always loved the temple, but now, the distant beacon was like a flashing neon sign that read No Vacancy.

An hour later, I lay in a running bath, covered in lily-scented bubbles, while my smelly bus clothes lay in a pile on the floor. After nearly forty-eight hours of nonstop travel, the hot water felt wondrous. My body went limp, but my mind flowed with the day's imagery—the heavenly vistas of Guatemala and every person I had met along the way. Each and every one of them deserved a warm bath more than I did. It had only cost me six dollars to travel from the Mexican border all the way to

Guatemala City, but now I was resting in a hotel that cost $150 per night. That was the price of a room on the ninth floor, safe and secure, with a clean, warm, king-size bed. I am a gringo brat, I thought, dreaming in my bath. I woke up after midnight, still lying in the cold and soupy tub, my fingers white and wrinkled, pointing me toward bed.

17

A PLACE WITHOUT GUNS

Day 7

"Looks like you're back!" Tony chuckled with relief.

"Yep, I'm here!" I kept smiling, just as my PR friends had instructed me over and over: Smile 'til it hurts and don't stop smiling 'til you're off the air.

"Looks like you had some technical difficulties for a minute there, but we're glad you're with us," the anchor said. "You must be somewhere very warm and exotic!" I answered the flurry of softball questions from Tony: "Yes, I am still riding a bus to Antarctica. Yes, I have traveled across nine states and across all of Mexico. No, it is not as dangerous as the media makes us believe. Yes, as you can see, my beard has grown longer since I left seven days ago!"

"Now today you're calling us from—and I hope I'm saying this right—Guatemala? Some of our viewers may not know that there is such a place." Tony led me along and I picked up each cue like shells on the beach.

"Why yes, Tony, there really is such a country called Guatemala. It's a small country just south of Mexico and really beautiful—filled with mountains and high volcanic lakes." I was bursting with positive energy, suddenly a cheerleader for one of the poorest countries in the western hemisphere.

"And the capital is also called Guatemala?" Tony kept prompting me for a geography lesson, and so I gave it to him.

"That's right, I'm in Guatemala City right now in fact, and it's sunny and warm!"

"Send some of that sunshine our way! We've been reading your blog, and *gosh*"—he chuckled—"it sounds like you've met some interesting people!" Someone over at Fox had done their homework. They had been watching my Twitter feed, had highlighted anything they found interesting, and in some early morning meeting, they had compiled a long list of questions for the host. I played the game and gave them the little anecdotes they wanted, then waved good-bye as they left me for a toaster strudel commercial. My fifteen minutes of fame were over in less than five minutes—gone with a computerized *bleep* from my screen. I had gone from half a million viewers back to a party of one, staring out the large square picture window that framed Guatemala City like a muted TV show. A wall of smoggy green volcanoes reminded me that I was far away from Washington, DC.

Down at breakfast, huddles of slick-haired businessmen surrounded me, laughing confidently as they stabbed triangles of watermelon with their forks and plotted the day's strategy. Not so long ago, I had been one of them, sitting in this very same dining room, stiff and scratchy inside a stifling wool suit, dripping with hair gel and sweat, pontificating about post-conflict business development before a day of meeting with bored government officials who felt patronized by our visits, if not offended by my bad Spanish.

This time though, I wore shorts and flip-flops—and I had come by bus. Pushing away the fruit plates and teacups, I unfolded my table-size paper map of Central America. With the spread of my hand, I measured out the distance left to Costa Rica—at least a hundred miles more in Guatemala and beyond that, three more countries to cross: El Salvador, Honduras, and the whole of Nicaragua. Four countries in two days—I disliked that I would have to rush through this wide span of map, broken up into tiny nations like a shattered plate, but my editor wanted me in Costa Rica fast.

Yesterday's chain of chicken buses had shown me Guatemala in slow motion, but for the countries ahead, I would have to upgrade to something faster, and safer. To make it on time, I would have to take *el bus privado.*

¡Conductores Altamente Capacitados! ("Highly Capable Drivers!") read the signs at the station. As promised, a highly capable driver filmed each of us boarding the bus, solemnly pausing his camcorder on my uneasy face. Once we were all on board, an armed guard entered, hand on gun, then locked the door to the bus. As we made our way down the CA-1, our guard was always the first to exit and the last to reboard.

This was no Greyhound—Tica Bus was clean inside with soft new seats that smelled like a car dealership. Cool air-conditioning blew steadily on my forehead, and anytime I wanted, there was a ready bottle of cold, filtered water near my seat. This was the added luxury a few more dollars could buy, catering to a different demographic than that of yesterday's chicken bus.

Señor Luís Enrique Menendez introduced himself as a Guatemalan *empresario* who lived and worked in El Salvador. All the while he spoke to me, he never looked up from the computer game on his Blackberry. Much of the rest of the bus was filled with gringo backpackers— Americans, Canadians, and Germans. Bits of English and German banter floated up to my seat, while outside, barefoot Indians walked up the steep and winding road. Gaping potholes kept us from driving in a straight line and twice we stopped for road construction, idling for twenty or thirty minutes before passing through dusty gravel pits where workers in hard hats sucked red popsicles in the shade. It was hot outside—the dry season of January, a time when the land glowed green with banana plants and reached up to the thatched roofs of ramshackle huts. Blue-green hummingbirds buzzed around bright-purple flower vines that covered every fence post and concrete wall.

Such a fast bus made me feel like I was traveling in a different country—in three hours we traveled seventy-five miles before reaching the border at Río Paz, the river of peace. The bus rolled across a narrow, one-lane bridge and into El Salvador, pulling over into a gravel parking lot. "*Documentos, dinero,*" the driver spoke into his microphone. Then he switched off the engine and left the bus to chat with a pair of customs agents in dark-blue uniforms.

The Canadians were the first to complain about the heat, whining from the back.

"I can't breathe!" one girl cried to her boyfriend, who tried calming her down but finally joined in her lament. I was unsure which was more insufferable—the heat overtaking the air inside the bus or the pair of whiny backpackers. Luís Enrique passed on their complaints to the stern guard, who opened the door and let in a nice bit of mountain breeze. He remained stone-faced, blocking the entrance of the bus with his gun across his chest.

Outside, an unseen band of young girls cried out, "*¡Hay pupusas!*" over and over again, like birds in the rain forest that just won't quit. The guard nudged them away, but like bees to a flower, they kept crowding around the front door of the bus and sounding their sirens' call: "*Pupusas, pupusas—¡Hay pupusas!*"

Their high-pitched call triggered a Pavlovian response in me—my mouth turned wet and I felt my stomach twist with hunger. I looked down at the Dorito bag in my lap with dissatisfaction. I would rather have *pupusas*, I thought—extra-thick, hand-patted tortillas stuffed with melted cheese, refried beans, or stewed pork. As warm smells floated through the bus, the other passengers craned their heads like curious giraffes, searching for a glimpse of the cooked food. Yet nobody dared move from their seats. I was the first to cave, walking up to the front of the bus and poking my head over the shoulder of the armed guard.

"How much?" I asked a little girl in a pink shirt and frilly apron. I might as well have poked a beehive. Before she could answer, twelve other girls rushed the bus, holding up their steaming platters like waitresses on roller skates, all shouting, "Buy mine! Buy mine! Mine are the best!"

I folded an American dollar in half and handed it to the little girl in pink, who quickly lifted up layers of moist paper towels before peeling away three too-hot-to-handle pupusas. I squatted low down on the steps of the bus, reached around the statuesque guard, and received the food. For two seconds, the girl's hand touched mine, her brown eyes stared up at me, and she lit up with a bashful smile. No matter the road signs and flagpoles and border guards, she was my real welcome to El Salvador.

I would never learn her name or know the details of her life, and she would never know mine. I only imagined this girl's gray-haired grandmother cooking those pupusas over a blue gas flame in any one of the slanted shanties scattered like Legos on the surrounding mountains. I imagined her days, shouting earnestly at every bus that crossed the river, and I imagined what she thought of all the foreigners she encountered and the money they slipped her. Beyond our humble transaction from basket to bus, the moment held nothing of great consequence, and yet, for those few seconds in time, our two lifelines had met. This was the tempo of bus travel—to go slowly and meet so many. It is a great gift, yet it carries a strange pain—the pain of leaving too soon; the pain of never really knowing the humans we pass by.

Back in my seat, I broke off the fried corn cake and watched the dripping cheese ooze from the center. Then I dipped the sloppy mess into hot sauce and pickled-cabbage *curtido*, pushing the warm food into my mouth.

"That smells *sooooo* good," mumbled the Canadian backpacker to her boyfriend.

"Yeah, it does," he agreed. "But it's not safe." I listened to the two of them talking about me behind my back, literally. "He's gonna get sick," the boyfriend whispered. "You can't eat street food here, period." But I was eating street food on the bus, no longer nervous like I had been back in Mexico. The stench of my supper filled the bus with the smell of hot oil and cheese, and as I was finishing my last few bites, Enrique walked to the front and bought himself three pupusas. Then some of the Germans followed suit. One by one, the backpackers scurried down the aisle, paying the pupusa girls, then returning gleefully with food.

Like falling dominos, every other passenger followed, including the whiny, overly cautious Canadians, until our bus privado had bought out the entire pupusa supply at the Las Chinamas border station.

The bus smelled more like a greasy diner kitchen than a new car dealership, but everyone was in a much better mood, relaxed and fulfilled. The driver came back and twisted the key in the ignition and our back tires spit gravel as we pulled away from the enclave. I looked out the window, and the young girls all grinned and waved good-bye while balancing their empty baskets on their hips.

Twenty minutes later we rolled into the city of Ahuachapán, the name spelled out on a billboard over a wishful slogan, *un lugar sin armas* ("a place without guns"). How I wanted to believe that sign, though I imagined that a sufficient number of firearms were floating around these streets. An hour later, we entered the country's capital, and in the dark of night, the city glowed with starry, white constellations—single houselights scattered across the steep, black hillsides and a rush of red taillights shot through the city streets like a million blood cells pushing away from a beating heart. Gazing at the shopping malls and cheery backlit signs for Pollo Compero and Mister Donut, I could see no hint of the notorious violence of these streets.

I do my best to ignore the State Department's travel warnings, but I had been to San Salvador before, on business, and I had been briefed: "Shootouts are common. Travel on public transportation, especially buses, is risky and not recommended." At the time, El Salvador boasted the second-highest murder rate in the world, right after its next-door neighbor Honduras. Most of the Salvadorans I knew back home had fled the uncontrolled violence in their homeland for the relative safety of America. "No," counseled one friend, "do not take the bus in my country, and whatever you do, do not walk around San Salvador at night. Always take a legal taxi."

In the dark of night, the private bus station resembled a miniature castle with heavy black bars on the windows, spiraling razor wire, and a circle of ten guards holding heavy semiautomatic weapons while facing our bus. With my backpack in front of me, I pushed through the line and hopped into a "legal taxi"—the kind that are licensed, numbered, and traceable.

"Do you know that six million people live in El Salvador?" asked my taxi driver, Carlos, pausing for my answer. Traffic blocked us on all sides, and though it was dark inside the taxi, I saw his eyes blink at me in the rearview mirror.

"*Sí*." I had been to San Salvador twice before.

"Did you know that if all the Salvadorans around the world returned to El Salvador, we would have twelve million people?" he said. "*My people* are the greatest export of El Salvador."

Since the revolution in the 1980s, millions of Salvadorans had fled their country for somewhere else in the world, including my own neighborhood in Washington, DC. Today, one and a half million Salvadorans live in the United States, and worldwide, Salvadoran émigrés send home more than a billion dollars per year.

"I am proud of my people," Carlos told me. "But I am ashamed of our government and the way things are in my country."

"*Entiendo*," I said. "Sometimes I feel the same way about my country." Traffic was moving now, and outside my window, the city lights made the place seem safe and carefree.

"Oh, but America is not as dangerous as here. You must not go out at all," said Carlos.

"It's all right," I said. "I'm not even staying. Tomorrow I leave for Honduras."

But the next morning I discovered that because of the recent coup d'état in Honduras, there were no buses going to Tegucigalpa.

"You cannot go to Honduras," said the ticket agent behind the counter, who seemed to enjoy blue eye shadow. "*Es demasiado peligroso*," she said. "But we do have an international bus—*es seguro*—and that goes straight to Nicaragua. No stops in Honduras, you just go through." I paid her my thirty dollars for a ticket to Managua.

Behind me in line was Jorge, a slicked-back businessman in a navy-blue suit and spit-shined black shoes. He held a briefcase emblazoned with a cartoonish-looking eagle and he was selling. Whatever it was, it led to a new life, improved health, and my becoming unimaginably rich. All I had to do was purchase an overpriced bottle of aloe vera juice.

"No thanks." I declined his miracle juice a dozen times, but Jorge was persistent. He kept pushing his business on me, then followed me into the waiting room and sat next to me, gazing right into my face.

"See how tired you look." He made circles with his index finger around each of my eyes.

"Yes, I am very tired," I agreed. Too many nights on the bus and 3:00 a.m. wake-up calls.

"*Mira*. Look at me," commanded Jorge, setting down his briefcase. "I am *never* tired! If you drink some of my aloe juice then you will never be tired, either."

The man was relentless, but he also did not know who he was dealing with. I had been a Mormon missionary—I knew all about haggling people and convincing them to do things. What's more, I used to live in Utah, which is the mecca for pyramid schemes. I would bet my bus ticket that there was some shady Mormon behind Jorge's company.

The security on this bus was even tighter than before—first a man switched on the lights, then walked down the aisle filming each of our faces. Then two guards boarded and bolted the door behind them, before we commenced our early morning journey across the eastern half of El Salvador.

I slept until sunrise, when the sky turned a flaming pink and peach, outlining a silhouette of angled volcanoes before us. I wiped my eyes and sipped some water from a bottle, then said hello to the American guy next to me. He was scruffy and sandy-haired, with skinny jeans and canvas shoes.

"I'm Andrew," I said.

"I'm Adam." He shook my hand. Adam was from the Philadelphia suburbs, and at that moment, he was between organic farms.

"I get school credit for my work down here," he said, admitting that he was actually a student at Princeton. "Last month I was in Guatemala—now it's off to Nicaragua."

"So what's your major, then?" I asked, but he never told me.

"Essentially, I study indigenous farming methods," he explained in a very serious tone, as if it was too complex for me to understand, all the while tugging at the many braided wool bracelets around his wrist. I wondered how Adam's parents felt about paying college tuition at an Ivy League school while their son played subsistence farmer in Central America. Then I remembered how National Geographic was paying me to play explorer. We were both white guys from the East Coast, chasing our own exotic dreams while enjoying the status of the blue passports in our pockets and all the safety and bottled water and air-conditioning that money can buy.

I had no trust fund to indulge my wanderlust, nor did I have any academic purpose to validate my wanderings, but I was traveling for fun just the same. Suddenly, sitting on this bus in El Salvador felt wildly luxurious.

"So, what is your dream?" I asked Adam. "Where do you want to go and what do you want to do once you're done here?"

"Own my own farm," he shot back without any hesitation. He wanted an organic farm in the hills of Pennsylvania, one that employed the same ancient methods he'd seen down here in the tropics. He was a boy from the big city with a bucolic dream, a longing to change the world into the same endless cornfields from which I had escaped back in Ohio.

"What about you?" asked Adam.

"I want to go to Antarctica," I replied frankly, imagining blue icebergs as the tropical sun shone into my eyes. Both of us wanted the thing we never had—for Adam, it was a farm, and for me, the frozen bottom of the Earth. We sat silently, both of us staring out the bus window that framed each second of El Salvador like a scene—the glistening roadside trash, a wall of tangled cactus with a sign that read Keep Out! and, next to it, a chubby woman in a pink camisole sobbing uncontrollably. The scenes continued like a rippling film strip—women balancing plastic buckets on their heads, gracefully sidestepping the mud puddles in the road; derelict nightclubs with goats outside; and cinder block walls spray-painted with political graffiti for and against presidential candidate Rodrigo Ávila.

The bus went slower and slower until it stopped altogether. Through the windshield I saw the line of trucks and cars stopped ahead of us, and above the clouds of morning dust, I saw two nearly identical flags flying side by side—El Salvador and Honduras.

18 | ENGLAND

I know you, and you know me. We are as different as the sun and the sea." The children sang the words like a roaring chant. Some swayed vigorously in their little chairs, their miniature bodies bouncing up and down with the jaunty rhythm of the song.

I used to be just like that, I thought—caught up in the music, singing on command, singing louder to please whoever was listening. Now I was the one listening, the grown-up at the front of the room, bending low enough to lock eyes with the youngest kids in the front, waving my arms like I was painting the sky in 4/4 time. Some of them looked so lost, gazing off into the corner, too fascinated by their own fingers or shoelaces to pay attention to the music that swelled from the piano.

"*I know you, and you know me, and that's the way that it's supposed to be!*"

I made them sing it three times, three different ways: super loud, then standing up, and finally, whispering as quiet as they could. If you want children to pay attention, you must pay attention to them and switch things up. But I also wanted them to remember the words—of all the songs in the approved LDS children's songbook, "We Are Different" was my favorite. The page was illustrated with two boys—one white, one black—building a sandcastle together. Another page showed a small girl in a wheelchair, smiling next to her able-bodied, nonjudgmental friend.

The song finished and the kids collapsed back into their seats with gusto, fidgeting until the primary president stood up and put one finger up to her lips, hushing some thirty-five children with a single *shhhh.*

"See how lucky we are to have Brother Evans as our new primary chorister?" she said, projecting her voice to the back of the room. "I know that *I'm* excited to see all the songs he will teach you—are *you* excited?" she asked, nodding her head until the children began nodding back.

"Now let's show Brother Evans how reverent we can be, *hmmm?*" She folded her arms and the children followed suit, then the pianist began tinkling out a slow rendition of the peaceful hymn "I Am a Child of God." Row by row, the children left the room in single file, quietly trotting off to their respective Sunday school classes. I waved good-bye to them, then began collecting my music and homemade posters.

"Hey, Andrew!" A friend called me from the hallway of the church. Ronan was a fellow student at Oxford—tall and broad-shouldered with hair the color of pumpkins. He was English, married with children, and a scholar of Ancient Assyria. His ability to read cuneiform ensured our Sunday school class never got too dull. He was also my home teacher, making monthly personal visits to my rooms at Christchurch, checking up on my spiritual welfare. On his last visit, I had been very frank with him: I was gay and I was in love with Brian.

"The bishop wants to see you," said Ronan. "He's up in his office."

Getting summoned to the bishop's office was never a good thing— at least not for me. In the previous month I had spent a fair amount of time sitting across from his desk, opening up to him with my problems and fears—how I was gay, how my family had stopped talking to me, and how my life seemed to be disintegrating in slow motion.

The bishop was a good man who smiled lots and greeted every member of the ward like we were all cousins at a picnic. He had converted late in life, a local man from the countryside who spoke with a rounded Oxfordshire accent that I loved. He was the one who had called me as primary chorister—a calling almost always held by women.

"I think you'll be good at it," was all he said, and I accepted the calling as I had always done. I had always been honest with my bishop—he knew my situation, that in the eyes of the church I was "unworthy" to participate, but he had given me a calling all the same. And now, after my first week in the job, he was calling me back in.

"How are you doing, Brother Evans?" he asked, though he meant it only as an opening line—a blank page that needed turning.

"Fine. Today was good," I said, and it *was* good. My heart was light and the shy sun of England was glowing through the windows. Even with all the complications in my life, I still found solace at church.

"That's great to hear . . ." The bishop paused, then stared back at me with a gray gaze, his eyes like those on a very old dog. He did not want to be doing this any more than I did.

"So that thing we discussed a while back? What you told me—about how you are gay. You know I think it's fine—you told me what happened at BYU, and I think it's so funny that they tried to make you change!" The bishop chuckled, hoping I might laugh with him, but I could not. My memories of those years of "reparative" therapy were not funny.

"Anyway," the bishop continued, "the stake president asked me to check in with the area presidency; in turn, they thought it best to check in with the leadership in Salt Lake." So our confidential chat had not been so confidential—my name had been kicked up the chain, all the way back to Utah. No matter where I traveled in the world, I could never escape Utah.

"I know I told you that this was just your nature." The bishop hesitated. "But the brethren are very concerned that your feelings are not simply for men . . . but perhaps for children, too?" He paused again and stared right at me, perhaps waiting for me to speak, though at that exact moment, I could not even breathe. I only felt sick—too sick to sit up straight.

"Do you? Do you feel sexual attraction to children?" he asked. "I need to know."

Several long seconds passed. The overhead lights hummed in the small square office, a watch was ticking, and my own forehead was hot with shame. My own bumbling bishop was asking me if I was a pedophile.

"No," I answered. "I am not a pedophile." Simply saying the word was loathsome.

"And you've never had those kinds of feelings?" he asked again. "For children?" The way he repeated the question felt even more humiliating, like he was forcing me to fess up to something I had never been or done. I got upset.

"No! I have never been attracted to children *that way*. I am gay, which means I like men—adult men—and like I've told you, I have a partner."

The bishop tried to calm me down, told me that of course, *he* knew I was not a threat, but he was compelled to check, "because of the brethren." Though at that point I was barely listening—I only heard the thumping of my heart and felt a tightening pain in my limbs and fingers.

"You understand that I have to release you from your calling," the bishop continued. "It's not my choice, but the area president said that either way, we can't have you around the children. It just looks bad." In the eyes of the church, I was a monster.

"The primary president already knows—I spoke with her this morning," he said. I nodded to the bishop and said nothing, then handed over the songbook, the sheets of music, and the binder of lesson plans that I had prepared for the coming months. Then I stood up, desperate not to cry in front of a man I had once respected.

"I am sorry, Andrew," he offered. "But I have to look out for everybody in the ward."

I turned away as a few tears tumbled from one eye, then I bit my upper lip and turned the doorknob. From the chapel came the intense discussion of Sunday school, and when I got downstairs, I could hear the youngest children playing a game in the nursery. Some of the kids were laughing; a few were crying, calling out for their mothers. A minute later, I was at the back of the parking lot, hiding behind the family-size cars and sobbing hoarsely, ashamed by what had just happened—ashamed that I was crying. I tried to calm down by sucking in the cool air, breathing slowly, in and out. Fall had come, the river was full and brown, and the trees hung with yellow-brown leaves. Everything was wet and hopeful, and I was alone, standing in my blue shirt and sun-flower tie and watching the blank white sky of middle England.

"Andrew!" cried Ronan, jogging out to me at the far edge of the lot. He held his jacket in one hand—the bishop had sent him out to check on me.

"Are you all right?" he asked, stepping closer. He had a pained expression on his face, half-frowning with an eyebrow raised. Clearly, I was not all right.

"Come back inside—we need you!" Ronan said, and I sighed. This was the Mormon way—the false pleading and condescending pitch, the relentless push for inclusion. Had I not said those same words to other members? Had I ever really meant it? Mormons seem to believe that saying something enough makes it true, but no matter what Ronan said, at that moment, I did not feel particularly wanted or needed by my church.

"I can't," I said to Ronan, wiping my face with my hands. "I'm sorry but I just can't go back in today."

"Well, I can understand that," said Ronan. "But it's going to be all right. I promise you. We're here for you."

"The bishop asked me if I liked children," I said bitterly. "Do you think I'm a pedophile, too?"

"Andrew, you just have to forgive us!" Ronan pleaded. "The church just isn't ready yet. We don't know how to deal with this yet, but some-day they will and when that happens, we're gonna need you."

"I don't think I can wait that long," I said. Then I stepped away and walked down the street, steering my way around the black puddles. Ronan lingered in the doorway of the church, waving back at me like a good friend assigned by the church to keep me in check. I walked a few more blocks, then ducked into the red metal booth, waiting for the bus to come.

19 MILKMAN

Day 8

While my bus rolled across the sunbaked southern corner of Honduras, former president Manuel Zelaya was hiding out at the Brazilian embassy in Tegucigalpa. He had been trapped there for months, waiting to take back his office after he was ousted in a coup d'état and then exiled. Zelaya had sneaked back into the country curled up in the trunk of a car, which must have been a lot less comfortable than my *autobús de lujo* with its cooling flow of AC and the sonorous melodies of Air Supply played over the bus speakers.

Strict curfews were in place across the country, and all roads in and out of Tegucigalpa were heavily guarded with several thousand troops. When we reached the turnoff at Jicaro Galan, the road was lined with at least a hundred soldiers dressed in olive-green uniforms and gripping black metal guns. A sign with an arrow pointed right toward Tegucigalpa, just three hours north, where at that precise moment, people in the streets were getting shot, stabbed, and beaten. Our bus turned left, and after we cleared the military checkpoint, we continued down the CA-1 past the terracotta roofs and shadowed porches hung with drying laundry.

This section of road was empty, like a blank space in the Pan-American Highway. Only a few trucks passed us by, while dozens of unused yellow school buses sat parked along the roadside, next to piles of light-green melons. The heat of the sun beat down on the red earth, and the entire country felt eerily quiet. Unlike El Salvador and Guatemala, there were hardly any people outside. Now and again I saw a child's face poke out the window of one of the pink or turquoise houses, but they disappeared just as quickly, retreating back under the blue plastic sheeting used for a roof.

It cost ten dollars to enter Nicaragua, where skinny chickens bobbed back and forth across the border. Moneychangers and food vendors preyed on our stagnant state, and while we waited for various officials to process us through, I made friends with a stray dog. The red mutt was smeared from paw to snout with dust, and he sniffed at my feet and whimpered until I dropped to my knees and began petting his head and then his ears. He did not run away but stepped closer and nuzzled his chin against my knees, earning all my sympathy. There is nothing more heartbreaking than an unloved dog, and I rummaged through my pack for any food I might have. My little dog gobbled the peanut butter granola bar in three bites and just like that, I was surrounded by a pack of miserable hungry dogs. I had nothing left to give, but the dogs followed me like paparazzi until I locked myself into the lone outhouse. The toilet seat was missing and the tiny closet swarmed with flies, but I waited a few minutes, holding my breath before stepping back onto the road.

The farther south I traveled, the slower time moved. Nicaraguan life was the opposite of urgent, and the bus seemed to roll in slow motion, letting me mindfully watch every mile of the country. I tapped out another tweet:

Roosters, hammocks, goal stands, bottles, beehives, bricks, ponies, dirt, thatch, oxen, palm fronds, bicycles, crosses, corn, coffee, sun.

While Honduras had felt stark and unwelcoming, Nicaragua was alive with wild, green mountains and busy humans—women broke stones with pickaxes and men with straw hats raked coffee beans across huge concrete slabs to dry in the sun. After the jungle came the cattle ranches, where cowboys gathered brahman bulls into corrals, and the cattle fences fluttered with diaphanous plastic bags hooked on the barbed wire, colored pink, white, blue, and green.

Nature reigns supreme in Nicaragua—the shining silver lake was so immense, the city on its shore looked miniature, though two million people lived within the expanse of scattered concrete blocks. Bromeliads sprouted from the tangle of electrical wires, and the emerald earth swept steeply to the pointed volcanoes above. Our bus turned into the tight streets of the capital, past belching trucks and horse-drawn carts. Graffiti covered crumbling concrete walls with the slogan *¡Viva FSLN!*, while the telephone posts had been painted red and black—the bold communist colors of the Sandinista National Liberation Front.

We arrived at the bus station at 6:00 p.m.—after the ticket office was already closed. A brigade of cleaning ladies was busy mopping the floor with lemony chemicals that stung my nose, while the other passengers dispersed quickly with their bags.

"Be back here tomorrow at 8:00 a.m.," the bus driver said, locking up the bus.

"I thought this bus was continuing onto San José?" I asked. The bus driver was heavy and humorless, and he shook his head with gusto, as if I had just asked him to work overtime.

"No, no, no," he said. "We do not drive at night in Nicaragua—*es muy peligroso*. We stop here for the night, and tomorrow we go to Costa Rica."

Tomorrow was too late—it would take us all day to get there, and I had to be in San José the next morning, ready to join up with the expedition group from National Geographic.

"Go find a hostel," urged the bus driver. "Get some sleep, eat some food, and then come back in the morning."

"That's too late for me," I said. "I need to get on the next bus to Costa Rica tonight!" I felt embarrassed by my tone—aware that I was losing my patience and frantically demanding something that did not exist.

"*No se puede*," said the driver. "The last bus left for Costa Rica three hours ago. Besides, we never drive at night down here—too many *bandidos* on the road."

Bandits? I imagined a Nicaraguan version of the Little Rascals brandishing slingshots and toy guns, sporting overalls and Zorro masks, but the truth was more frightening: gangsters with AK-47s and machetes, T-shirts pulled up over their faces, blockading the road and demanding ransom money.

Still, there had to be a way to get across the border tonight, I thought, even if I had to drive myself.

At the back of the station sat a few lingering taxis, and while most of the drivers ignored my request to reach the *frontera* before it closed, one did not—an elderly man with a full head of gray hair and a wrinkled face that was brown from the sun. His name was Panfilon and he looked like my grandfather.

"You want to get to the Costa Rican border tonight?" he checked.

"*Sí,*" I replied.

"This is very difficult," he said. "There is too much traffic in Managua now and the way is long—more than 150 kilometers. And then, *los bandidos.*" He paused. "*Es posible . . .* the others will say *no es posible,* but I can do it."

"Fantastic," I said, relieved.

"Eighty dollars," he said. "Do you have it?" Eighty bucks was a lot of money. More than I had spent on all my buses for the last four days— but now was not the time to quibble over the price. Eighty bucks was the price of a cab to the airport in Washington, DC.

"Yes. Let's go!"

"*Vámanos,*" said Panfilon. I threw my bag on the backseat of his banged-up Toyota, then crawled into the passenger side with my knees pressed against the plastic dashboard. There was no seat belt, and so I clung to the door and the edge of my seat as we spun through the aggressive Managua *tráfico.*

"You will see—I am very fast. I hope I can get you there in time—I think I can!" Panfilon gave himself his own pep talk while revving his engine at every red light and attacking every city block like its own unique drag race. Like me, he craved the challenge ahead—to beat the odds and achieve the impossible. We had one hundred minutes to drive one hundred miles, and the minute we broke free from the stilted traffic,

Panfilon shot the car into top gear, tearing down the CA-1 at a break-neck speed and passing cars and trucks and cows in the dark. This was too fast, I thought—if we hit the slightest bump, a forgotten water-melon, some discarded muffler—then this scrappy Toyota would fly right off the road and into the depths of Lago Nicaragua. I guessed we were doing eighty miles an hour, though the speedometer was lifeless, jumping only with the bumps in the road. I had invented my own little death trap.

At 8:37 p.m., Panfilon slowed the shaky car and pulled over in front of the border post.

"Go, go now! Hurry!" he said, urging me to cross before it closed. I handed him a hundred dollars and kept repeating "*gracias*" over and over as I waved good-bye and walked backward toward the border. The night was warm, and on the side of the road a group of shirtless men was drinking beer and shooting pool. All the adrenalin of racing through Nicaragua evaporated in the calm jungle evening that now enveloped me.

The Nicaraguans stamped me out of the country with ten minutes to spare—then I walked alone in the darkness for half a mile, caught between countries in a strange international limbo. For a moment, I imagined bandidos hiding in the darkness of the trees, but then I saw the sign announcing Costa Rica, painted with an italic subtitle: *Dios Guardara Su Camino* ("God Keep Your Way"). Then I spotted the single lightbulb hanging in the distance. Mosquitoes floated around my head and the unrelenting heat forced me to stop and sip water. As I reached the light, I saw two women and two men sitting behind a wooden picnic table. The four immigration officers wore polo shirts and all of them were smiling.

"Welcome to Costa Rica," the older man said in English.

"Thank you," I said, feeling more relieved than ever—amazed by the day's adventures and shamefully glad to be upgrading to a more developed country. A laptop and a laser printer sat on the table and my passport was stamped and handed back to me without delay—two seconds versus the two hours it had taken for me to enter Nicaragua.

"Is there a bus?" I asked.

"No, no—not until morning," the man said, checking his watch. "In nine hours."

In nine hours I had to be in San José—two hundred miles away. Now that the border was closed, there were no taxis or even cars—only the narrow lanes of the Pan-American Highway and a long line of northbound trucks waiting to cross.

I walked on, alone, rocking back and forth with my pack, listening to my boots crunch against the gravel shoulder and the idling engines of heavy cargo trucks. Then I heard a different engine—a moving engine—and I saw my own shadow grow taller in the bright headlights. It was the last southbound truck to cross that night—I spun around and stuck out my arm and began waving it like an anxious volleyball player. The eighteen-wheeler slowed and then braked in front of me. The driver rolled down his window.

"¿Adónde vas?" he asked.

"A San José," I answered.

"I'm going to Puerto Limón," he said. "I can take you there."

He opened the right-hand door; I climbed up into the cab and the driver helped me stuff my bag into the back. Then he put the truck into gear and steered us onto the highway, chugging slowly up the hill.

"I'm Marvín," said the driver, reaching out his hand to shake mine. He pronounced it with a rolled r and a long i: Marrr-veen.

"My name is Andrew," I replied and shook his hand. Six days spent in six different Spanish-speaking countries had done more for my language ability than any amount of study.

"I am carrying milk from Nicaragua," he explained. "This milk"—he nodded backward to the container behind us—"we ship it to Venezuela, then I drive back to Managua carrying oil from Venezuela." Milk for gas, I thought, smiling to myself. I was inadvertently participating in the "Oil Diplomacy" of Hugo Chávez.

"Why are you going to San José?" Marvín asked.

"I'm just traveling—I am on my way to Antártida," I confessed. I had left Washington, DC, more than a week ago, I explained, and I was traveling overland, all the way to the bottom of the world, something I had always wanted to do.

"*¿Es su sueño?*" said Marvín, and I nodded, pretending I understood. He repeated the question, pointing from his heart and then right at me. "*¿Es su sueño?*"

"What is this, *sueño*?" I asked, but no matter how much he tried to explain the meaning of the word, I did not understand.

"Yes, this is my *sueño*," I said, not knowing if I was talking about my shoes or the sweat on my forehead. The truck puttered onward and Marvín balanced the steering wheel, wrapped with tight, red plastic string. His cab was decorated with extraordinary color, with framed pictures of his wife and daughter and flowery velvet fabric over the dashboard. A plastic Virgin Mary dangled from the mirror and a half-dozen CD cases clacked against one another.

"You like music?" he asked, and I nodded yes. Then he popped in a CD and began singing along to Celia Cruz. Marvín swayed to the merengue and kept checking on me, stiff and silent in my seat, not even tapping my foot.

"You gotta dance!" He nudged me with one hand. "Like this!" Marvín began swerving his hips from side to side in his seat, left foot tapping madly while his right foot stayed steady on the gas. Sweat beads rolled down his tattooed shoulders and soaked his white cotton tank top. He kept nudging me until I began snapping my fingers, reluctantly.

Marvín smiled, and when Celia began crooning some of her highest notes, he slipped into a warm harmony.

"This is how I stay awake," he explained. "I don't ever drink coffee— I have to stay up all night every night, and if I drank coffee all the time my heart would go *loco*." Marvin pulled up a gallon jug from the floor of the cab.

"I sing and I drink water," he said, taking a long swig from the plastic jug. He offered me a drink but I declined. Though I had broken the rule about accepting rides from strangers, I was still not accepting drinks from strangers. That's exactly how my cousin got drugged and robbed on a bus in Uganda. And yet Marvín was drinking from the same jug he was offering me, so would it have mattered?

My exhausted brain tried to gauge the risk at hand, while my eyes fluttered shut as I fought to stay awake. If I fell asleep, I thought, then I might wake up handcuffed and blindfolded in some rusty shed in the jungle with a few missing vital organs—or worse, a political prisoner of the Chávez regime. I did not want to be an urban legend, I did not want to become a cautionary tale for the State Department, and I did not want my face on CNN. But I was not the only one fighting sleep. I kept turning to Marvín, who was nodding off himself. We puttered up and down the hills of northern Costa Rica at twenty-five miles an hour—the only vehicle on the road at 2:00 a.m.

The languorous nightclub melodies of Vicentico Valdés now sang from the truck's speakers, but Marvín's own voice kept dropping off as his head leaned closer and closer to the steering wheel. Now it was my turn to offer him water and keep him dancing in his seat.

"So what is the difference between salsa and merengue?" I asked Marvín. He mumbled back at me and counted out the beats in Spanish, tapping the wheel, but then grew silent once more.

"I don't feel very good," he said, suddenly. "My stomach hurts." He grabbed the side of his belly and moaned. Was this real? I wondered. Was this part of some act? Is this where he overpowered me and stuck a chloroform rag over my mouth? Now Marvín was slowing the truck, pulling over to the shoulder of the road and stopping beneath a canopy of tropical trees. He shut off the engine and coughed a little before unlocking the doors in the cab.

"I just need a minute," he said, getting out. "You wait here—I have to *hacer pis*." No surprise there. If I had been drinking gallons of water for four hours straight, I would need to *hacer pis* in the woods, too. I sat quietly in the truck, wondering how far we had traveled—no more than a hundred miles, I thought. Sally the trusty GPS tracker was still blinking her happy green eye at me, but I had no cell service in Costa Rica—and so I had no idea where I was. The jungle was dark and silent—I only heard the sound of trickling water from Marvín. Soon he returned, moaning and leaning against the side of his truck, where he began to vomit violently. Milky water gushed from his mouth like an erupting geyser, splashing down the side of the truck and onto his own seat. He continued to vomit until there was nothing left to throw up, and then he began dry heaving like a wild animal in pain.

I retreated into the cab, a bit horrified, holding my breath from the stench of stomach fluids. Then Marvín climbed back into his wet seat, panting heavily.

"I'm fine—everything is fine," he said, shutting and locking the door. Then he closed his eyes and passed out in his own mess.

I waited, on guard, for Marvín to jump up from his phony sleep and lunge at me with a knife—that's how it happened in the movies. Instead, Marvín began to snore loudly, sucking in air, and then exhaling, sending sputtering bubbles out his nose. I waited a minute, then five more minutes—Marvín was definitely asleep, and I was definitely locked in his truck in the middle of the night, deep within the Costa Rican jungle, miles away from any kind of civilization.

Clearly Marvín was not well, but I was not going to hang around until he slept if off. I had another hundred miles to go before dawn, and there was no way I would get there by sitting around inhaling residual vomit.

With the deft hands of a thief, I reached into Marvín's pants pocket and pulled out the keys. He had a soccer ball key chain with six different keys, and I tried each one until I popped the lock on Marvín's door.

Working in slow motion, I pulled my backpack from the rear and set it in the passenger seat while straddling Marvín's sleeping body. Using all the muscles in my back and arms, I lifted my backpack and slowly pulled it across Marvín, then dropped it to the ground. Once I shut the door, I never looked back. I just kept walking ahead in the dark, not knowing where but hiking onward, farther south, believing I would get there.

The all-night trucker café was nothing more than a slanted tin roof propped up by a few wooden boards, but it was open. I sat down because I had nowhere else to go—I was tired, and I could not remember the last time I had eaten a meal. The waitress and I were the only humans in the world, it seemed, and she brought me a pile of beans and rice with a big bottle of Salsa Lizano.

"You're walking?" asked the waitress, who was tall and thin, with European features and a blue apron around her waist.

"No." I tried to explain, but I was too tired and my Spanish had collapsed into gibberish: "Truck driver Nicaragua sick sleep now me solo me airport today."

"You're going to the San José airport?" she asked.

"*Sí*," I said.

"Don't worry, *hombre*," she said. "I can help." She walked out into the road and waited for almost ten minutes, watching for a passing car in the darkness. Then she began waving both her arms in the air. A small blue car swerved into the gravel lot, and through the window, the waitress chatted with a young man.

"This is my friend, Jorge. He will take you where you need to go," she said. "*¡Buen viaje!*"

And like that, I was zooming back down the Pan-American, this time at seventy miles an hour in a blue sports car driven by a slick businessman who asked no questions but let me sleep until we reached San José, where I would meet up with our group to catch a bus to our ship in Herradura.

I had made it to the meeting place with two hours to spare. I sat cross-legged on the polished floor at baggage claim, slumped against my backpack, panting wildly. Then my eyes closed once more, and I fell asleep on the floor—a bum with his bag.

20 PANAMA

Day 12

Eight laps in the pool—no biggie. In high school I had swum the same distance in less than two minutes, but that was in clear, chlorinated water with bright lights, antifog goggles, and bleachers filled with screaming parents.

The Pacific seemed so dark and forbidding—like crinkled foil reflecting the gray storm brewing on the horizon. Some guests went back in the zodiacs, but the captain said we could swim back to the ship. I kicked my legs in the soupy sea, trying not to think of the likely creatures swimming with us, namely crocodiles and bull sharks. They lived here in Golfo Dulce, hanging out in the mouths of coastal rivers, feeding on fish at dusk. It was dusk now.

I took a few light strokes and turned to check on Chris. She was floating on her side, head held high, her right hand extended like a flying superhero.

"I'm doing sidestroke," she said, spitting out saltwater. "That's the one I do best." Chris kept her rhythm steady, stroking and pulling, while I hung back, hovering in the black water.

"If I get too tired, you'll get one of the boats to pick me up?" she asked.

"Of course—but you can swim this, no problem."

Chris was thirty years older than me—a retired Latin teacher from North Carolina with the haircut of a Soviet male gymnast and an accent from *Gone with the Wind*. As the only single travelers on the ship, we clung together like two girls at summer camp—I was her younger sidekick in the jungle, always stopping to point out the toucans or two-toed sloths in the cathedral canopy of trees, and she was the one who stopped me every twenty minutes to slather sunblock on my face and shoulders. Now I felt so greasy, I was sliding through the water, wishing that sunscreen was shark repellent.

"Are we halfway there?" asked Chris, gasping just a little.

"I think so," I said, though I could tell the ship was pivoting on its anchor line, turning away with the current, doubling the distance from the beach.

"I can't. I can't swim any more," she said, hitting the top of the water with her hands. I called over a zodiac to pick her up, and though they had enough space in the boat for me too, I stayed in the water.

"I'll swim," I said, determined to make it to the ship, even with my heart beating and the scary realization that I was alone in the ocean. I plunged onward, closing my eyes and pulling at the inky water as if climbing an endless ladder. With every kick, I imagined a shark or croco-dile close behind, nipping at my bare toes with their teeth. I was the solitary figure in the water, alone beneath the darkening sky. I looked back to shore and saw the last few tourists in their swimsuits and life-jackets, preparing to head back for a leisurely evening of dinner and drinks aboard the *National Geographic Sea Lion*.

I was floating untethered in the largest ocean on Earth with only my cold muscles to pull me back to the dry refuge of our boat. I was swimming for myself now, without any cheering parents or online audi-ence. There was no prize for winning first place—only the ship in the distance and my own fear that kept me swimming, kicking, paddling, closer and closer until I was finally there, hugging the steel hull with my long, naked limbs.

Over the next five days, we sailed south, hugging the tropical shore-line so closely, I could hear scarlet macaws screeching in the trees. A decade spent living with a biologist had armed me with enough knowl-edge to show off in front of Chris, pointing out roseate spoonbills and the scarlet-rumped tanagers with back feathers the color of grenadine and silver beaks like a tin whistle. When seedpods and sticks suddenly rained down on our heads, I rushed Chris under shelter and pointed out the howler monkeys overhead.

"When they feel threatened, they throw things," I explained.

"Like high school students," she said, shading her eyes with her hand.

"Except when howler monkeys run out of projectiles, they'll start throwing poop," I said, speaking from my own experience.

"In thirty-five years of teaching, it never came to that—fortunately." Chris laughed.

When we finally entered the Panama Canal that night, she invited me up to the highest deck, so we would not miss a single second of the action at the Miraflores Locks.

"This is the whole reason I came on this trip," she said. "I had to see the Panama Canal." The warm night air blew over us, and Chris stood there, pensively, in love with the awesome mechanics in play. The gates opened, and our ship slowly pushed into the measured box of seawater and steel.

"My grandfather worked here, back in 1912—he helped build this canal with his own two hands," said Chris. "It's something that he always talked about—the heat and humidity, the gargantuan scale of it all—but nobody in the family ever got to see it for themselves. Now that I'm here, I feel like I'm visiting a part of his life." Chris paused to take in the tremendous engineering that now swallowed us. The gates began to close behind us, while under beams of bright lights, the linemen ran back and forth at the edge of the lock.

"My ex-husband never wanted to go anywhere—and now that my sons are grown, I'm worried they're too much like him. All they do is work," said Chris. As the water swelled in the lock and the ship lifted upward, we talked about our respective families—the love and admiration, and the damage and hurt.

"Believe me, as a mother," said Chris. "Your parents love you more than you will ever understand."

"I know that," I said.

"Give them time," she urged. "It will be hard for them, but they will come around." We stayed on deck until after eight, when the ship was slipping through the calm, brown water of the Río Chagres. I pointed out the faint lights of the small town of Gamboa, flickering like a nest of fireflies in the jungle.

"That's where Brian works," I said. "He's probably there right now." After four thousand miles and more than two weeks apart, I would see him. Somewhere out in those shadows, down below the dark forest, Brian was probably walking around with his flashlight, following the peeps and croaks of the tiniest frogs as they woke up to the moon and the living night.

"Well, I hope I get to meet him," offered Chris.

"I hope so, too," I said, but when I looked at her, she had turned her face and was wiping her eyes.

"I'm such a silly old lady," she said, sniffling. "I can't believe our trip is almost over. I think I am going to have a hard time saying good-bye to you."

"Me, too," I agreed. Traveling together does this—forges sudden bonds between strangers.

"I'll be following you online, young man," she said. "You better stay safe!"

❉

Brian met me on the dock in Colón, next to a mess of cranes and containers. It was hard not to kiss him.

"Not the place," whispered Brian. We stuck out enough as it was—a pair of tall white guys in shorts, standing at the gates of the most reviled city in the Caribbean.

"Don't you dare walk out of this place," said our Panamanian expedition leader. "You go outside and you'll be robbed in five minutes." Brian had booked us into a hotel near the sea, but the view was hardly romantic. The water was gray green and filled with debris: plastic garbage, dead fish, and floating tree trunks. Iron gates and fences fringed with barbed wire cordoned off the free-trade zone from the more substantial and decrepit side of Colón, inhabited by unsavory people.

"Why does everybody look like a pirate?" I asked.

"Because they are," said Brian. "The Panamanians think everybody in Colón is a criminal. Mostly, they're just unemployed." The city streets were heaped with garbage, and raw sewage flowed in the gutters. A century ago, old Colón was beautiful. Ornate fragments and historical paint jobs clung to the rows of dilapidated architecture with hints of Old Havana and the palaces of Venice, but now all these buildings seemed lifeless.

"*Lonely Planet* calls it 'a sprawling slum of decaying colonial grandeur and desperate human existence,'" I read out loud from the screen on my phone.

"That's why you hate *Lonely Planet*," said Brian.

"I know, but maybe for once, they're right," I said, before checking Twitter, where a friend of mine was begging me not to leave the hotel. She had published a different guidebook to Panama, one that described Colón as "rife with poverty and crime—provokes shock, sadness, or a very uncomfortable feeling." While her description was apt, I had come to Colón with a quest. Though it stretches from the top of Alaska to the end of Argentina, the sixteen-thousand-mile-long Pan-American Highway skips a beat for about a hundred miles, near the border between Panama and Colombia—a notorious no-man's-land known as the Darién Gap. Here the road ends abruptly and the jungle takes over—swamps and mountains make it almost impossible to pass through without an experienced guide, not to mention the swarms of paramilitary groups and narco-terrorists dueling out their differences in the rain forest. Bad things happen in the Darién Gap—people get shot or kidnapped and held hostage. Only a few travelers manage to make it through, either by blind luck or by paying off the right people.

While on assignment for our sister magazine *National Geographic Adventure*, journalist Robert Pelton was kidnapped while attempting to cross the Darién Gap in 2003. He and two other backpackers were held for ten days by the United Self-Defense Forces of Colombia (AUC), a right-wing paramilitary group. In the end, they made the crossing—albeit at gunpoint—after which Pelton called the Darién "the most dangerous place in the Western Hemisphere." That is saying something, coming from a man who specializes in the world's deadliest places.

In light of Pelton's kidnapping, my editor at *National Geographic Traveler* asked me kindly to please skip the Darién Gap. "I don't wanna have to call the State Department," he said. I reassured Keith that I had no intention of trying to hike into Colombia—I did not have the time or the gear or the contacts, nor did I have a death wish—but I still felt determined to travel overland.

Jumping on a plane felt like cheating. I wanted the line to remain unbroken—from the front steps of my apartment all the way to Antarctica—without ever letting go of the earth. I did not want to miss a single inch of the globe I was crossing.

I asked around at the port, shouting to sailors aboard their ships, "Where are you going?" followed by, "When are you leaving?"

"*¡No pasajeros!*" they shouted back at me, even when I offered them money. I left Colón without success and Brian drove me along the Caribbean coast in search of a charter sailboat that might be headed to Colombia.

I found my boat at the very end of the road, an hour past Portobelo, where the one-lane asphalt stopped and the murky swamps took over. Mangroves gave way to the muddy saltwater and farther out in the milky green waves bobbed several small sailboats, their rigging slapping furiously against the masts.

"Which one is it?" I asked, pointing, but the white lady shook her head.

"Not those boats. It's a different one," she said. Her accent was German, and her head was piled high with blonde dreadlocks. She was the one who greeted me at the shack in the swamp, smiling at me with missing teeth when I told her I was looking for a boat.

"Yes, yes. We have a boat leaving for Colombia!" she said, clutching a naked baby on one hip. She was practically naked herself, sporting a loose bikini top over a flat chest and a stained miniskirt wrapped around her frail torso. "Come in, come in," she said, disappearing behind a makeshift plywood door. Brian shook his head at me and shot me his most disapproving look. "No way," he whispered.

Still, I walked inside the shack that smelled of pot smoke and dirty diapers. I followed the German back to the kitchen, where her husband was repairing an old boat motor on the linoleum floor. He was tan but scarily emaciated and his hands were covered in black oil. A red cotton sash was tied around his mass of dreadlocks, and he barely looked at me as he tinkered with the busted engine.

"These guys are dodgy as hell," Brian whispered in my ear. He had followed me into the squalid hut and was appalled by the putrid garbage on the floor and the buzzing flies that hovered over the rotting food in the sink. I thought back to our life in the British Virgin Islands, when we were young, barefoot, and broke—how happy we were just to eat fruit off the trees and fish from the sea. Back then it all seemed so hopelessly romantic, while these dirty German hippies made poverty seem grim and unfortunate.

"Seven hundred and fifty dollars," said the lady, when I asked her how much.

"That's a lot of money—just to sail to Colombia?" I asked. Besides, her boat would not be heading straight to Cartagena but hugging the coastline all the way to the border, where I would have to hike or thumb a ride on an illegal speedboat into Colombia.

I left the hut and walked down to another cluster of shacks, where a bunch of crusty yachties sat draining cans of beer.

"Yesterday, a boat got towed back in. Snapped its mast three days out!" said one of them. Another one chimed in, "It's January, *amigo*, the winds have shifted, so it's all chop. You can hop a boat to Cartagena, but you'll be sorry you did."

Disheartened, I sat on a dock over the muddy shoreline and stared at the rolling whitecaps in the distance. Colombia was only one hundred miles ahead of me—only a few hours by bus, if there was a road, but seemingly out of reach by sea. I heard the sailors muttering in the background, hinting at the obvious—how these sailboats running back and forth to Colombia were in fact smuggling narcotics. Taking my chances on a sailboat could easily derail my chance at riding the bus to the bottom of the world.

Brian handed me a cold can of ginger ale, then sat down next to me. For a while he said nothing, dangling his legs over the water and sipping a Coke. He knew the turmoil I felt—how I always wanted things a certain way, and how critical it was for me to complete this journey without any airplanes. Then he held my hand and spoke.

"You're flying," he said and then turned to look me in the face. "I don't care what you say—this situation is dodgy as hell and you're not sailing. You've made it all this way, Drew—why do you want to risk it all for a hundred miles? That's stupid." I was disappointed by the truth but glad to have Brian with me, stepping in as the voice of reason.

"You can waste another week trying to figure this out, or you can fly to Colombia and get on with your assignment," he said.

"But I wanted to do this without flying . . . ," I whined.

"I know. But you're flying. I just decided for you." Brian jumped up on the dock and offered me his hand. It took us three hours to drive to Panama City, where I bought a one-way ticket to Cartagena. We said good-bye in Brian's herpetology lab, surrounded by shelves of giant glass jars filled with dead vipers and pickled boa constrictors.

"I'll see you in March," he said—two months away. I hugged him once more, tightly, and he pecked me on the lips.

The plane peeled away from the runway, and as we climbed into the sky, I kept my face stuck to the oval window, watching the smoky-green jungle give way to the turquoise Caribbean and the enormous piles of clouds. Cartagena is about one hundred miles north of Panama City, so I was flying north to South America, waiting for my first glimpse of the continent. Then it appeared, immense and green, pulling us all the way in, until our plane skidded down the runway. I clicked my stopwatch. Flight time: twenty-six minutes.

21 THROUGH THE PLEXIGLASS

You just don't bleed that well," said Sheila, standing in her lab coat.

"I get nosebleeds almost once a week—at least I did when I was younger—and once I got punched in the face and dripped blood all the way to the hospital."

"That's not what I mean," said Sheila. "I have to take a blood sample every day—and right now when I prick your ears, there's barely any capillary action." Sheila spoke with a Midlands accent, so that *capillary* rhymed with Hilary. It was Hilary term now—the second term at Oxford University, from January to March. We left in May. I needed the money.

"Can't you take it from my finger?" I offered up my hand, but Sheila shook her head.

"No, the whole point of the experiment is to calculate blood oxygen levels in the brain—bleeding the ear is the most accurate reading we can take." This was her doctoral thesis—to study the effects of long-haul flights on the human body—and it involved locking students in a gas chamber pumped full of altered levels of carbon dioxide.

"Brian bleeds fine. I can use him," said Sheila. But that wasn't enough. The pay was five hundred pounds per person. If we both completed two weeks of the experiment, we would earn enough to spend the whole summer in the Caribbean.

"Give me one more chance," I begged her. Being a guinea pig in the physiology lab was the most lucrative student job at Oxford. Sheila slathered my ears with red pepper gel. Tears squeezed from the corners of my eyes; I felt the quick sting of the needle in the fleshy edge of my earlobe. Three drops of my own red blood brightened the floor.

"There you go," said Sheila, placing a tiny glass tube against my ear and then pinching the wound. She laughed, relieved. "Brilliant. Think you can do this every day?" Her tone mimicked a teacher praising a slow kindergartner who's finished the school day without peeing his pants. I nodded yes and signed the contract.

My transparent prison cell was nine feet long and four feet wide, with enough room to stand up and reach the ceiling. I had a sturdy cot with a mattress, pillow, and blanket, along with a rigid plastic chair and narrow desk that I stacked with old leather-bound books I borrowed from the geography library: *Outer Mongolia, The Antarctic, Africa's Gold Coast, Life among the Esquimaux.* None of the books had anything to do with my thesis, but they were far more interesting.

Every morning, Sheila entered my cage to prick my ears and bleed me into a pair of tiny glass tubes. At night, another technician stuck a series of cloth electrodes to my chest and a breathing mask that measured the gas I exhaled. Sometimes the mask fell off, and I would hear a knock on the glass wall with a swift gesture to reattach the long tubes to my face.

Brian was just across the room from me, asleep in his own plexiglass box. Sometimes I tried getting his attention by waving or jumping up in the air, but the scientists said I could not exert myself too much—it might affect the results. The lab was just one block away from where Brian and I first met—at a college dance that grew so popular the fire marshal had blocked anyone else from entering. Not one to be turned away at the door, I sneaked around to the back of the building and climbed through an open window, working my way through the college kitchen and onto the dance floor where I first saw him: tan, lithe, and laughing.

"You want lasagna or chicken curry?" Sheila asked me every night, holding up two boxed frozen meals against the glass.

"Whichever one Brian doesn't want," I said, but Sheila could not hear me. I pointed to the lasagna, because I already knew Brian wanted the curry. Born and raised in Africa, Brian could not comprehend a meal without meat, and here in the lab, they fed us like pets, handing us our microwaved meals through the trap door. If ever I needed to go to the bathroom, I was released from the chamber and ushered down the hall with the instruction "Be quick." Each time I awkwardly presented the warm jar back to Sheila, who quickly sealed it up and dashed back to the lab to get an accurate carbon dioxide reading.

On day 3, we were permitted a shower. The technician released both of us from our cells and led us down another hallway to a rarely used men's room, equipped with a pair of tiled shower stalls most likely built in the 1930s. Then he checked his watch.

"You've got five minutes before I have to lock you back up in the chamber," he said, handing us two towels before leaving. The door shut behind him. Brian was quick, dropping his clothes to the floor and pulling me into the warm stream of water. We only had four minutes, but it was four minutes together. We made the seconds count, arms wrapped around one another, the soapy foam pouring from our skin.

I wondered which of us was the control group, and which the experimental—only one of us was breathing normal air. At that moment, an entire team of young scientists was studying our very heartbeats, printed out on a long coil of paper through the night.

"See all those squiggles?" the technician pointed out that morning, unfurling the roll in front of me. "That's a dream—you're dreaming. And let's see, you had, one, two, three—four of those episodes last night. Four dreams, at least." The squiggly line rose and fell, then jumped, like a cross-section of the Himalayas. But my dreams could never hide my own reality—how I was locked in a box in a lab in a drab brick building at the edge of Oxford University, how I was so depressed and paralyzed with uncertainty that I had suspended my doctorate indefinitely. A nervous breakdown, they whispered in the college dining room. Psychosis, said my family back in America—that could be the only explanation for coming out to them as gay.

They had tried to intervene. First, my sister flew to England and offered me money if I left Brian and moved back to America. Then my father stopped by after a business trip to London. After lunch in college, he told me, "Don't ever make me sit with you and Brian in public. I want to spend time with you, but I do not want to give even the slightest impression that I approve of what you're doing."

"Dad, the only impression you gave is that you were having lunch with your son."

"You have free agency, which means you are free to destroy your own reputation," he replied. "But I am a high priest in the church. I choose to live by a certain standard. Every day I strive to set an example and live a Christlike life."

I believe the whole of Christianity can be defined by who Christ would sit next to in any school cafeteria—alas, one did not argue with my father and expect to win. He argued professionally for work, and at home and church he argued for righteousness and the world he believed in: black and white, male and female, laws and punishment.

"You may think this is fine now, but what are you going to do a year from now? America is not like Oxford. I can tell you now, nobody's gonna want you as a neighbor. If a pair of homosexuals moved onto my street, I'd be grabbing my kids and getting out of there so fast." My dad's face flushed red and purple, and he paced back and forth like a boxer, throwing out threats like punches. "And let's be honest, Andrew—you'll never get a job. Ever. You think any respectable company's gonna hire a homosexual? Forget about ever working for the federal government."

My father's words became shouts. I saw the panic and fear in his eyes. He had grown up in Washington, DC, in the 1950s. He had witnessed the McCarthy Era firsthand. My grandfather knew colleagues who were fired from their jobs, whose lives were ruined overnight simply for being too swishy and suspect. Now his son's son faced that same dismal future, along with eternal darkness and damnation forever after. My father was fighting for me, and I was fighting for me, too. My mother fought in her own way. She cried and sent pleading letters across the Atlantic. On my fourth day in the airtight chamber, I received her e-mail: *Dear Son,*

I'm so glad to hear you're feeling better. Hopefully you can use this time of quiet and calm for prayer and meditation.

Brian sent me a letter, too, which Sheila carried across the lab. Inside was a printed map of the British Virgin Islands with scribbled notes about each place. "Great diving here," he wrote over one island, and then next to another arrow, "Rainforest." The tiny speck of Sandy Cay was circled, along with the note "Uninhabited." Uninhabited sounded so nice.

"All we need is a little escape," wrote Brian, and that was our plan: to leave England with its gray moments, to go live on the beach and not wear any shoes, to be happy together. I was tired of fighting the entire world, my family, and the church—I was tired of hating myself for who I was. I just wanted to be me, wherever I could do that in the world.

I longed for silence and calm—for a quiet place that had no words for what I was, a place far away from the others, a place that would never kick me out. For now, I could only wait and dream, alone in my tiny glass box, measuring each breath.

It was raining on the sixth day when we stepped outside. Neither of us had an umbrella, so we got wet, raindrops falling on our faces, walking hand in hand through the park, underneath the stained English sky.

"You're bleeding, honey," said Brian, turning toward me. I wiped the side of my neck and stared at my hand, pink with blood and rain. Then I pinched my earlobe tightly and waited until the bleeding had stopped.

22 DEATH IN COLOMBIA

Day 18

Silky colored stripes waved at me from the top of the street—the first flag I saw in South America was a flashy rainbow that heaved and flopped in the languid breeze.

I followed the big gay flag to the stucco building on the corner—three stories high, with paneled French doors and balconies on every floor. The man at reception was young—and gay, I presumed. His T-shirt was so tiny and tight, it revealed the scant geography of his chest, punctuated by two boyish nipples. His eyes were blue, his smile bleached white, and a cloud of cologne hovered around his tanned face.

"We only have one room left," he said, leading me up the creaking stairs and down a sloped hallway. The rectangle room was old and immense, with a stone fireplace and high ceilings, and an antique bed that looked positively seaworthy. I had never stayed at a gay hotel before, nor was I sure what makes one hotel gayer than another. Besides the rainbow flag, the pretty, twink receptionist, and the disco ball in the lobby, the gayest thing about this hotel is that I wanted to stay there.

"This room is more than four hundred years old," said the receptionist. He offered me a welcome cocktail but I was eager to wander through the old city before dark.

Cartagena is such a dazzling place that I walked slowly, examining every building like a piece of framed art. The oldest homes had been gracefully remodeled and painted with the brightest shades of yellow, pink, orange, and blue, while other buildings decayed in the sun, their loose stones crumbling beneath the untamed boughs of fuchsia flamboyant. Dark-haired children ran in and out of the ruins—they lived here, while the larger palaces had become vacation rentals.

Loud and obvious tourists pushed through the streets, sidetracked by the jewelry and souvenir shops and the spectacle of costumed peddlers and the dancing ladies in the square. This was all a show, I thought—a kind of life-size theater set with beautiful backdrops and an endless supply of Romeo-and-Juliet balconies festooned with beautiful flowers. No matter, Cartagena was so beautiful and calming that I felt reenergized—as if my journey had begun all over again. The northern shore of Colombia was my new starting line—a green light and a gunshot before I plowed my own slow race down through South America.

Inside La Iglesia de Santo Domingo, I thanked God for letting me get this far, then lit a one-thousand-peso candle and asked for a safe and uneventful passage through Colombia. I stared at the quivering yellow flame and then looked upward to the pastel orange walls and the ceiling painted a soft baby blue. Plaster saints looked down on me with compassion. Their pious poses matched my own mood—as if together, we were dancing in the same spiritual ballet.

As the day cooled, I walked along the tops of the old city walls, constructed from square blocks of coral stone in a time when pirates used Cartagena like a beachside ATM. The sea was like blue-green milk, churning with the wind. Iridescent pigeons hopped along the blockade, and vendors sold green mangoes from their carts. As I walked further down the wall, two teenage boys approached me, their skin like dark chocolate. They set down a heavy cooler in front of me and begged me to buy a drink.

"¡Coca-Cola, naranja, agua fresca!" they shouted at me. I paid for the water and drained the bottle in two gulps, then wiped the sweat from my face.

"Are you Spanish?" asked the younger one, with a baseball cap balanced on his skinny head.

"No. I'm American," I confessed. The boys smiled back at me.

"Your president—he's just like us!" he said, pointing at his own bony chest and then that of his friend. "*¡Negro!*" He rubbed his black forearm in the sun.

"Yes—he is," I said.

"Do you like Obama?" he asked, though he was really asking how I felt about black people.

"*Sí. Me gusta Obama*," I said. I had covered his inauguration for a lifestyle magazine and still remembered shivering on the steps of the Capitol as our first African American president was sworn in.

"Someday, I might be president of Colombia!" said the shorter boy.

"*Verdad*," I said, shaking both their hands in farewell. I had hoped to move south into Brazil, crossing the Amazon at Manaus. I longed to see the great river—a single highway crossed the great green void of the world's largest rain forest, but that meant detouring through Venezuela, where things were dicey. Too many foreigners were getting robbed, shot, or kidnapped, and public transportation was a common target. Riding a bus to Caracas was simply asking for trouble, though the same could be said for Colombia.

"At night, the robbers throw a huge log across the road and then wait," my friend Fernando explained. "When the bus hits the log, it breaks the wheels and the bus must stop. That's when they board the bus and take everything, or shoot everybody." That was the Colombia he knew, but things were changing.

"Did you get robbed last night?" my taxi driver asked as we sped through the modern outskirts of Cartagena to the bus station.

"No."

"What? You did not stay at the hostel?"

"No," I replied from the backseat.

"The hostel was robbed last night," he said. "About forty guests—they just lined them up in their underwear and took everything—passports, money, cameras, jewelry. The bandidos had machine guns, but they didn't shoot anybody this time." He talked about the robbery like it was last night's baseball game, and I was suddenly very glad that I had stayed in my little gay hotel.

The "luxury" bus to Bogotá cost sixty dollars, which included security and air-conditioning. I was frisked before boarding the white Mercedes-Benz painted front and back with the Colombian flag. Inside, the bus attendant ushered me to my seat, wobbling on her stilettos. She looked barely twenty, with jet-black hair beneath a fading bleach job. Her miniskirt and crisp white shirt were ironed with geometric perfection, and a navy blue scarf was knotted around her neck.

The landscape opened up near Río Magdalena, with rivers and ponds shining as far as I could see from my window. Green cattails bordered the riverbank, and thousands of pure white calla lilies grew wild in the marshes. The road seemed to float above the rivers, where whole families balanced on narrow dugout canoes, digging long poles into the mud and pushing up and down the riverbank. The currents below left almond-shaped islands of sand, where humans walked, fished, bathed, and washed clothes. Lacking any dry, rectangle field, a posse of young boys played soccer, kicking up clouds of dust that rose up, then disappeared in the heat.

We stopped frequently, in small villages and military checkpoints. First came a platoon of Colombian marines behind a barricade of sandbags. The soldiers waved us through with their machine guns, and we rode onward, past the clotheslines hung with their camouflage shirts drying in the sun. The farther we traveled, the more military we encountered, patrolling the highway and checking every vehicle that passed. That afternoon, six policemen stopped our bus while a cowboy tried to pull a stubborn cow across the road. Our bus driver shouted directions from behind the windshield, but the cow never moved. Even when the police began kicking the animal in the rump, she only looked up and waved her head from side to side, all the while standing her ground, horns in the air. Finally we detoured around the cow, as did the long line of cars behind us—a dusty parade around the tenacious beast.

The road switched from paved to unpaved and back again. *Vallenato* music blared through the bus as we zigzagged up and over each new wave of charred hillsides, where ranchers had burned their pastures for new growth. Flimsy stick fences marked out each property, and bushy trees sprouted like broccoli from the hilltops.

As dusk fell, we entered a town so small that I counted only three lightbulbs shining in the dim street. Young boys swerved their bikes in the dirt, and old men with beer bellies swung in their front porch hammocks waiting for the warm, dark night to take over.

After 10:00 p.m., the two bus drivers swapped seats, sending one to sleep in the back, while a younger balding man, perky and refreshed, buckled into his seat and drove us down the dark road, past more military checkpoints. I slept in my seat like a fitful child, waking and stretching, shifting my legs one way, then another. I felt nervous and on edge—I was riding a bus at night through one of the long, empty gaps in Colombia. Bad things happened here. That's what everyone said.

BLAM! The explosion shot me forward, smashing my face into the seat back in front of me. I grabbed at my nose as the bus dropped to one side and then slid off the road, tilting dangerously to the right.

Eerie silence filled the bus. Every passenger had been jarred awake, but nobody spoke out loud. I wondered if our driver was alive—but he was only in shock, gripping his steering wheel firmly and gazing out into the thick blackness. Nobody moved from their seats and there was not a breath or a whisper to be heard. When a lady began to cry, the others shushed her.

"*¡Silencio!*" they whispered. This is how buses were robbed in Colombia. Right now, the bad guys were outside—paramilitaries poised with guns, ready to fire. The night was deep and clouded, without a star in the sky. I checked my phone—4:09 a.m. At any moment, some lunatic might charge through the door and shoot us. This was the worst game of hide-and-seek ever.

I was the first to move—perhaps I was the most naïve. I had never lost family or friends in these kinds of attacks, but when I stood up from my seat, the other passengers gasped and one of them grabbed at my pant leg and said, *"¡No, no!"*

But something didn't make sense to me. If a group of road thugs wanted to rob and murder us, wouldn't they have done it by now? The silence was too big and all-consuming—I had to find out what was out there.

I couldn't find my pocket flashlight, so I slung my camera around my neck and walked up the aisle toward the bus driver. He tried to stop me, but I slowly pushed my way out the door and stepped onto the soft shoulder of the road. I waited for the push of a cold metal gun in my ribs, but nothing happened. The air was warm and wet; the moon was dark and the road entirely empty. An insect chorus seethed with the tenor of a million chanting crickets. I shuffled my feet in the gravel, guiding my hand along the slanted front of the bus.

I felt the shattered headlights and heard the crunch of broken plastic under my boots. The entire front of the bus had broken into sharp, angry pieces and the bumper hung on by a tangle of electrical wires. I backtracked alongside the bus, feeling my way, gently tapping the ground with my feet, searching for a clue. I flipped my camera to its most powerful flash and hit the shutter—white light splashed in a circle and then disappeared. A second later, the LED screen showed nothing but my boots and the gray gravel beneath. I walked another yard and snapped the same image. Over and over, I pushed my nervous feet forward, snapping empty frames. After five minutes without my being shot dead, the bus driver emerged from the bus and followed behind me. Then my boots hit something large and warm.

Whatever it was now blocked my path, emanating warmth. With shaking hands, I aimed my camera and snapped the shutter. The photo showed an immense brown beast, her backbone arched like a mountain range, dead as hamburger.

"Vaca," whispered the bus driver. A cow. We had only hit a cow—but now he had forty people on a broken-down bus, in the middle of nowhere, in the dark. He started to swear, then ushered me back to the

bus and closed the door. Like a child who knows too much, I spread the news through the bus, "A cow! A cow!" The other passengers laughed, a few babies cried, but the mood was joyful. An hour later, the patrolmen arrived.

"You—come here." They pointed at me, and I followed them off the bus.

"You have a camera?" they asked.

"Yes," I replied.

"We need photos of the cow for *evidencia*."

I waited for the sunlight to photograph the death scene before me. They wanted every angle, and they wanted the number branded into the cow's back: #30233. Apparently, killing a cow is a crime in Colombia, and the guilty party cannot leave the scene until the animal's owner has been contacted and paid in full. My whole life, I had strived to work for National Geographic, and now here I was, on assignment, playing coroner to a dead cow.

The heaping carcass was free of flies or any sign of blunt force trauma. She was merely sleeping on her side, it seemed, unbothered by the passengers who ventured past to gawk at raw death. Her life had ended quickly—one second she was chewing grass on the roadside, and the next she was gone—off to cow heaven, which I imagined looks something like Montana, minus the fences, cattle grids, and steakhouses.

The full heat of midmorning chased me into the shade, and I wandered into the nearby pasture, where I sat beneath a tree and uploaded over thirty pictures of the dead cow onto a spare thumb drive. I turned the evidence over to the police, who were busy trying to move the victim's body into the back of the rancher's red pickup truck. I joined in, along with soldiers from a nearby military camp and a dozen other passengers, as we attempted to lift the one-ton cow.

It was the rancher's wife who made us stop. We had only inched the dead animal across the gravel, making a mess of it. She shooed us all away, and with the help of her husband, they stoically butchered the cow right there on the road.

I felt sad for the expired cow, the rancher's wife, and the distraught bus driver, who was sitting on the road while a mechanic worked on the bus. After four hours, the police let us go, and the driver sat down in his seat and started the engine. Looking up in the rearview mirror, the driver did a quick head count to make sure he had not left any of us out in the fields.

"Everybody here?" he asked.

"Wait!" a man cried from the back of the bus. "You forgot the cow!"

The bus boomed with laughter and all the drawn-out tensions of the morning disappeared. Our driver was not amused. He merely drove our injured bus toward Bogotá—another five hours climbing higher and higher into the mountains.

CLOSE CALL

Day 20

The road cut through an endless field of cherry-red carnations—more flowers than a human could smell in one lifetime, planted in perfect rows, like the corn in Ohio. The vast bleeding landscape was alive, and come night, these long and slender stalks would be executed one by one, stacked in a box and flown to the United States by morning. This is the land where Valentine's Day begins, a million little blossoms for hospital vases and grocery store bouquets and school dance boutonnieres—small, decaying bundles of affection.

In junior high school, we sent carnations every February—white carnations to friends and red carnations to lovers. I remember in seventh grade when flowers were passed out in homeroom to every student except me. The next year, I paid a dollar and sent myself a single white flower. All I wanted was a single friend. Now I had both love and friends— thousands of friends, according to Twitter and Facebook—more friends than this field had carnations.

A long time ago, Sarah and I had sat next to each other in AP English. Together, we suffered through our final year of high school, and now, after all this time, she was living in Bogotá and it happened to be her birthday.

Happy birthday, dear Sarah, happy birthday to you!

I sang along in English with the five women I had just met—all of them lawyers, diplomats, or human rights workers. Meanwhile, I had spent the last twenty-seven hours riding a bus from Cartagena and looked like it.

"How crazy was that bus ride?" Sarah asked. Though we had not seen or spoken to one another in seventeen years, we still chatted like two kids at the back of the class.

"Well, last night our bus got knocked off the road and I thought we would all be kidnapped or murdered, but it was just a cow—and let me tell you, dead cows are *heavy*. We ended up butchering it on the road, then we ate breakfast on a military base, and on the ascent into Bogotá, the lady sitting next to me filled up three carsick bags."

"Gross," said Sarah.

"I know, right? I didn't even know a person could throw up that much!" I said.

Sarah's friends stared down at the rare steak on their plates. Perhaps I was not a very good dinner guest. Three weeks on the road and I had already forgotten about all of this—how one dressed, acted, and spoke in polite company. Theirs was a world of office hours and happy hours, and mine was texting haiku on Twitter and using empty notebook pages for toilet paper.

"Why don't you just fly?" asked one of Sarah's friends—as if she had just discovered the solution to all my problems.

"Because I'm taking the bus," I said. "That's kind of the whole point." I felt silly trying to explain my quest to these people with responsible lives and full-time jobs. Why spend three weeks driving when Bogotá was just a five-hour flight from Washington, DC? I tried laughing along with them, but I felt too fragile and exhausted.

I spent two full days in Colombia's capital—I needed a break from the bus. I slept and blogged and did laundry, then headed outside for a run. Dodging traffic was difficult, as was breathing at nine thousand feet. So I wandered through the flea markets instead, snacking on grilled *arepas* and wandering for hours in the Museum of Gold, dazzled by the brilliant collection of trinkets and armor and masks that the Spanish had carried away.

In Plaza Bolívar, I watched the changing of the guard—about a hundred soldiers in camouflaged uniforms marching in formation, slapping their guns in their hands as their commander barked through a megaphone. All the while a construction crew was dismantling the city's gigantic artificial Christmas tree right in front of the cathedral, dropping each metal piece onto the back of a truck with a clang. On the church steps, a blind woman sat wrapped in a bundle of filthy skirts, picking swiftly on her beat-up guitar and sending the most haunting Andalusian melody across the square. Gray pigeons flocked and flapped upward, soaring in an arc before floating gently back down to the ground. If I could trap that scene inside a snow globe—with the palace façade and the double bell towers—then the snow would be tiny plastic pigeons, shaken and floating down, filling the square with feathers.

I loved Bogotá and its wild urban feel, an explosion of people and cars fenced in by rocky pinnacles. The thought of leaving so soon irked me, but that night, I asked the concierge to recommend a safe and reliable bus to Ecuador.

"¡Ay! you should fly, señor," he said.

I shook my head no and unfolded my map, upon which Colombia was the size of a dinner plate. A bellhop walked over, and then another. They both shared their opinions with the concierge. Then a security guard chimed in, crossing the marble lobby to weigh in on the subject of buses traveling south. Five minutes later I had six different men all arguing about the best way to Ecuador. It took me half an hour to pry myself away.

Like my previous bus from Cartagena, this Bolivariano bus looked brand new, with side-view mirrors that stuck out like butterfly antennae. We traveled with two backup drivers, along with two armed guards, and a clock-size overhead speedometer showed the driver's current speed with big, red digital numbers. Anything faster than eighty kilometers per hour was *prohibido*.

I dozed through those first few hours of Fusagasugá, an area of terraced coffee plantations and fields of magenta, orange, and white flowers. Expansive colored mansions sat on each hill, each with a swimming pool in the back and an array of sports cars and hefty SUVs parked in front. After the poverty I had witnessed on the coast, this kind of conspicuous wealth seemed out of place—apparently there is money to be had in agriculture, whether you're growing flowers, coffee, or something else.

Our bus climbed even higher into the Andes, whipping around dozens and dozens of hairpin turns, scaling a wall of stone that shot straight up from the green valley below. Impatient trucks passed on the left, forcing us out on the far edge of the narrow lane. Clinging to one truck's rear bumper was a teen boy on a bicycle, getting towed up the mountain at the edge of a two-thousand-foot precipice.

Afraid of heights, I focused on the screeching Colombian telenovela that played on the TV screen above my seat. The exaggerated eyebrow penciling and grotesque breast implants pulled my mind away from the fact that we were skirting the edge of a cliff. After the lady in the teal silk cocktail dress shot the bad guy with the beard, the series ended, and one of the reserve drivers opened a bag filled with pirated DVDs. Seconds later, a young Dakota Fanning was flirting with her horse on-screen.

It happened in slow motion—the stove-size chunk of granite dropping right down in front of us, crushing the truck in the opposite lane and toppling it over, followed by a rush of rocks and debris.

The hard brake jerked us forward, stopping at the pile of rocks. Our bus driver leapt down from the bus and began kicking at the windshield of the wrecked truck, turning the glass opaque with stars. Gripping the rubber lining with his bare hands, the driver peeled away the entire windshield, then reached inside and yanked the keys out of the ignition.

A bit shaken, I got off the bus, along with all the other passengers. We approached the cab of the truck, expecting to see two bloodied corpses, but surprisingly, both the driver and passenger climbed out unscathed. They patted our bus driver on the back and then the growing band of spectators all began clapping.

I was too shaken to cheer—a second or two later and the boulder would have smashed our bus and hurtled us down the deadly drop-off, but there was no time for what-ifs. We all got busy lifting rocks away from the road. Soon my hands and clothes were covered with fine, gray dust, but with everybody working together, we cleared the right lane in about thirty minutes. Our little landslide had shut down the Pan-American Highway and traffic was backed up for miles in both directions. Once clear, we reboarded the bus and continued our slow ascent into the clouds.

A ridge of glowing green mountains melted into the mashed potato skies. Evening came, and the headlights of our bus lit up each bend in the road as we began to descend. In Quindío, I gained a new seatmate—a girl dressed from head to toe in pink, traveling with the rest of her family. Her name was Jenny and she was thirteen, and though I tried to chat with her, Jenny never spoke a word to me—she only rolled her eyes and looked away. To be fair, if I was a thirteen-year-old girl, and I had to spend the night on a bus next to a strange man with shards of plantain chips stuck in his beard, I would have rolled my eyes, too.

At around 7:00 p.m. we neared the city of Tuluá and stopped at a heavily guarded control post. A pair of policemen boarded our bus and rode with us for the next half hour while we passed through a *zona de alta seguridad* (zone of heightened security). Jenny and I sat silent in the front seat, inches away from the squatting guard whose sinister weapon was poised at the windshield. I doubt either of us liked the idea of bullets spraying through the glass before us, and unconsciously we found ourselves dropping lower into our seats. Even after those guards left, our bus was hitting military checkpoints every ten or twenty miles. This was El Valle del Cauca, a simmering battlefield for several narco-militias, while the heavy military presence was part of President Uribe's plan for "Democratic Security"—an attempt to take control of the country's highways after a decade of violence and insecurity.

Road signs pointed to Cali—a city I remembered from the news, and not in a good way.

After all the stopping and waiting at military checkpoints, Jenny had dropped off to sleep, unconsciously resting her head on my left shoulder. I felt both awkward and touched, and I barely moved so as not to wake her as we rumbled down the road in the dark. I looked down at her limp hands and saw the cheap gold rings on her fingers and her teenage attempts at glamor with nail polish. Then came another stop with more guns. This was her normal life—the only kind of family vacation Jenny knew, so different from my own family's road trips through the Midwest. Back then, my biggest concern was whether the next McDonald's would have shamrock shakes, or if our hotel would have a swimming pool. I never had to sit next to strangers on an overnight bus or worry about masked gunmen shooting at me through the windows.

Our bus never stopped in Cali—at least, not officially. We drove right past the bus station with its bright lights and Friday night crowds, past the neon bar signs and all-night markets, then slipped off into a grid of dark alleys, turning right, then left, then right again, backtracking the opposite way we came. Finally we stopped on a lonely, unlit corner.

"You have five minutes," said the bus driver through his speaker. A team of private security guards positioned themselves around us, and any passenger who needed to use the bathroom was ushered into a small shack in the far corner of the vacant lot. I was too impatient for the long line of women, so I found a dark corner against the wall. Sounds of the city—laughter, music, and car horns—erupted from half a mile away.

For whatever reason, stopping at Cali's bus station was too dangerous, and within ten minutes, we had left the city. All through the night we got stopped, either at military checkpoints or by the police, who would board and walk up and down the aisle, studying each of our faces.

Surely, I had encountered more soldiers and tanks and guns in Colombia than any other country on my trip, but I had also crossed the country in a cocoon of security, wherein the only violence I had witnessed was hitting that poor brown cow in Boyacá.

I was glad that I had made it this far and glad that morning was coming. Soon the night split in two—the black mountain silhouettes against the indigo sky. Then came the hint of dawn with its welcome warmth and a new light on the pointed volcanoes around us. Jenny and her family left me in Pasto.

"*Adiós*," I said, but Jenny offered me nothing, hiding her sleepy face in her mother's chest.

"*Adiós*," said her mother, reaching out to shake my hand.

In Ipiales, the air was cool and filled with dust. Old women with green paper facemasks swept the streets and men in woolen ponchos drank coffee in doorways. I gathered up my cold canvas bag and thanked my driver over and over again, then paid sixty-five cents to ride a *colectivo* to the pair of colonial customs buildings down below.

I crossed the Rumichacha Bridge on foot, stopping halfway across and asking another passing traveler to snap a picture of me. "Welcome to Ecuador!" declared the sign above me, and below it: "Use your seatbelts!"

24 COURT OF LOVE

The church doors were all locked, but after waiting around, some smiling man in a suit and tie cracked open a glass door and welcomed me in, as if this were a furniture store and I had shown up too early for a sale.

"You must be Brother Evans!" he boomed, shaking my hand and shutting the door against the bitter March wind.

"That's me." I attempted to share his enthusiasm, though I was fairly certain that he would be among my accusers that evening. Mormons are the nicest people in the world, especially when they don't like you that much.

"It's still a bit early, but let me show you downstairs," he said, leading me into the darkened church basement, so quiet on this Wednesday evening. Another awkward young man was already waiting outside the room—slightly older than me, his neck bulging from his white-collared shirt, with heavy glasses, and a brown briefcase covering his lap.

"Brother Lafar, this is Brother Evans," he introduced me. I shook his plump and sweaty hand and my gaydar soared—this dude was a homo: overzealous and repressed. I knew the type because I had been the same—dressing the part, volunteering every spare hour at church. Perhaps they had invited him here to scare him straight—to witness my own execution and set him on the right course. Meanwhile I saw Brother Lafar as a cautionary tale—a more righteous version of myself, so good and obedient, thirtysomething, and desperately virginal.

We were strange twins, matched by odd fate in the Maryland suburbs.

"What do you do?" I asked.

"I'm an editor," he said, his eyes darting side to side.

176

"Cool," I answered. "Who for?"

"I work at the Heritage Foundation," he replied. "I edit all their publications. You know them?"

"Yes," I said. "I do." The Heritage Foundation is probably the most conservative think tank in Washington—an institution that at the time was actively leading the fight against gay rights and same-sex marriage, an institution that claimed homosexuals were depraved deviants scheming to destroy the nuclear family and the whole of human civilization. They had just released a paper about how legalizing gay marriage had led to the rapid demise of the family in the Netherlands. And this guy had probably edited the thing.

"What do you do?" asked Brother Lafar.

"Fair trade and labor rights in the developing world," I explained—I might as well say I was a communist. Perhaps we belonged to the same church and sang hymns from the same pews, but we came from such opposite worlds. Brother Lafar seemed nervous already, as if he were fraternizing with the enemy. He pulled out the Book of Mormon and began to read, while I went looking for the drinking fountain.

The court began at 6:00 p.m. They asked me to open with a prayer, and I complied, rote-like, speaking the words out loud but saying a different prayer in my head: *God, help.*

"Are you comfortable?" began the presiding priesthood leader.

"Yes," I answered. I sat on the lone chair in the room facing the table where the four of them sat facing me. These were my judges—lay leaders from the church and disciplinarians by night, and by day the head of the local power company, a gynecologist, and one Bush appointee, fresh from Utah. Brother Lafar took notes.

The Bush appointee was presiding, and he launched right into the scriptures, reading from Leviticus, and then on to the book of Romans in the New Testament. I knew the verses too well—verses that blatantly condemn homosexuality and say that all fags must surely be put to death. The president read the words as if he were throwing the law at my face.

"So the scriptures are pretty clear on this issue," he said, peering over his reading glasses and nodding to his assistants on either side. They nodded back. He talked about my betrayal of the church, my family, and God. He talked about my mission to Ukraine, and how I had betrayed all those people I had served. He talked about the imaginary woman I had not married—the children I had not fathered who were now stuck in heaven, without physical bodies or a chance to come to Earth. He reminded me of all the pain I had caused my family, the great humiliation I had brought upon my parents, and the bad example I set for the church. Was I not ashamed?

He played the role of grand inquisitor, and one by one, he asked me about my beliefs: Did I believe in God? Did I believe Joseph Smith was a prophet of God? Did I have a testimony of the church?

"Yes," I answered. "My testimony of the gospel is the only reason I am sitting here tonight." Already, the tears stung my eyes. I was too exhausted and too frightened not to cry. The man backed off on his interrogation. One of the counselors took over and asked me to tell them my own experience—what had led me to this point. And so I told them everything, starting from the age of eight, when I was baptized into the church: how I always felt different from all the other boys; how I already knew as a teenager that I was gay; how I served a mission, and how afterward, I underwent a full year of "reparative therapy" at BYU.

"I could not marry a woman—that would be deceitful," I said.

"Oh, but you can marry a woman—you should!" said the other counselor. "Trust me—I'm a gynecologist. I know more about these things than you do! God made men and women to fit together . . ." The president hushed his counselor.

He asked me about sex—did I ever masturbate, and if so, how often? Did I have sexual relations with any other men? What was the actual nature of my relationship with Brian? Did we share a bed? Had I ever confessed to these sins before?

"Excuse me, but that really is none of your business," I said, shaking a little, yet refusing to answer any of his questions. I loved the church and my family, but I had no love for these men.

"But it *is* our business," he countered. "As leaders in this church, it is our duty to determine how repentant you are, and right now, you are not being very cooperative, Brother Evans. In fact, you're acting a little cocky." I wiped the tears from my eyes and cleared my throat.

"My sex life is between me and my partner," I said. "And besides, that's not the real issue here, is it?"

"What do you mean? If you are engaging in homosexual behavior, then you are violating your covenants and should be disciplined," said the district president.

"Maybe. But there are plenty of gay Mormons having sex in this city who are not facing disciplinary councils. The only reason I have been called in is because I am living openly as a gay man, in a long-term relationship, at the height of a national debate on same-sex marriage, which the church opposes. This is a political issue—not a religious one."

"Other members struggle with this same affliction—yes," the district president replied. "But if they come to us and confess their sin and repent, then we do not discipline them. It's only those like you, who are confused and think somehow that what you're doing is not a sin—you are damaging the reputation of the church," he said, raising his voice. The niceties had vanished. There was no more pussyfooting—he was laying down the law now.

"Let me be clear with you," he continued. "We are asking you to leave this man . . ."

"Brian?" I offered.

"Yes—if that is his name. Is he a member of the church?"

"No," I said.

"Never mind—if you leave him and come back into the fold and repent, then you can be forgiven. It's that easy." The president looked at me smugly, his arms folded. "Essentially, the choice is up to you." He paused, and I waited. I felt angry and fatigued—my head ached with a slew of rebuttals. Don't say it, I thought. Don't say it out loud.

"What if I asked you to leave your wife?" I asked. "If you were forced to pick between your wife and the church, which would you choose? Which do you think she would choose?" Mine was an insolent question and Mormon men are not used to having their authority challenged by lesser members—but I had stopped caring. I was not going to let them bully me.

"But I am married, and you are not," said the president. "My relationship is validated by God, by nature, and the government!" He was furious now, as if he'd been waiting all this time for a sparring partner with whom to argue his point. Now that I was here, he was throwing his punches.

"You're absolutely right—for now—and I know that you do not see it this way, but Brian is my husband, and we intend to spend the rest of our lives together."

"Marriage is the union of a man and a woman only!" His voice grew louder, his face flushed red, and his eyes bulged. "Once the Federal Marriage Amendment passes, you will be outlawed by the Constitution of the United States. What will you do then?" I did not answer. I only stared back at him, silent.

"I'm not like your bishop over in England who just let you get away with it—we're not a bunch of liberals here. We are members of the Church of Jesus Christ of Latter-day Saints and we obey God's law. Do you understand that you are violating God's law? Do you?" Now the district president was shaking.

"I believe God made me this way for a reason," I said. "I believe God led me to Brian. I know I am supposed to be with him, and I believe God wants me to be honest with myself." The president sighed, then whispered something to his left. Brother Lafar scribbled into his notebook.

"Well then," he said. "I don't think I have any more questions for you." He turned to his counselors. "Anything else you think we need to add?" One counselor shook his head no; the other nodded yes and turned to me.

"I just want to remind you, Brother Evans, that we have nothing against you personally. We love you, and we are here to help you regain your path to your Heavenly Father. We are not here to judge you—that's why we call it a court of love, because everything is done with the spirit of the Lord present. I hope you have felt that same spirit that I have felt here tonight." When he was done speaking, Brother Lafar escorted me out of the room and back to my chair in the hallway, where I awaited their decision.

An hour passed, and I got up and began walking through the empty rooms of the church basement. I stopped in the primary room and began flipping through the songbook. These were the same songs I used to teach the children back in England. I looked up at a homemade poster that clung to the wall with masking tape. "I Am a Child of God," it said. Yes. I am a child of God, and I am gay. And this is what hell will feel like, I thought—me, totally alone, trapped inside a darkened church basement, dressed in poly/wool blend for all eternity, waiting forever to be excommunicated.

After more than two hours of deliberation, I was called back in. I took my seat and tried to read the faces on the council for a clue, but the men behind the table were expressionless.

"We apologize for the wait, Brother Evans. This council is made up of different individuals, and there are many things we have to take into account." The president turned to his counselor. "But, in the end, after much discussion and prayer, we have reached a unanimous decision." He paused and breathed in. The clock on the wall ticked closer and closer to 10:00 p.m.

"Brother Evans, it is hereby decided that you be excommunicated from the Church of Jesus Christ of Latter-day Saints." There. He said it. The words fell down like a guillotine—words that I had feared my whole life—the ultimate punishment that established me as an outcast in this life and the life to come.

I felt the air being sucked from my lungs, felt my stomach drop. This was no surprise—I had known all along that this would happen, but that did not soften the blow. My life in the church flashed before my eyes—age eight, dressed in white for my baptism, the sensation of the water flowing over my face as I made that holy promise to God, then passing the sacrament as a twelve-year-old deacon, knocking on doors as a missionary, doing service projects, teaching Sunday school, writing tithing checks, playing the piano for priesthood meeting, going to hear General Conference with my grandfather. All of that was over now. I had given my life to this institution, and now, after four hours, they had cast me aside.

"Brother Evans, is there anything else you would like to say, for the record?" asked the kinder, gentler counselor.

"Yes, please," I said. "Thank you for sacrificing your time to come here tonight. I do have one question for you, though."

"Yes," said the president. "Go ahead."

"Gordon B. Hinckley has stated very plainly that he loves the gay and lesbian members, and he also said that there is a place for us in the church. He is the prophet, so what he says is true. And that is my final question to you—that is what I am curious to know—where is that place? Where is *my* place in the church?"

The men did not answer—they had no answer to give. The only answer was the one they had just delivered—the only place for gays in the church was to be excommunicated.

My auto-da-fé ended with a short prayer, and several strong hand-shakes and pats on the back, as if we were slapping hands on the soccer field and mumbling, "Good game, good game."

"Do you need a ride home?" asked the counselor, but I said no, I would take the bus. Brother Lafar and I ended up riding together. He sat on one side, and I on the other, neither of us speaking. He tried not to look at me, but for a mile or so, we traveled together, staring out opposite windows.

I was sad and yet relieved, too. Now the church could not hurt me anymore. There was nothing left for them to do. In a single moment, I had joined the ranks of all the other people who had been excommunicated through history—heretics, apostates, men of science, and criminals, too. Now I was one of them.

And I felt real joy—a wave of happiness pulsed through my body and I became hyperaware of the world around me. The streetlights shone like torches in the night, and I walked home from the station feeling free and exuberant. There was no more shame, and perhaps most surprising, I felt love—real love, pouring down from above. God still loved me—I felt it. I had just been kicked out of the community of saints. Yes, I had just been deleted from heaven's list, but God was still there. That was my testimony—the church had left me, but God had not. He was by my side, guiding me home.

I walked up Seventeenth Street, past the little gay steakhouse lit up like a TV. Inside sat two morose drag queens with blonde wigs, wet from the drizzle outside. They each wore tiaras in their hair, gossiping tête-a-tête over half-eaten steaks. Those were my people—two disheveled angels, taking a break from the demands of the world, reapplying their makeup for the new day to come.

A week later, the letter arrived in the mail.

You are hereby effectively excommunicated from the Church. Excommunication means complete severance from the Church. You are no longer a member of the Church. As such, you no longer have any privileges of Church membership. You may not wear temple garments or pay tithes and offerings. You are no longer entitled to the constant inspiration and companionship of the Holy Ghost.

The letter did say I could attend church—but only as an observer. What it did not say is that I was spiritually severed from my family—for now and all eternity. We would not be together in the next life, case closed. I skimmed the letter once, then filed it away in my folder labeled REJECTIONS. It was the same red folder that held all my rejections from *National Geographic* and other magazines, short forms from disinterested publishers, and letters from agents saying, "Thanks but no thanks."

I went back to church one more time—to say good-bye, or perhaps to make a point. Mine was an inner-city congregation, mostly recent African American converts, and few of them understood that getting thrown out of the church was much easier than joining. Soon they began to ask questions to the local leadership—"What happened to Brother Evans?"—and when they found out, they became upset.

No, I could never worship here again. For so much of my life, my church had determined my thoughts, decisions, and feelings, but now they had lost that power. I could not attend a church where I had been made invisible; where I was treated like a diseased man, waiting for a cure that would never come; where so many members went out of their way to avoid me or else lavished me with phony fellowship while secretly abhorring my kind. No, the church did not know how to deal with me, but I knew how to deal with them, and before the second hour of services began, I walked out the front door and never looked back.

25 MIDDLE EARTH

Day 24

"¡*No gracias*! *No quiero* guinea pig," I said to the guy with smiling silver teeth and a face like horse leather. He tipped his straw hat and wiped his brow with his sleeve, then grabbed my elbow and dragged me toward the smoking barbecue, trying to convince me that what I really wanted for lunch was a plump pink rodent.

The creepy-looking carcass was the size of a cat but missing its eyes and fur as it sizzled on a spit. His little legs were crumpled up and his buckteeth stuck out, as if ready to bite. An army of tourists picked at the barbecued beasties on their plates like a band of ogres eating Alvin and the Chipmunks.

My personal travel rule is to eat whatever I'm served, but right there, at Quito's biggest tourist trap, eating guinea pigs seemed gratuitous, especially when none of the Ecuadorians were having any. Indeed, there was nothing particularly native about this whole jamboree at La Mitad del Mundo. The "Middle of the World" offered a tatty gathering of souvenir stands and T-shirt shops, cheap trinkets and ice-cream parlors, unrelated museums, hustlers, blaring loudspeakers, and a center stage filled with a dance team of half-dressed women trying desperately to move the bored crowd with the sway of their hips. Like the ladies' frayed denim shorts, the roasting guinea pigs were only around for titillation— I was unsure what any of this had to do with the equator.

It cost two bucks to see the imaginary line on the ground, marked conspicuously with a line of orange paint. I walked along the manmade equator as if it was a steel girder suspended high above Manhattan. A

185

fellow American tourist offered to take my picture, and I smiled while straddling the Earth's halfway mark, a foot in each hemisphere, arms raised upward in triumph. Hundreds of others were doing the same little dance, all of us enthused and amused by this little mathematical line and how it offered some sort of definition to our planet, making the incomprehensible infinity of space feel a little more finite.

The equator is defined as 0.0°0.0′0.0″ latitude, but when I checked my phone, Google Earth gave me a reading of 0°0′4″ S. So, even though I was standing on the official, recently repainted equator, I was at least a hundred meters south of the actual equator. La Mitad del Mundo was a fraud.

Thus I clipped Sally the GPS to my belt, and following a compass I walked due north, watching my coordinates shift closer and closer to zero, before running into a cinder block wall. The real equator was outside this unamusing amusement park.

Cars and buses blew past me as I walked along the highway. Taxis honked for my attention, thinking I was a lost foreigner heading in the wrong direction. My GPS guided me closer to my goal, but I was still half a second off. I thought back to the much-maligned explorer Robert Falcon Scott, who used a sextant and the stars to approximate the South Pole in 1912. He posted the Union Jack within six hundred feet of the actual South Pole. A century later, a GPS the size of a stapler could give me an almost 100 percent accurate reading as to my exact position on the planet.

Sally was telling me that the equator was inside a dusty brick yard: 0°0′0″ S, 78°27′12″ W. I took one big step north, and the phone flickered to "N," then I stepped back and the "S" returned—I had found the equator. At that very moment, I was traveling at a higher velocity than any other human in either hemisphere, because the equator is the fastest part of Earth.

I scribbled out math on the free notepad at the hotel—I had left National Geographic headquarters with a starting position of 38°54′18.64″ N, 77°2′12.27″ W. Using a measurement of sixty-nine miles per degree of latitude, I calculated that I traveled 2,684.47 miles due south, even though my indirect route through Mexico and Central America had nearly doubled that distance. According to Sally's data, I had clocked a clean five thousand miles. Measuring due south to the Antarctic Circle (66°33′39″ S) left me with 4,592.73 miles to go. The equator was my halfway point.

As a city, Quito resembles Legoland—as if a team of sugar-fueled kindergartners were let loose with a million bits of colored plastic. Blocks of peach, blue, and yellow houses lay scattered across the hills, swathed in the moist mountain fog. A cold and drippy rain was falling, and when I tried to go out, the hotel guards at the hotel said it was not safe.

"Too many pickpockets," they said, but I pushed past them. By now I was feeling a bit immune to all the scaremongering in South America, and I was hungry for a meal that did not involve corn chips or fluorescent soda. At a nearby café, I dug into a bowl of chunky ceviche doused in fresh lemon and sprinkled with purple onion. I snapped a picture of my food and tweeted it to the world. A minute passed, then another.

"Andrew? Is that you?" called a muffled voice from the street. A short man with a baseball cap peered at me through the foggy window of the restaurant. He did not resemble anyone I knew, but he spoke English and wore shorts and a T-shirt.

"Yes?" I said, looking up from my meal.

"I knew I would find you here! See? What did I tell you?" The man nodded to the woman on his right.

"Hello," I said, extending my hand.

"Hello! And welcome to Ecuador!" he said, shaking my hand and not letting go. "I am Luís," he said, "and this is my girlfriend, Isa." Isa was squeezed into a tight, gray sweater with a gold pendant that dangled in her bosom, and she seemed very concerned that her hair might get wet.

"Excuse me—I'm sorry," I said, a bit shocked. "Do I know you?"

"Yes! From Twitter!" he shouted, still holding my hand with the grip of a desperate man. "You chatted with me!" I could not remember his Twitter handle out of several thousand followers. I stopped responding in person after Panama—I didn't have the bandwidth. Granted, a few of them had become friends—there was the sixth-grade schoolteacher in Texas who had turned my journey into a day-by-day geography class for her students, and then dear, sweet Chris back in Costa Rica—but Luís had just appeared out of nowhere and claimed we were the best of friends.

"You and I have so much in common," he said. "You like ceviche, just like me! And we both love to travel."

"How did you find me here?" I asked, a bit surprised.

"Easy! I followed your tweets. Remember, I am from Quito—for me it's easy. This whole time, I knew exactly where you were!" he said and finally let go of my hand. I reluctantly agreed to have coffee with them, and though Luís offered me a ride in his car, I insisted on walking the four blocks to the café. We sat around a wooden table under a covered patio, watching the rain fall and cupping our warm mugs with both hands, while Luís explained his Twitter handle. "It's because I ride my bike all the time—and I'm like a monkey!"

"You like to ride bikes?" I asked flatly.

"No—I LOVE to ride bikes," said Luís with a laugh. "That's my job. I am a professional tour guide in Quito. I do bike tours all over Ecuador, too." He took out his phone and began flipping through a cascade of photos taken at various points of interest around the country. Periodically, he checked to make sure his car had not been stolen.

"You've gotta be careful here," he said. "Thieves will take your car in the middle of the day!"

Luís wanted to have a picture with me, so I smiled at the camera while the rain fell hard on the slanted concrete sidewalks. Everything seemed slanted in Quito.

"Tomorrow I will show you the old city," explained Luís. "Plus a few days to see the other parts, and after that, I will take you all around

Ecuador!" He flung his right hand in the air, as if brushing away the horizon.

"That would be great, Luís," I began, "but I'm afraid I just don't have that much time. I still have a long way to go." I was only halfway to the bottom of the world.

"No, Andrew, you can't miss Quito." Luís ignored me and kept right on making plans, telling me what to pack for our adventure and not to worry, from now on, he would take all the photographs. "I take very good pictures, you will see—wait, let me show you!" And he returned to his phone, pulling up photos of Andean sunsets and pre-Colombian ruins in the grass. "See?" he said. "Just like *National Geographic*!" Luís was not simply offering to be my guide—he wanted my assignment.

"These are beautiful pictures," I said, still trying to be polite and thinking I could just excuse myself and walk away, but when I tried saying good-bye, Luís and Isa followed me onto the sidewalk.

"I will go with you to Peru as well. I have lots of time right now," offered Luís.

"No, thank you," I told Luís. "I always travel alone." That was true—when I was working, I traveled alone. It was better that way.

"No, Andrew. You cannot travel by yourself. I have heard your Spanish and it's no good. Nobody will understand what you're saying," said Luís. I felt a little insulted. Frankly, this guy was starting to annoy me.

"Thank you so much, Luís, but I really have to go back to work now," I said. I shook his hand one more time, and then waved good-bye to Isa, who stayed silent.

"But where are you staying?" asked Luís, following me down the sidewalk. "And when are you leaving? It's no problem. I will make all the arrangements. We're going to be partners, and you'll want me to come on all your other trips, too! You'll see."

"No, Luís," I spoke to him directly. "You can follow my journey on Twitter, but I travel solo. Good-bye." I walked away and did not look back. The storm was growing darker, and I picked up the pace until I was safely inside the hotel lobby. Three hours later, I emerged for dinner and found Luís still standing on the curb.

"Oh—the Holiday Inn is a very nice hotel," he said. "Do you like it?"

"They have good Internet," I answered, wondering if he had really stood in the rain for three hours waiting for me to show up again. "Why are you still here?"

"Oh, I thought I would just hang around a bit longer. And then tomorrow I will pick you up right here," he said. "What room are you in? What time should I be here?"

"Luís, you can't travel with me. I work alone. Besides, I'm leaving tomorrow—early."

"What time?" he asked.

"Eight o'clock," I lied, deciding to check out by seven.

"Then I will be right here at quarter 'til eight," said Luís, pointing to the front door of the hotel.

"Fine," I said, taking a different approach. "¡Hasta mañana!" If Luís did not understand me saying no, then he would figure it out on his own, tomorrow. I kind of hated to stand him up, but the dude was starting to creep me out. I shook his hand one more time and then walked away, checking over my shoulder to make sure he wasn't following me.

Twenty minutes later, I heard his voice again. "This is a good restaurant," said Luís, walking right over to me and sitting down at my table. "Have you ordered yet? Here, give me the menu." He grabbed the menu from my hands. "I will tell you what to eat here."

"Luís, leave me alone," I said. "I'm tired; I need to eat and then go to bed." What I really wanted was to scream at him to fuck off, but I found myself still speaking to him in that polite, sweetly condescending Mormon voice.

"Two for dinner?" asked the waiter, holding up another menu.

"No—uno, just me. He's not eating here," I said, but Luís took the menu and began to order, so I simply stood up and fled the restaurant, sprinting back to the hotel bar. Waiting for room service, I noticed Luís pacing outside, watching me through the window. That night, I blocked him on Twitter.

The next morning I packed swiftly, then looked down from my balcony at the sprawling city. There was Luís, still standing in front of the hotel doors. It was barely 6:00 a.m.—had he really hung around my hotel all night long? I called security and ordered a cab to meet me at the back door.

On the way to the bus station, I found myself checking the faces inside the cars stuck next to us in traffic. I was being chased by a crazy man. I stayed silent on Twitter and ordered a one-way ticket to Guayaquil.

I boarded the bus and slumped down in my seat, relieved to be getting away from Quito. Only when we pulled out of the gate did I peer out my window and look back. There on the corner stood Luís, frantic and bewildered, searching up and down the street, with a full pack on his back.

26 BANANAS

Day 25

"*¡Climatización!*" someone shouted from the back. Others echoed the call, begging the driver for more air-conditioning, but he was lost in his own world, swaying his body gently and tapping the steering wheel as he watched the swerving road. A poster of Jesus was glued to the driver-side window, right next to a decal of Daffy Duck, and fixed to his dashboard were two silver dragons and a plush hippopotamus holding a cross. The screams of dying teenagers blared from the TV, with the movie's body count rising faster than the temperature on the bus.

I tried ignoring the ghastly horror movie, locking my eyes on the glorious view outside. Gauzy waterfalls flowed from every vertical slope and colorful birds flitted about the jungle treetops. We had left the coolness of the high Andes for the warm and sticky lowlands of the tropics. The bus was getting stuffy, and I was still on edge after escaping my stalker back in Quito.

"*Climatización. ¡Ahorita!*" people began shouting. "And turn off the damn movie!" shouted a middle-aged woman sitting nearby. A minute later, the AC kicked in, sending a welcome rush of cool air upon us. Then the bus attendant hit eject, ending the bloodbath on-screen. The people on the bus began to cheer and then settled down into the quiet hour of banana fields and slow, brown rivers that flowed like chocolate milk.

The man sitting next to me woke up, rubbed his face, and said, "Hello." Milton was on his way back from the Amazon where he worked for an oil company. Once a week, he climbed on this bus and rode twelve hours into the jungle. Then every weekend he came back to Santo Domingo to be with his wife and three *niños*.

"I never tire of the trip. It's nice to see the mountains," he said. "And it's a good job—other people in Santo Domingo don't have any work at all. We have a house and my children go to a good school."

"My dad works for an oil company," I offered. Milton was only slightly older than me, and I imagined my own father at that age, working day after day and keeping us safely middle class. My own father had eight children before he turned forty—a fact that shaped his entire life. After I was born, he quit Exxon and left the urbanity of Houston for a tranquil corner of Ohio, where in ten minutes, he could be home for dinner or cheering from the stands at a high school swim meet. Talking with Milton felt like talking to my own dad as a young man—someone as determined yet fallible, wrapped up in the great demands of life and love.

Since crossing the equator, people had stopped balking at my notion to reach Antarctica by bus. Antarctica was closer than Europe down here, and an older couple on the bus nodded to me, as if riding the bus to the bottom of the world was a very normal thing to do.

"At our next stop, if you sit on the bus and watch our things, then we will come back and watch your things so that you can go eat."

"Deal," I agreed, happy for a chance to enjoy a paper plate of *gallo pinto* without holding my backpack at my feet. Joseo and Rosita were brother and sister, and every year she flew home from Toronto to see the family.

"Where will you stay in Guayaquil?" Rosita asked. "And which bus will you take after that?"

"I don't know," I replied, because I really did not know. All I knew was that I had three weeks to cross South America.

"Guayaquil is a big city—and it will be night when we arrive. You won't be safe!" she exclaimed in English. Rosita thought I was foolish and that I would end up stabbed on the banks of the Río Guayas. And that's exactly what she said to her brother in Spanish.

The afternoon came with a swell of sunshine that lit up the green quilt of banana fields all around. Hours and hours went by with nothing but banana stalks loaded down with curved green fruit. I had come full circle, back to the land of my breakfast bananas, complete with a flimsy scarecrow fashioned from bamboo and a curly wig. Did these children play hide-and-seek in the banana groves, like we used to play in the Ohio cornfields? I wondered.

Guayaquil glowed orange with streetlights and the humid evening air. Rosita cried with delight as her family smothered her with embraces. Children tugged at her shirt and an older man thrust a wrapped bouquet in her hands, while another sister just hugged and hugged her without letting go. Then she turned to me and said, "Wait! We are going to help you."

"No, no," I said. "I'm fine, really." But Rosita dispatched Joseo to guide me to the bus company's offices, where he jumped the line and rushed back with information.

"There is no bus to Peru—not here. You have to go to another part of the city," he said, handing me a piece of paper with a written address.

"Thank you, Joseo." I shook his hand to leave, but he stopped me.

"We will take you there," said Rosita, then she pulled me over by hand to introduce me to the entire family.

"This is Aunt Lourdes," she explained. "And this is Cristina. And this is Jorge. And this is . . ." I tried to remember all these names and faces, but it was impossible. I could only remember the little girls, Rosita's nieces Fiorella and Samantha.

"I will get a taxi; you really don't have to take me over there," I said, but Rosita ignored me.

"Guayaquil is not safe for someone like you. This bus station is far away, and you will need somewhere safe to stay," she said. "We will take you—it's not a problem." Tiny five-year-old Fiorella took my hand and began showing me her best dance moves. Then she wanted to go through my backpack and see all my gear. She switched the miniature flashlight on and off, laughing when the light came on, so I gave it to her.

Nine of us crammed into a Honda Civic with me sitting shotgun and the two girls on my lap. Bouncing on my knee, Fiorella practiced her kindergarten English while I practiced my kindergarten Spanish. She and Samantha began singing Spanish Christmas carols, and as we raced down the dark highway, I felt a wash of calm that everything would be all right. I did not know where I was or where these people were taking me. I was completely at the mercy of strangers but only felt their kindness.

The smaller bus station was a little storefront operation on the far eastern outskirts of Guayaquil, and while Joseo checked to make sure there would be a spot available for me on the next day's bus, Rosita called around to all of her friends asking for a "safe" hotel in the area. Safe meant a hotel where the family knew the owner personally. I listened to her negotiating on the phone.

"Do you have bars on all your windows and doors?" she asked. "I have a good friend with me—*un extranjero*—and I want to know if your hotel is secure." The family drove me over to the pink stucco tavern, and Rosita followed me in to interrogate the manager. She inspected the room herself, even checking the locks.

"They say you can stay here for ten dollars," she said. "Is that OK? This is a safe hotel. My sister knows the son of the owner. They will take care of you, and they will make sure you get on the bus tomorrow morning." I thanked Rosita and Joseo, then bid good-bye to the family. Fiorella rushed over and kissed me on the cheek. Samantha gave me a hug. I had known them for less than an hour, but the entire family joined in, hugging me tightly and wishing me well on my journey.

"Have fun in Antarctica!" said Rosita. "And be careful—don't trust any strangers!" she added, but I had trusted her from the bus and she had helped me hugely, offering me the warmth of a family's love in a strange city. Trusting strangers is the only way *to* travel, I thought.

My trip to Tumbes was quick—about four hours—and the double-decker bus was a step up from the other buses I had ridden so far. The AC was blasting and when lunch came, bus attendant Kelly handed out cold drinks and small Styrofoam boxes filled with rice and ham. I ditched my assigned seat and went up to the lounge, where a few upholstered seats were fixed around a long oval table with a panoramic view out the top-level windows. Here was a kind of jungle like I had never seen before—a tangle of wide and muddy rivers, shirtless men attacking plants with long machete blades, and open-air huts perched on high stilts and covered with corrugated tin roofs.

I had left bananas behind and was now traveling through the land of chocolate. Thousands of cocoa trees grew straight as lampposts, with branches loaded down with cocoa pods—some green, some yellow, and some red. Joining me in the little lounge were Julián and Joán, ages nineteen and twenty, who were busing from Colombia to Argentina. The journey would take them six days, whereas the six-hour flight would set them back eight hundred dollars.

In line at the Peruvian border, Julián asked to see my passport, and so I traded mine for his red Colombian one. He had never left South America and much of his passport was so clean. Mine was curved and worn, stuffed with extra pages and tattooed with too many airport stamps and oversize visas.

"Woah! You've been everywhere in the world," said Julián.

"Not really," I said, taking back my passport. The world is infinite and travel is not a contest—to tally up countries like the basketball score is perfectly meaningless. Attempting the trip is the only thing that matters.

The gap between Ecuador and Peru was in fact a wide ditch filled with years of smelly garbage. Skinny stray dogs crossed freely between the two countries, sniffing through the plastic-wrapped trash for a scrap to munch. As we drove over the bridge and into Peru, I realized the ditch was actually a river—a kind of South American Styx clogged with floating refuse that marked a hard line between the two countries.

In my atlas back home, Ecuador was green and Peru was purple. In real life, Ecuador still shone green—an outrageous peacock green with tiny emerald dewdrops on every leaf—but in real life, Peru was brown.

Rolling into the town of Zarumilla felt like changing channels from Technicolor cartoons to some early western shot in sepia. My first few miles in Peru were beige and barren, with desperate trees that scratched at the overcast sky.

The bus dropped us all in Tumbes, in a station so crowded, I had to elbow my way to the ticket counter. There were no more buses to Lima, they said, at least not until the next day. I would have to spend the night in Tumbes, an almost-ghost town lined with crumbling concrete streets and roaming with zombie chickens that pecked in the dirt dispassionately.

"Can you help me?" cried a voice. On my left side stood a girl from the bus, pushing against the counter with both arms to keep from being crushed by the crowd. She looked so small and fragile—but she was holding back the rush of frantic travelers.

"Hold on," I yelled, gripping her forearm and swinging around so that she could hug my backpack. Step by step, I fought my way back through the sea of standing bodies while the young woman hung on tightly.

"I'm Gabriella!" she yelled back at me.

"And I'm Andrew!" I said.

"Where are you going?" she asked.

"Lima, hopefully," I said, then turned my head around to see her. "But there aren't any buses tonight." The sheer force of the crowd spit us out onto the empty street and we both stopped to catch our breath.

"So what will you do?" she asked.

"I'm gonna go find a place to stay."

"Do you mind if I come with you?" she asked. The sky had dimmed to gray and I could tell she did not feel comfortable walking around Tumbes on her own. Together we hiked south on the Pan-American Highway, for a mile, and then another. Taxis swung and honked at us, asking if we wanted a lift. Gabriella waved them away in Spanish and we continued along the road, side by side. Just then a double-decker bus trundled toward us with a sign in the window that read "Lima."

"Stop the bus!" I yelled to Gabriella, and we both jumped into the road, waving our arms above our heads like we were signaling a plane. Miraculously, the driver slowed to a stop and opened the door. This was the six o'clock bus—running an hour behind schedule. As it happened, the bus had exactly two remaining seats in the farthest row back. Gabriella and I each paid our one hundred soles (about thirty-five dollars) and then squeezed ourselves in place. Both of us were sweaty and coated in gritty, tobacco-colored dust but laughing because we had actually caught the last bus.

Night came down like a blanket, swallowing up the final light of day and leaving only a white gibbous moon. As we climbed upward, the Pacific Ocean appeared—vast and electric blue, sweeping into the desert shore. Though the rest of the bus settled into sleep, I remained awake at my window, watching each new mile of Peru. Here was a new inch of the globe that I was finally meeting in person.

A sign declared 1,100 kilometers to Lima—another long night. I envied the sleeping babies swaying in their mothers' laps, but the snow-like sand was too impressive for sleeping. Distant city lights sparkled like gold chains laid out beneath the southern sky, and I watched Orion cartwheel through the heavens. A shooting star blazed overhead—I blinked and breathed a wish.

27 MEDZHYBIZH

Embrace pain with joy.

BAAL SHEM TOV

He spoke no English and I spoke no Hebrew, and so we spoke French.

"I grew up in France," said the rabbi. "*C'est ma langue maternelle.*"

"And I studied there," I said, "when I was younger." We chatted about Paris—how the twentieth arrondissement had changed so much—but the small talk ended too soon and the man with the long beard glared at me, blocking the doorway with his portly frame and wide black hat as I hovered in the cold with my heavy boots in the slush.

"How can I help you?" he asked politely, though his eyebrows seemed impatient.

"I am searching for the Baal Shem Tov," I said. The rabbi's face relaxed, and his beard opened in a half smile.

"Are you Jewish?" he asked.

"No," I said. "*Je ne suis pas juif.* I am a writer. I am writing a book about Ukraine . . . a book for travelers. I want people to know about this place and why it's important." I was rambling now, but he cocked his head to one side and kept listening.

"*S'il vous plaît*, I would like very much to see the grave of the Baal Shem Tov." I sucked in a deep breath and waited.

"Right now?" he asked.

"*Oui*, if possible."

199

"You can't come back later?" He gazed beyond me, looking for my car, but I had hitchhiked to Medzhybizh from thirty miles away. I had a train to Kiev that night.

"I don't want to bother you . . . ," I begged.

"No, it's really no bother, it's just that I have guests here—pilgrims from Israel—with a lot more coming tonight," the rabbi explained. He whipped around to grab his coat and join me outside.

"Let's go then," he said, stepping into the muck with his black leather shoes and leading me to the white mausoleum in the compound.

Once inside, I took off my boots and shuffled across the white marble floor, curling my toes in hopes that the rabbi would not see the holes in my socks. He nodded toward the polished tomb, inscribed with glossy black Hebrew letters. I felt the reverence one feels at any grave site, heightened by the knowledge that underneath the stone box lay the bones of the founder of Hasidism.

Every faith has its holy man, and every holy man his shrine. I remember distinctly when my parents drove all of us kids through two days of cornfields to the far side of Illinois, first to see the final bloodstain of the prophet in the oak floorboards of the Carthage jail, and then on to Nauvoo to see the final resting place of Joseph Smith, first prophet of the Church of Jesus Christ of Latter-day Saints.

This quiet Jewish grave in Ukraine felt the same, only with a bit more marble and grandeur. I was not convinced that the holiest man in Hasidism would actually appreciate the explosive show of finery. From my own scant research, the Besht sounded more like a forest hippy—a kid who enjoyed running around shoeless in the Carpathian Mountains and who grew up to be the kind of rabbi who taught "To pull a friend from the mud, don't hesitate to get dirty."

We both got pretty dirty that afternoon, as Rabbi Gabbai guided me through the mushy unpaved streets of Medzhybizh. It was not enough for him to merely show me the grave—he wanted me to know the life of the Baal Shem Tov and what it meant today.

"Do you believe in God?" he asked point-blank as he led me through a field of last year's wheat.

"*Oui*," I said, following the rabbi's footsteps through the dark earth, dodging the gray patches of lingering snow. Late March only felt like the prolonged winter, with warm sunshine peeking through the slate clouds and black crows hopping around the sleeping fields.

"That is good." He turned around to smile, then pulled me by the hand into the *beth midrash*, with its low wooden beams and spectacular hand-carved decoration, all made to match the original "house of learning" that stood on this exact spot in centuries past.

Rabbi Gabbai told me how he had raised the money to rebuild the place, how he'd followed the original plans and archival photos to be as true to the original as possible.

"It was completely destroyed, but now it has come back to life." He invited me to stay a few days for the celebration they would be having. Already the faithful were arriving from all over the world.

"The rest of the world sees us all dressed in black and they think we are boring and serious, but actually, it's the opposite!" the rabbi said, smiling with his teeth.

"Hasids know how to party," he aded. "Stay for the festival and you will see—singing and dancing, eating and drinking. We can sing and dance and not stop for hours!"

I wanted to stay and see that—to be in the midst of hundreds of happy Hasids, all jumping and sweating in dance; to step into that world that always seemed so guarded and separate and severe; and to know how it felt to be wrapped in the warmth of joy and tradition. Traveling the world had shown me that once you get past all the costumes and lyrics, all religions feel the same on the inside—and yet with any religion, most of us are outsiders. In New York and Paris and Zurich, I had seen Hasidic Jews move through crowded airports or on the subway, but they were clearly separate from the rest of the world. They were forever traveling—all of them fellow travelers—and their journey had started right here, with the voice of one man in muddy Medzhybizh.

"Now stand right here." The rabbi pushed me behind the hand-carved pulpit. I held either side with my hands, just as I had done as a child in my own church, bearing my testimony to the congregation or singing "Jesus Wants Me for a Sunbeam."

"This is where he stood—the Baal Shem Tov," he said. "This is where he taught everybody—not just the rich or the educated elite, but all people, you know, like shoemakers and farmers."

I gazed into the empty room—a room filled with too many ghosts—and inhaled the tickly scent of carpentry and newly stained wood. I watched my own breath escape my lips and hover for a moment in the cold room, then disappear.

The world is new to us every morning—this is God's gift; and every man should believe he is reborn each day.

The Baal Shem Tov first spoke the words in Yiddish, some three hundred years ago, perhaps on this very spot. Now everything was silent except for the sound of a distant truck and some disturbed geese back in the village.

"Let me show you something else." The rabbi led me outside and locked the door, then took me down a pathway lined with naked linden trees. He was an odd man, this French-speaking Israeli, wrapped in his oversize coat that hung to his knees like a dress over his short pants and black stockings, his shoes clumped with mud. For a moment I felt as if I was touring Medzhybizh with the Jewish mystic himself.

Rabbi Gabbai greeted every Ukrainian we passed, addressing them in his sloppy Russian and consistently using the informal *ty*, even with the elderly *babushki* of the village.

"We are all equal in God's eyes," he said, explaining his attitude toward the villagers out loud on the street, like Tevye breaking the fourth wall in a production of *Fiddler on the Roof*.

"No one is more important than another."

Beyond the houses and haystacks lay a cemetery with rows of weathered gravestones all askew. The rabbi motioned me closer, then slid his finger into the grooves of Hebrew lettering on one stone.

"I did all this." He waved across the field of a hundred graves. "Every one of these I lifted back up from the ground; I repaired them all. I had to re-chisel and repaint every letter." The graves dated back to before the wars, before the revolution, when Medzhybizh was three times larger.

"When I first came to Ukraine, this was all forest," said the rabbi. "The people here, they said, oh, there's a Jewish cemetery over there somewhere, but I had to dig around for quite some time before I found it. It took a year just to remove the trees and roots—basically, every forest you see is a cemetery. It's the only place they won't plant crops."

But he was only talking about the official cemeteries from long ago and not the unmarked graves of Jews murdered in the war. The Germans had kept them alive just long enough to build the road into town, and when the task was complete, they gunned them down in the ravines outside the village. Nobody knew the exact number, but at least three thousand bodies lay hidden beneath the mud of Medzhybizh.

Even now, in winter's fading grasp, this place still felt dead, with its tired donkeys and coal-heated houses plopped around the broken ruins of a Polish castle.

"Today I am the only Jew in the village," said the rabbi, and then he asked rather unexpectedly, "Are you married?"

That question again—the older I got, the more I was asked it, though usually only by Mormon mothers with available daughters.

"Yes," I lied, because that was the easiest answer to give. I felt married to Brian but if I tried telling the truth, this whole moment would be ruined. The Hasidic rabbi would leave me in the cold or cast me out as an imposter, shutting my window into his secret world. I panicked with the fear of rejection, even by this stranger.

"What's your wife's name?" he asked, calling my bluff.

"Brian . . . Brianna." I invented an unconvincing woman's name and wondered how grave a sin it was to lie to a rabbi.

"How long have you been married?"

"Seven years."

"How many children do you have?" he asked, then waited for my answer.

"No children . . . yet," I said, staring down at the ground.

"Seven years and no kids? What's wrong with her?" The rabbi shook his head, as if my childless marriage was the greatest misfortune a man might suffer.

"What's wrong with her?" I thought, fighting a smirk.

"By now you should have at least have four or five children!" he said, showing five white fingertips like bobbing heads on his fingerless gloves. I nodded, imagining me now, a penniless guidebook writer, with five kids to support.

"Have you brought her to a doctor? He might help you find out your wife's problem!" He really was not going to let this go. I had lied to the rabbi, and now that lie was turning into a tangled tree of ridiculous lies. I imagined Brian spread in stirrups as the gynecologist delivered the diagnosis, "Well sir, it seems your wife is unable to conceive—because he is a man."

The rabbi saw my discomfort and felt sorry for me—a nebbish without sons, married to a barren woman, who at that moment was all alone at home in America. I did not try to correct the picture he had imagined.

"Come. Eat," he said, leading me back into the heated synagogue. I took off my boots and followed him down the stairs into a steamy kitchen, where a dozen Hasid women sat waiting to be fed, each of them with heads covered and wrapped in shawls and skirts. Over in the corner, a *mashgiach* was sorting through a pile of dead fish. For every one he kept, he discarded two.

"He is looking for worms," said the rabbi. "If there are worms, then it's not kosher. Every few months he flies up from Tel Aviv to check our kitchen."

I was grateful for the plate of fish and potatoes and greens—the food was plain, but it was fresh and hot, and the best I had eaten in days. After lunch, the rabbi showed me around the place. Besides the kitchen and dining room, there were rooms for prayer, a separate synagogue for women, and a library—aside from the candlesticks and Hebrew banners, it felt a lot like a Mormon church. All they needed was a basketball court.

"This is our *mikveh*," said the rabbi, leading me into the warmest room of all, which was covered in white tiles with steps leading down into a deep, square pool that glowed aquamarine with crystal clear water. The bath resembled the font where I was baptized back in northern Ohio, oozing warmth and purity.

"This is rainwater—we collect it from the roof and purify it ourselves. Why don't you go in? Just dunk yourself into the *mikveh*! It's quite nice," the rabbi offered.

"Thank you, but no," I declined. All day I had felt so cold and gritty, wearing the same clothes that I had worn three days before. I felt dirty— too dirty to bathe in such a clean and spiritual place.

"Really, you should go in the water. This is all that it takes to be Jewish. You are already circumcised?"

I nodded yes. The rabbi was getting personal.

"Well, then, you just bathe in the *mikveh* and . . ." He snapped his fingers. "You're Jewish!" He smiled and extended his hand toward the water, like an usher pointing the way to my seat.

I had always thought being Jewish was a bit more complicated than that. You had to have the name and the mother and the family, the aunts down in Florida, all the holidays and languages and bread, the sarcasm and tragedy, some piece in the history of suffering, and a lifetime of otherness in a world of steepled churches and Santa Claus.

I was not Jewish and I was no longer Mormon—I was a gentile to both tribes, wandering through a land where I had once been a missionary myself.

"Bathe in the *mikveh*," the rabbi insisted, nearly pushing me in, but I was still afraid.

It was God, I thought, staring into the glassy blue water before me—I was afraid of God. After my friends, my school, my church, and my family had rejected me, I was waiting for God to do the same. I was waiting for him to lash down at me, to cut me off from everything I loved and then fill my life with punishment and hurt. I had come to expect the worst from life, except . . . what if God had led me to this place?

"All right," I said to the rabbi.

"Just take off all your clothes—everything off." The rabbi motioned his own hands down his body. "Go down into the middle of the pool and then dip yourself under the water three times," he said.

"That's all?" He smiled and nodded, then left the room and shut the door. I squatted down to test the water with my hand—warm, gentle water that rippled around my fingertips. Then I began stripping off my layers of clothes—first the dingy gray cashmere with holes in the sleeves, then the shirt from my rowing days and my jeans that smelled like the smoky filth of overnight trains. I removed Brian's ring and dropped it safely into my pants pocket, then finally kicked my way out of my long underwear.

I stared at my toes, pink from the cold, then broke the water with one foot. Falling slowly forward, I slid my naked body into the warm essence of the *mikveh*. The heated rainwater surrounded my shoulders, then washed over my head as I knelt down, eyes blinded with blue. I dipped myself under twice more—*splash, splash*—and then rose up, standing chest deep in the pool.

The water dripped from my face, and though I was alone, I felt warm, clean, and secure. My heart swelled with that rare and calming energy. There was no towel, and so I simply wiped myself dry with my sweater and reluctantly stepped back into the gray clothing of the outside world.

The rabbi met me at the door, and I thanked him, shaking both of his hands. Like me, he was a stranger in a strange land, but he had shown me kindness—he had fed me and let me bathe in the cleanest pool in Ukraine.

"Have a safe trip," he said. "And take your wife to the doctor! Find out her problem and fix it—I think if you do this, you will have many children."

"I will," I lied once more.

"Good-bye, my friend," said the rabbi in the doorway. His eyes looked elsewhere—his mind had moved on to the next task of the day.

"Good-bye." I waved back and trudged with my boots into the slush. I heard the door close and then walked a mile across the emptiness of western Ukraine, back to the main road, where I hitched a ride in a little white Lada all the way back to the city, where I waited by the tracks for the train to come.

28 A THOUSAND MILES OF SAND

Day 27

The sun rose at six, sending light up the mountains and changing the colored slopes from yellow gray to salmon pink. White fog dissolved over the glistening ocean as our lonely bus sailed along the edge of the empty shore. The desert was still there—blank and omnipresent—as if God had run out of green and left Peru unfinished.

After riding the bus all night, I had reached the great Sechura—a lifeless landscape as big as Florida stretched out over 1,500 miles of barren coastline. Splintered fence posts poked up from the swirling dunes, vaguely separating the ever-blowing sand that buried the edges of Ruta 1 Norte. The roadside dunes held a trove of broken human objects—shattered silver CDs, smashed plastic bottles with sun-bleached labels, fluttering paperbacks, shredded tires, and plastic bags that rippled in the wind.

Rare humans quivered in the air like a mirage. A leather-faced woman in a clean white dress tipped a watering can on the only tree in her brown yard, a young boy fought the wind with a red cloth kite, and a mother washed her crying baby in a plastic bucket of water. How these unfortunate humans lived in such isolation was beyond me. They were quite literally a hundred miles from anywhere, their lives no more than a scratch on the ground. A bit more wind and they would all be swallowed up by sand.

At times, the Pan-American Highway clung to the edge of the steep and massive dunes like a penciled line upon an empty wall. From my seat at the back, I could look straight down to the rushing waves some three hundred feet below. A scampering desert fox chasing a rodent could easily kick-start a sand slide from above that would shove our bus right over the edge and into the gray ocean—or crush it like a soda can on the rocks below. The road seemed built on hope, rather than solid engineering.

It took hours to admit that I was bored. Only after I had listened to a day's worth of music and composed descriptive tweets about the monotonous dirt outside did I accept that boredom had found me. The dead landscape offered zero distraction, while curled up next to me, Gabriella the Argentine seemed locked inside a drug-induced coma. Traveling the world in slow-motion did not equate to constant thrills and adventure—often it meant rolling slowly, mile after mile, with nothing but my wandering thoughts to populate the distance.

Why do this, then? I stared at my own reflection in the window and felt my beard with the back of my fingers. What was I trying to prove? The whole world was watching me now—several thousand readers were checking my status every few minutes, asking where I was exactly, how I was feeling, and when I would arrive at my goal. They demanded more pictures than my phone would allow me to send. I had turned my longing for Antarctica into a kind of vaudeville act, and now, skimming the copper coast of Peru, I had no dance left in me. I could only switch off my phone and watch the scenery like a static TV screen that never turned off.

It took the whole day to reach Lima, which appeared out of no-where, with painted box houses and concrete towers set among so many brown hills—like a great oasis flowing with murmuring traffic instead of water. After discovering for myself that most of Peru was empty, I was amazed that ten million people lived in the capital, crammed together by geography—mountains to the east, desert north and south, and the cold Pacific on the west. At our first red light in fifteen hours, I watched a shirtless man juggling machetes while a young child hit up the waiting cars for spare change. It took our bus an hour to move just two miles through the city, and another hour to reach my hotel by taxi. By the time I lay my head down on my pillow, I hated all cars, the exhaust they belched, and the rabid drivers behind the wheel.

The next day was cool and overcast. Lima reminded me of San Francisco that way—though it was summer, the wind was cold and constant. Fog appeared and disappeared, while seals slept on the rocks offshore. Far below, surfers in full wet suits dotted the beach like black ants, making their way into the slate-gray ocean and bobbing in wait for the next big wave. At a skate park in Miraflores, I watched a pack of jean-clad youth spin and jump on their skateboards, crashing and sliding down the polished concrete ramps and bowls. It seemed so normal— teenagers skateboarding in the big city—and I began talking to one of the girls on the sideline. Angelica wore canvas Converse shoes and a baggy flannel shirt, and though her hair was long and black, she reminded me of my blonde and blue-eyed sister Emily. She pointed out each skater and told me their names while sucking on a red lollipop the size of a ping-pong ball. The skaters liked that I was taking photos and began showing off, attempting more and more daredevil tricks, then running over to see if I had captured them in action.

Perhaps it was hanging out with teenagers, or working out at the gym, or that I ate a whole octopus by myself, or that I sent my one thousandth tweet—whatever it was, Lima cured me of my fatigue. On my last night in the capital, I sneaked up to the hotel's fifteenth-story roof and watched the burning orange sun set slowly over the Pacific Ocean. The chaotic city turned yellow, then pink, and I felt a renewed sense of calm and ease. I had traveled all the way to Lima—by bus. I was closer now than I had ever been to my goal.

Alas, January was the height of the rainy season and all the roads to Cuzco were closed. The TV news showed mudslides and massive flooding in the Andes, ending my hopes of getting to Machu Picchu. I consulted the various routes of Peru's largest and most luxurious bus company. Ormeño still manages the longest commercial bus trip in the world, with weekly service from Lima to São Paulo, Brazil. The 3,700-mile journey takes ninety-six hours and crosses over the Andes and much of the Amazon—an overland journey equivalent to driving from Chicago to Anchorage. Had I a week to spare, I would have gladly made the trip—one-way tickets cost only $175—but I had only seventeen days left to make the ship in Ushuaia. So I bought a second-class ticket to La Paz instead.

"You know that it will take you twenty-four hours to get there," said the lady behind the counter, gripping her phone to one ear and checking her long, red fingernails.

"Yes, I know." After a month on the road, a day and a night on a luxury bus did not seem too difficult a challenge.

"*Pasaporte y dinero*," she ordered. I had five different national currencies in my wallet, so I just handed her my credit card along with my passport. She cackled on the phone while typing up my ticket, christening me Señora Evan Andrews. I pointed out the mistake, and she crossed out the *a*, relegating me back to male.

Lima filtered away to a few scattered adobe shantytowns, as our driver mumbled into his microphone, "Fasten your seatbelts." Second class meant sitting on the upper level of the bus, and whenever we made a stop, vendors crowded the bus, if only for a single minute at a red light. All of them carried long sticks lashed to the bottom halves of plastic Coke bottles. Passengers opened their windows and pointed, shouting their orders before dropping money into the plastic bottle held up next to them. The poles went down and then were lifted again, filled with corn chips; *galletas*; or iced bottles of Inca Kola, the Peruvian soda that resembles the urine of a dangerously dehydrated man but tastes like bubble gum.

I was tired of eating junk food, especially in a country like Peru, where the real food is outstanding. I paid instead for *choclo*, a steaming cob of corn on a stick, with plump yellow kernels the size of human teeth.

The city was gone with its life and lights and now the land was dead again. Dust tornados twirled through desert soccer fields with rusted goalposts and squinting donkeys munched desperately on fallen cornstalks blown here from a greener elsewhere. This was Ica, where it rained less than a tenth of an inch per year. Rippling dunes surrounded us and a vapor of hot swirling sand blew across the road with phantom fury. Here was scenery in motion—where wind moved mountains— the opening act of the Atacama Desert.

Few realize that Antarctica is the largest desert in the world—the entire continent averages less than two inches of precipitation per year. Nevertheless, that measly snowfall has been piling up for a few hundred thousand years, adding layer after layer to the polar ice cap, which is nearly nine thousand feet thick at the South Pole.

Seeing the Atacama was like seeing Antarctica naked, without any ice or snow—a dead place ruled by wind. Once upon a time, giant penguins lived here, too—scientists had only just discovered the fossil of *Icadyptes salasi*, larger than the emperor penguins of today and only a foot shorter than me. That was over thirty million years ago, and those monster penguins and the water they swam in were both gone. Today, the only giant animals in this area were all manmade, tattooed in the sand by an ancient culture.

I had read about the Nazca Lines in *National Geographic* and seen the mysterious images scraped into the landscape: dogs, whales, birds, and monkeys. Now I was here, traveling through the real-life pages of *National Geographic* but unable to stop and see the dried-up mummies and the lines in the sand for myself. Road signs pointed to exits that led to the different figures and billboards advertised sightseeing flights with a better vantage point than the back of my double-decker bus.

Once again, I had to accept that I was not touring Peru but merely traveling through. My purpose was to reach Antarctica, even though it meant brushing past the Nazca Lines. I was tracing my own lines in the earth—a lifeline from start to finish marked by GPS and tire tracks from my own home to the coldest place on Earth. Now I was racing at forty miles an hour through this dry land of mysterious art, redheaded mummies, and old penguin bones.

The desert changed from red to gold to pale violet blue. The final light of day detailed the rolling Pacific, and after a thousand miles of sand, we turned left, away from the coast. I looked back once more at the ocean, so dark and infinite, teasing the edge of the silent Atacama. Then I closed my eyes and felt the wheels of the bus turn eastward, uphill toward the wall of the Andes.

THE LAWS OF PHYSICS

Day 30

Tiny pinpricks of light hinted at faraway villages high up in the mountains as our bus zigzagged upward. My velvety inflatable travel pillow cushioned my neck, but I failed to sleep. At midnight, Eva the bus attendant brought around a tray of teacups filled with green leaves steeped in boiling water.

"It's coca—so you don't get sick," she said, handing me a cup. Everyone else on the bus began sipping their tea, but I hesitated, passing the hot tea from one hand to another. I had never touched tea, let alone coca. I had never seen the leaves in real life, though I had seen the pictures in *National Geographic*. Coca grew on bushes, and it was the chief ingredient of cocaine. I had just been served cocaine—on a bus!

"Just drink it," said my seatmate, Igor. He was much older than me—a father and a husband, traveling with his wife and two daughters. "It will make you feel better later on tonight." I knew that in the Andes, people chewed on coca leaves to alleviate the effects of altitude sickness, but at thirty-four years old, I had never touched drugs in my life, and that included coffee, tea, and alcohol. Why would I break from that standard now? What if it made me ridiculously high and I did something stupid, or worse, got my bag stolen?

"If you start drinking the coca after you are feeling sick, it won't help as much," explained Igor, a Bolivian psychologist who taught at a university in Cochabamba. "Trust me, I'm a doctor!" He laughed.

I took a tiny sip. It tasted like dried leaves. I took another sip. It still tasted like raking leaves—coca tastes like October in Ohio.

"*¡Bueno!* Now, drink this cup, too. You're a big man, you'll need two," said Igor, handing me his own cup. I sipped the tea and felt no different—only I was tired, so I laid back into my neck pillow and dozed off to sleep. Hours later I woke up to the groaning sound of sick passengers. A few of them vomited into their sick bags. There were people in the aisles, hugging their stomachs, and one lady was crying and rocking her head from side to side.

"How are you feeling?" asked Igor, gazing at my face in the dark.

"Fine."

"We are going too fast up the mountain," explained Igor. "We have to acclimatize slowly." Our bus had traveled from sea level to fourteen thousand feet in about six hours. I felt a twinge of pressure in my head. I pinched my nose and tried equalizing like when I go scuba diving, but the headache did not go away. It felt like car sickness, only worse.

CRACK! An explosion pushed my head forward and startled me awake. I felt the back of my neck and pulled away the flaccid remnants of my inflatable neck rest. The pillow had popped—*poof*—just like that. Here in the Andes, atmospheric pressure was nearly half of what it was at sea level, where I had inflated the pillow right after finishing off a bag of Doritos. When it exploded, my own stale, warm Dorito breath blew right back into my face.

An unpleasant sound hit the air like a gunshot, and I raised my head to see what it might be, but nobody moved. The sick were still sick, while the others laid back and prayed for dawn to come. Another muffled gunshot popped the air, followed by a delayed staccato. It was the sound of someone ripping cotton sheets, the sound of a slowly deflating party balloon—the sound of an elderly man gently farting in front of me. Like my neck pillow, the high-pressure gas had escaped from inside him in a kind of sad and disgusting lament.

"Dad, I can't—I just can't," whined Igor's eldest daughter. "Why didn't we fly? This is *repugnante!*" Any smells from the man were over-powered by the abundant vomit on our own level and in first class.

Sara's own sister had moved to the front of the bus with her mother to sip some cold water and sooth her sickness.

Soon the bus had crossed the highest pass and descended onto the *altiplano*, a broad and scrubby plateau that opened up like some dead, flat wasteland, except at an altitude of twelve thousand feet. The faintest hint of blue morning had begun to creep across the shadowed land when another explosion rocked the bus. Sara screamed, and I hugged the seat in front of me while the driver cut the bus engine and rolled us with a limp to the edge of the road.

"Everybody off the bus!" shouted Eva, the attendant, motioning to us like nursery schoolchildren. Her pine-green polyester uniform had lost its shape and her shiny pumps were scuffed. The farting man remained asleep in his seat—farting away like a buzz saw. The rest of us huddled outside in the dirt, jarred awake by the cold air of the altiplano.

The bus driver was bent over the back wheel, studying a worn tire as tall as his chest. The mechanic seemed flustered, but it suddenly made perfect sense that we would have a mechanic traveling with us.

"Too much tire pressure," said Igor, explaining that before climbing the Andes from sea level, trucks and buses need to release enough air so the tires can expand.

"If you don't, then *boom*, the tire pops." He smiled.

"The same thing happened to my neck pillow," I said.

"And that farting man on the bus," said Sara, who huffed off to be alone in the endless dirt.

"I could have flown to this psychology conference in Colombia, but if I took the bus, then I could bring the whole family," explained Igor.

I was not very fond of psychologists—the only other psychologists I knew had all tried to cure me from my homosexual "disorder"—but Igor was a marriage counselor.

"This bus is just like a marriage," began Igor. "See how they're fighting right now, the driver and the mechanic?" The two men were arguing over the popped tire—each blaming the other for not decreasing the tire pressure before our ascent.

"At this point, it does not matter whose fault it is," he said, taking on the tone of a college lecturer. "What matters is that they fix the problem—and fast." Igor scanned the horizon, deep in thought. "I know couples who will fight and fight forever, each blaming the other for every broken-down thing, and in the end, they walk away from the bus and their marriage never gets fixed. Those two can blame each other all the want, but if they want to get the bus moving and their sixty passengers out of the cold, they're going to have to shut up and fix the wheel."

And like that, Igor walked away from me and went to counsel the troubled bus driver and his mechanic. Their conversation grew heated, but a few minutes later, the mechanic walked away and came back with his toolbox. One by one, he removed the lug nuts from the wheel, and together, the three of them began to change the tire.

Despite the cold and a minor nagging headache, I was overcome by the stillness and piercing blue skies of the altiplano. In just one night, we had driven to the moon. Our broken-down bus leaned in the dirt like a sad spaceship on the lunar surface so that I half-expected a crescent Earth to appear above us in the sky. Once more, I had reached a part of the planet that few ever know—most people fly over in planes, all of them busy watching sitcom reruns on tiny screens, oblivious to the emptiness and colors of the land below.

I was glad for the breakdown, even if it took more than three hours to replace the wheel and adjust the pressure in the other tires. That was three hours that I was able to spend in a spectacular spot of Earth, bathed in silence and sunshine—three hours to meet all the other passengers with whom I'd been traveling for the past twenty hours. None of us cared that we were six hours behind schedule. We were glad for a break from the long drive and a chance to stand and walk. In the open air, the sick recovered a little, the farting man reached equilibrium, and my own small headache disappeared.

Whether the multiple cups of coca worked or not, I was hit with a burst of euphoria when our bus reached the shores of the great Lake

Titicaca. More than any other landmark, Titicaca felt like the greatest triumphal arch in my journey—I had come to a place that I knew only by name and reputation from a lifetime of encyclopedia entries, magazine articles, school textbooks, and the Internet. To finally see that lake in person was an astounding moment of excitement and recognition. My first glance at South America's largest lake was no more than a glance—a tiny triangle of blue that emerged between two mountains as our bus descended toward the shoreline. Then it disappeared until we arrived at its marshy fringe, where boats made of bundled reeds bobbed on the surface. The Quechua women looked so distinguished with their piles of colored skirts and red wool shawls, two long hair braids tied together at the tips beneath their brown bowler hats.

There were llamas, too—and kids running across the packed brown dirt into squat, square mud-brown huts, and fields of pretty yellow flowers that shone brightly against the blue expanse of Titicaca. Once more I longed to jump off the bus and stay awhile, to go native at twelve thousand feet and take a reed boat out to the famous floating islands in the lake. I imagined sleeping in a grass hut built on a raft of reeds, hovering on the surface of the nine-hundred-foot-deep lake the size of Cyprus and making best friends with the rare Uru people whose blood is black, they say, which makes them never feel the cold.

At a rest stop in Puno, I drank several more cups of coca and scowled at the tourists. I disliked the way the city was overrun with European and North American backpackers, part-time hippies who struggled under the weight of their behemoth backpacks and haggled with impoverished Indian women over the price of lousy trinkets. Seeing so many white faces upset me, in fact. They were a tribe of their own, sporting abundant bangles, braided bracelets, or manufactured dreadlocks and twee knitted hats. These were the travelers who played dress-up for a time—until their bank accounts ran dry, or until their new jobs began—the kind of travelers who dined at establishments with names like Machu Pizza and then flew back home to write anonymous and damning Yelp reviews in which they complained that the service was too slow.

Life had been getting slower ever since I had crossed into Mexico. The tempo in the Andes was like a slowing heartbeat and I saw absolutely no point in fighting it—my bus was running six hours behind schedule and I had stopped caring. Maybe we would break down again and again, and I would never make it to Antarctica, ever. All I wanted was to try, and that meant pushing on past Puno and pretending that I was somehow different or better than the patchouli bomb of backpackers who were busy destroying an ancient civilization one dollar at a time.

When we arrived at the border in Desaguadero, Eva called me outside.

"*¡Americano!*" she whispered and motioned me to come with her.

"You come with me and we'll walk across the bridge into Bolivia."

"*¿Por qué?*" I asked, wary of doing anything in secret.

Eva quietly explained, "The Peruvian police—they stop all the foreigners and try to take money from them. Just don't look at them. Look right ahead and keep walking—stay close to me. If you're with me they won't bother you."

A shakedown! I was grateful to Eva for steering me away from trouble, and I followed behind her, acting as if my backpack were weightless, checking my pace as we made our way across the single-lane bridge and the *Bienvenidos a Bolivia* sign. The minute we crossed, Eva disappeared into the crowd, leaving me to fend for myself at *migración*.

The air was dark and stale inside the small cement box on the border, with dusty swirls of sunlight and the scent of rotting wood. The floorboards creaked under the weight of my boots as I stepped up to the first window and presented my passport, bent in the shape of my front pocket.

"The other window," said Official #1, who motioned me on to Official #2. This man was shorter, with a mustache, but wore the same military uniform as the first official.

"*¿Americano?* That's not me—go to that window over there," he said, pointing across the room. Official #3 was much older, with a wrinkled face and no energy to deal with me. He nodded to a desk in the corner, manned by Official #4.

"Do you have a visa?" he asked me.

"No, I do not have a visa," I answered, like a kid who forgot to do his homework. "The Bolivian embassy in Washington, DC, said I could get a visa at the border." Well, the website of the Bolivian embassy said that.

"No—you must get a visa in Peru," said Official #4.

"But I already left Peru." Official #4 pointed down a long and dusty hallway, posted with tattered maps of Bolivia and a giant glossy calendar of the new president, Evo Morales. Official #5 said nothing, but pointed to a desk that was three feet away.

"WHAT?" asked Official #6.

"I need a visa. Please," I asked, trying to sound meek. That's the only way with bureaucrats—once you lose your cool, it's all over.

"Go back to Peru," said Official #6, nodding toward the bridge.

"No." I stood my ground. "I know I can get a visa here."

"Yes, you can," said Official #6, scooting his chair away noisily and leading me down another dark hallway before knocking on the door.

"You need a visa, right?" said Official #7, who was younger and smiled at me.

"Yes, please."

"One hundred and thirty-five dollars," he said, pulling out the paperwork.

"Can I pay with a credit card?" I asked.

"No," said Official #7, shaking his head. "No machine. Cash only—can you pay or not?"

"Yes, I can pay." Slowly, I slipped off my belt and unzipped my pants, turning around to remove my money from inside my underwear. My hundred-dollar bill looked like a failed piece of origami and I slowly unfolded it until Benjamin Franklin's head came back into focus. I laid it on the desk along with two crisp twenties. Official #7 stared at each bill carefully, then frowned and shook his head.

"No, no. I can't take this," he said, pointing to one of the twenty-dollar bills. "See this? It's too old and worn—I can't accept it."

"But this is real American money—that I carried from America. It's good!"

"No good. We can't take it," said Official #7.

"Can I pay you in soles?" I asked, pulling out a wad of colored cash.

"No," said Official #7. "But you can change the soles for twenty dollars."

"Where do I change money?" I asked.

"In Peru," said Official #7.

"But I'm already in Bolivia—I left Peru. *Perú finito*." I offered up my crappy Spanish.

"You only need fifteen dollars. Don't worry, I will keep your passport until you return—it's safe here."

"*Ha*." I kind of laughed. "I will keep my passport, thank you." Never trust an immigration official, even if he's young and handsome with dark eyes and intense cheekbones.

"I need it if I'm going back to Peru," I said.

"No you don't," said Official #7. "Nobody uses passports around here."

So I sloshed my way back across the mud puddles at the checkpoint and across the bridge, searching for the off-brand moneychangers that hover like pigeons at every border.

"I need dollars," I said to an old Indian woman with a wad of cash the size of a brick. Then I ran back past Officials #1, 2, 3, 4, 5, and 6 before opening the door to #7.

I was panting from lack of oxygen, exhausted by the high altitude, while Official #7 studied the new twenty-dollar bill. With a plastic pen, he began to fill in the visa forms, carefully creating each letter to fit inside the narrow lines, then handing me a dozen other papers to fill out for myself. With the care of a heart surgeon, Official #7 glued the rainbow-colored square of paper into the back page of my passport before stamping it three times—*bam, bam, bam!*

Official #7 handed me the passport along with two more forms and several sheets of paper, then led me to one more room, the office of

Official #8. It was clear that he was *el jefe*—the chief—who pulled on his mustache and reviewed all the paperwork carefully, then stamped my passport five times with five different stamps.

"Now make two photocopies of the visa page in your passport."

"Where do I get photocopies?"

"In Peru," said El Jefe.

"Señor, I can't go back again—they've already . . ." I made a hand motion of my passport getting exit stamped.

"*Es fácil*—everybody does it," said El Jefe, showing me the door.

"Andrew!" shouted Igor, rushing over. "Is everything all right?" he asked. "The bus driver is really upset. We've all been waiting for you."

I explained my conundrum to Igor, how I technically was not allowed to leave the border until I had submitted photocopies.

"Can't I just leave?" I asked Igor. "I already have my passport and visa, right?"

"Absolutely not! You must give them the photocopies or else you will have big problems when you leave the country," said Igor. "But I will help you. Let's go." Together, Igor and I walked back across the bridge into Peru, running to every shop with a sign that read *Fotocopias*. The first was closed, the second one lied—they did not have a copy machine. The third shop said they *used* to have a photocopier, but now it was gone. The fourth shop was closed. The fifth shop was a tiny pharmacy with high shelves nearly toppling over with packages and medicine. Their copy machine was busted, but they did have a scanner that could make copies.

Igor and I stood next to the pharmacist while the scanner warmed up. As we scanned my passport and printed out two copies, I thought of the bus driver and all the other passengers waiting back at the border, cursing the gringo without a visa.

"Three soles," said the pharmacist.

"*Ha.* I don't have any more Peruvian soles," I said. "I just changed them all for dollars, but I can pay you in bolivianos."

"No way." The pharmacist turned down my inferior currency. "Go change your money into soles—I only take soles." I had spent all my soles—and all my dollars. All I needed was a dollar and I didn't have it.

"Here." Igor opened his wallet and slammed three coins onto the counter. "My gift to you." I thanked Igor but felt embarrassed as we ran back across the bridge to Bolivia and past the seven officials to El Jefe's office. I handed over the two photocopies, breathless after sprinting a half mile at 12,500 feet.

El Jefe added the papers to a disheveled pile on his desk. Then he smiled, nodding smugly, before stating, "Welcome to Bolivia."

30 RAINY SEASON

Day 31

I guessed a hangover felt something like this.

My head pulsed with pain, as if malicious dwarves were hammering on my temples. Sitting up in bed, I felt nauseous and dizzy—it took me ten minutes just to lace up my shoes. I tried walking up the cobbled street but after fifty steps, I felt utterly winded, doubling over in a back alley and gasping for breath. I leaned against a gray brick wall and sucked in the cold, empty air, then wiped a watery streak of blood from my nose. My only relief was returning to my windowless hotel room and lying down, closing my eyes, breathing slowly and consciously, waiting for the pain to pass.

This was my own fault for rushing from sea level to La Paz—I should have ascended slowly, stopping off along the way, allowing my body a chance to adjust. Now I was paying the price for my impatience, strung out like a corpse on a coffee-brown bedspread, sipping copious cups of coca tea and wishing I was at sea level.

Sally the GPS had perished somewhere in the Andes—the last I had checked she was flashing green and happy, but come morning, she was gone. Lying in bed with my pounding head and nothing to do, I tried fixing her, but no tinkering or fresh batteries could save Sally.

No GPS meant that I had no more proof about where I had been. Beyond my tweets and photos sent from the road—none of which were geotagged—I had lost any scientific record that I had moved myself physically across the earth. The *Guinness Book of World Records* had a category for "Longest Journey by Bus" and I was nowhere close to breaking it, but I still wanted some kind of proof that I had traveled this road from beginning to end.

After a few more hours of bed rest, I threw my pale and fragile body into the spastic carnival of La Paz. Afternoon Mass had just ended, filling the streets with families—ladies in silver shawls draped over their shoulders, braids down their back, rustling past with bundles of bright skirts. Young kids wore polished shoes and their cheeks shone red from a lifetime spent at the top of the world.

Steel-colored storm clouds packed the sky, closing a lid over the urban valley and making the rainbow colors so much more intense. Spanish colonial homes were painted yellow and turquoise, red and brown, trimmed like wedding cakes and tangled up in a spiderweb of electrical wires. Piles of dyed wool filled the shops, along with burlap bags that overflowed with neon confetti. Rows of foam rubber masks smiled weirdly from window fronts, and vendors sold popcorn, chicken, deep-fried steaks, sacks of coca leaves, and heavy glasses filled with *mocochinchi*—dried peach cider.

White water rapids flowed through the streets, sprinkled with confetti. During the downpour, I holed up inside El Museo del Arte Contemporáneo, where a security guard followed me from room to room, stopping behind me as I lingered in front of a portrait of Che Guevara made from dominoes.

"Perhaps you would like to buy a painting?" he offered, leading me toward the gallery with its splashed canvas representing Bolivian president Evo Morales.

"*No, gracias,*" I said, wandering into another room, where a clumsy installation was labeled "*Viaje/Travel.*" The wall was pasted with National Geographic maps, including the bare white circle of Antarctica, winking at me—as if the artist had taken the walls of my Ohio bedroom and framed my lifelong dream in a museum. I knew the shape and contours of the continent, knew the ice-carved islands that spilled out from its long peninsula, and knew the names of all the seas and mountain ranges buried beneath the polar cap. I knew the largest runway on the continent

was nothing more than a mile-long ice cube and that the lowest temperatures in history (-128.6°F) had been recorded there. Antarctica was still
my great secret and I stared at its likeness with reverence and awe, as if
the actual continent was the most valuable painting in the world.

It still felt like a dream—Antarctica. The past month on the bus felt
like a dream, and as I walked back through the streets to my hotel in the
highest capital in the world, fluttering with hundreds of checkered rainbow flags, I was walking through a dream.

A knock on the door woke me from my dream the next morning.
There was Farley, standing in the hallway of my hotel with his collared
shirt, V-neck sweater, and sport coat.

"Hi," he said in his deadpan way—as if faraway friends meeting in
Bolivia was an everyday occurrence.

"Welcome to Bolivia," I offered, leading him into my tomb of a
room.

Farley and I first met at a book signing in New York, seated next to
each other at flimsy tables. He was selling his book about Prague; I was
hawking my guidebook to Ukraine. Over the years, we crossed paths in
various parts of the world—I crashed on his floor in the Village, and he
stayed at my place in DC. His most recent book detailed his journey
through Italy in search of the foreskin of Jesus Christ, a holy relic now
owned by the Catholic Church. That we now found ourselves in Bolivia,
together, in the same hotel, was pure serendipity. Farley's magazine had
sent him to La Paz last minute as part of a series where the writers only
discovered their destination on the way to the airport. He had sent me a
message the night before, asking if I might happen to be passing through
on a bus.

"I'm already here!" I texted back. "The altitude is really gonna knock
you down," I predicted, and now I was brewing him cups of coca tea.
"Drink this, then drink another. The more you drink, the better you'll
feel."

"You know, altitude never bothers me," said Farley, remembering
all the high places he had traveled of late—the Himalayas, the Canadian

Rockies. "I'm feeling fine right now—only a bit jet-lagged." The cup of tea grew cold on my desk.

"You may feel fine now, but give it time and you'll feel like hell," I said. Farley still refused any special care and asked me if I wanted to join him in search of an Aymara shaman. He wanted to get his fortune read, which sounded a lot more fun than sitting in my room.

The Witches' Market was filled with strange herbs and dead animals, among them armadillos and dried llama fetuses to be buried in the foundation of a house for prosperity. I stared at the baby animal that never lived, shriveled up in its fetal position with gigantic closed eyelids, bizarrely cute yet so freakishly disturbing. Surrounded by pre-Columbian talismans and magic potions, Farley was in heaven, except that he was also in pain. After an hour sniffing and poking around the magic shops, I watched Farley succumb to the same malady that had taken me.

"I think I better go lie down. I'm feeling a little bit horrid," he said. Returning to the hotel, he lay flat on his back, shut his eyes, and breathed in long, slow moans.

"*Oooooh*," Farley exhaled like a sad ghost. "I'm really not feeling well at all." He did not look well either, and though I wanted to be self-righteous and say "I told you so," I dutifully played the nurse, boiling up a steady stream of coca tea.

"Once it hits you, it hits you bad." I handed him some dry coca leaves to chew, then packed my bags in a hurry. I had a bus to catch, though I felt guilty leaving him in such a bad way. I sent him a text from the station: "What did the shaman say?"

"He said that I would get really sick—probably that I would die," Farley texted back, undaunted by the prediction but energized by his emerging magazine story.

The La Paz bus station was packed with more tourists than I had encountered anywhere else in my journey. Dozens of bus companies called out from their brightly painted booths, broadcasting upcoming buses and departure times, while Japanese and German backpackers rushed from one desk to another, trying to book a seat before the roads closed. Outside, the rain fell hard, sending waves of deafening thunder from the metal roof. I found myself shouting to the ticket vendor.

"I need one seat to Uyuni for tonight!"

"No seats," she said plainly. "We have another bus in two days. They might have seats." Both buses to Uyuni were full, packed with tourists headed down to see the Salar de Uyuni, the world's largest salt flats. I wanted to be one of those tourists, too, so I hung around the buses, begging for a seat. After an hour, a Japanese man sold me his ticket for twelve dollars.

"Daisuke?" the driver called out to the bus.

"*¡Aquí!*" I shouted back, raising my hand up high. For the next twelve hours, I was Daisuke, the tall, white American with curly hair, crouched into his window seat, trying to sleep against the cold window as rain pelted the glass. My seatmate was Jung Byong Sun—a Korean exchange student doing a year of intensive Spanish in Mexico City.

"Call me Víctor," he said. "That's my Spanish name."

"Call me Daisuke," I replied. "That's the name on my ticket." Víctor spoke no English—only Korean and some Spanish—but we chatted the best we could, while the attendant passed out wool blankets, ham sandwiches, and bubbles of pink yogurt wrapped in tight plastic baggies. The diesel fumes were overpowering, and right in front of us, a shaky TV showed determined Latino midgets playing basketball. The audience was in hysterics, laughing uncontrollably at the repeated gag of short bodies reaching to make a basket. It seemed like such cruel humor, yet the Bolivians on the bus thought it hilarious.

We stopped at an all-night café, lit by a single bulb in the mud-brick room, where a hunched-over Indian woman fried eggs for hungry passengers. Our bus had left the paved road some hours before and now the wheels were caked with mud. Dark water flowed along the road like an angry river, and when we reached Uyuni around dawn, the strange and solemn streets flowed with mud.

I joined a day tour to the salt flats, shaking hands with the other backpackers in the four-wheel drive as we splashed out to the great white horizon. For a while, I felt like I was back in college, or at some church activity, filled with youthful energy and the thrill of a chaperoned adventure that would finish with brownies and punch.

The largest salt flat in the world is the size of Connecticut, twenty-five times larger than the famous Bonneville Salt Flats in Utah. I stepped onto the white earth and looked all around me, as if I had been dropped at the edge of a blank piece of paper. The sun was high and hot, the sky clean and blue, bleeding like a mirage into the eternal expanse of white. Weeks of heavy rains had washed into the great basin, filling the empty miles with ankle-deep brine that floated with oozing amoebas of sparkling salt crystals. Together, the sun, water, and salt made a massive mirror that reflected the living sky and the scattered humans in the distance—shadowy stick figures that seemed to float on glass.

I took off my boots and walked barefoot through the sun-warmed water. Minutes later, salt crumbs coated my skin and the hair on my legs. I was alone—the other travelers seemed to disappear in the distance. I kept walking, farther and farther away from the people, and closer to the split reflection of sky versus sky. Mormons believe the highest level of heaven is the Celestial Kingdom, where the righteous live in the presence of God on "a globe like a sea of glass and fire." Now I was here, floating like a lone spirit on this salty sea of glass, feeling reverent in the midst of its odd serenity, my heart beating wildly. Bolivia was heaven—it was closer to heaven than most countries on Earth and closer to the sun and the stars. If the real heaven looks like Uyuni, I want to be there.

The most beautiful places on Earth have no phone reception—I had stopped checking Twitter. Followers around the world were waiting for my steady stream of stimulating dispatches but I had nothing. I had switched off my phone and buttoned it into my pants pocket—I had lost that urge to always be transmitting. Hours passed and evening fell without ever getting online. I accepted the silence and boarded the night bus to Villazón.

The road was unpaved and the ground soft. Twice we passed buses bogged down in the muddy floodwaters. Both times we stopped to help—the driver commanding us down to the water's edge, where we formed a human chain to assist passengers from their broken-down bus to shore. At one point I found myself waist-deep in water, gripping a woman and her child, fighting the current with my legs. The new castaways joined us on our mud-streaked bus, crammed onto laps and in the aisle. I awoke at midnight to the sound of a snoring man at my feet—a man as old as my grandfather, so delicate, his bare head jostling on the bus floor. I felt terribly guilty sitting in the seat that I had paid for while a man more than twice my age was asleep at my feet, but I did not wake him. I did not offer him my seat. I only tried to sleep.

"¡Todos empuje!" shouted the bus driver, tapping me on the shoulder. It was two o'clock in the morning and the rain had stopped. Our bus had stopped too and we were leaning dangerously to one side. Clear moonlight lit up the landscape, and one by one, we jumped from the last hanging step and into the mud.

The bus had gone off the side of the road and tumbled into a shallow ditch. The front tires had sunk halfway into the wet mud, and by the spray of dirt that covered the window, it was clear the driver had already tried and failed to reverse the bus. Now he was the comandante, barking orders to a dozen of us—all men. We all pushed and pushed, rocking the bus in the mud, but without budging it an inch.

"This is not going to work," I said out loud, in English, but we all kept pushing until the bus driver said it to us in Spanish, as if it were our fault, "This is not going to work."

I said nothing but went about searching for sticks and stones to lay behind the tires—the mud was too soft to steer through. We needed traction. Using my bare hands, I dug into the mud, pulling out clods of earth and then packing the ground with rocks. We all worked together— the old man at my feet was now at my side, rolling boulders uphill and then dropping them into the hole.

I was shivering in the piercing cold, soaked through and through, coated in mud and praying to the clear night sky, spattered with white stars. God, please, get us out of here. For two straight hours we worked, digging around the huge wheels and packing the dirt with anything we could find. The other passengers chipped in, bringing us bundles of twigs and grass or bits of cardboard. When it came time to push, I felt a swarm of hands pushing me from behind. The engine revved and then caught, and inch by inch, the bus moved backward, uphill, slowly lurching over the muddy shoulder and then back onto the road. We all cheered.

"YES!" I yelled out. Some of the men, as muddy as me, came to shake my hand. They said nothing but nodded their approval.

"*¡Bravo el gringo!*" shouted one of the ladies, who handed me a scarf to clean my hands. Unlike the previous night, I was now the only foreigner on the bus, and I basked in the approval of my new Bolivian friends. A shared triumph makes a forever bond, and though I would never see any of these people again, we had beat the odds and rolled our bus out of the mud.

A broken-down bus was no more than a night of adventure for me, but for them, this was a way of life. Less than 10 percent of Bolivia's roads are paved, and the rainy season can shut down whole regions for weeks at a time. Nine-hour bus rides turn into fifteen-hour bus rides—buses wash into rivers or fall off deadly cliffs. Every year, hundreds of Bolivians perish in bus accidents, but we had escaped those statistics.

Instead we greeted the morning—dirty and exhausted—glad to reach the quiet border intact. My pack had been stored under the bus and was now soaked through—luckily I had wrapped my computer and camera in plastic and stowed them with me on the bus. I bid farewell to my new friends and shook hands with the driver, who thanked me and wished me "*Buen viaje.*" Dripping a trail of raindrops behind me, I squished through the streets of Villazón in my soaking boots, and when I arrived at Argentinian customs, sunburned and salty, my face was still painted with the red mud of Bolivia.

31 ARGENTINA

Day 34

"Give me back my money."

The man blinked at me and the corner of his mouth quivered into a smirk. I said it again, a little more forcefully, "Give me back my money, dammit." My tired face and mud-streaked clothes did not make me look tough or forbidding—rather, I looked homeless and weird in the small square room with the spotless white tile floor.

"Next!" The man behind the counter gave me a little laugh and dealt with another customer until I stepped in front of him and persisted.

"I'm not kidding—*soy muy serio*. Money, now!" I was shouting now, slamming both hands on the counter, employing the ultimate Spanish word of urgency: *ahorita*.

The Argentine man was small and sneering, dressed in a well-ironed uniform of black slacks and a crisp white shirt bearing the logo of the bus company and his nametag: Miguel. He looked like a Mormon missionary with perfectly polished shoes and long, dark eyelashes, while I looked like a drunken bum who had spent the last two nights pushing a bus through the mud.

Miguel had sold me a ticket to Córdoba, and when I balked at the price—nearly $250—he assured me that Argentina was much more expensive than Bolivia. His credit card machine was broken, he said, and the once-a-day bus was leaving in five minutes, so I handed over the last of my American cash. Only when I boarded the bus did I realize that Miguel had sold me two full-fare, first-class tickets, round-trip, when I had specifically asked for a single second-class, one-way seat.

"I thought you wanted a seat for your bag!" he explained. "*Estúpido.*" I was only stupid to have trusted such a shyster.

"You stole a hundred dollars from me—give it back," I demanded. The bus driver honked his horn and the engine revved outside.

"We don't give refunds," said Miguel, waiting for me to rush out the door for the departing bus. But I stood still, my fists clenched and my face flushed.

"I'll call the police," I said. It was a weak threat and Miguel chuckled at me. The police would have no time for me, and I would have no time for the police. My bus was leaving and Miguel knew it. Losing a day at the border was not worth a hundred bucks, but I was not going to let this slimy bastard of a bus agent ruin my trip. For weeks and weeks I had been helped through strange lands by friendly strangers. I had never been robbed or cheated or harmed—things had always worked out. After surviving the threat of Mexican drug wars, Honduran revolutionaries, Nicaraguan bandidos, Colombian paramilitaries, Ecuadorian stalkers, and Bolivian floods, I was not going to let this jackass rip me off.

"Convenient bus routes for all South America!" said the large sign against the wall. A satisfied Caucasian family smiled in the same direction, preparing to board the bus to the future—or paradise. The sign was light, posted on light foam board, which I picked up easily and cracked in two.

"STOP!" yelled Miguel. "Are you crazy?" He rushed from behind the counter and tore the broken sign from my hands.

"Give me back my money or else *I will wreck this place!*" I yelled back at him—in English this time. "If you can't give me a refund, then I'll take it in kind!" I said, grabbing the computer from behind the counter.

"Stop! Stop!" yelled Miguel. He grabbed my arms and tried to pull me out the door, but he was a tiny man with small hands.

"What? You want to call the police?" I asked. Miguel pushed his whole body against my chest, trying to force me out the door. The other customers had backed into the corners of the room, clutching their purses and bags. Now Miguel was trying to grab my face, but for once I was the stronger opponent. I wrapped my fist around his starched white collar and lifted the man a foot off the ground. Then I slammed him against the wall and held him there, pinned between the concrete wall and my shouting red face.

I felt dizzy and hot. My heart beat wildly, my brain flooded with blood, and it all came back—all the mean and horrible people in my life: the kids that made fun of me on the bus, the kids who called me "girl" or "faggot" or "pansy" or "fairy," the kids in the hall who punched me in the chest and who tripped me on the stairs or kicked me in the back, the kids who mocked the way I spoke and walked, the phony friends who laughed at me in secret, the strangers in the street who yelled insults at me, that guy who threw a brick at my head when I was a missionary in Ukraine, the self-righteous bullies at BYU, the street gang in England who bashed my face and sent me to the hospital, the church leaders who made me cry, the bishops who made me feel worthless, the family who picked me like a scab from their lives, the African dictators, American warmongers, child abusers and gun nuts, the idiots who torture dogs, the wife beaters and hypocrite preachers and bike thieves, and that asshole Karl Rove!

I held all of them in my fists, ready to choke them gone from the world. I tightened my grip on Miguel's collar, felt his body dangling above the floor, his untucked shirt now exposing his bare abdomen, covered with swirls of fine black hair.

"You are crazy! Let me go!" he yelled. "Somebody help—somebody call the police!" Miguel looked around for help, but none of his co-workers intervened.

"Give me my money, and then I will leave," I said, suddenly calm. Miguel pulled my tightly folded hundred-dollar bill from his pocket. I held onto his collar with my left hand while I checked the money, then I released him and watched the blood drain from his face. He stepped away and smoothed his shirt, tucking it back into his pants.

"*Americanos*—so violent," he said.

"*¡Y los Argentinos,*" I answered, "*son ladrones!* All thieves."

"Not all of us!" said a lady who had been watching near the door. "Just the Italians—and he's an Italian," she said, pointing toward Miguel. "All the Italians are thieves," she added, and Miguel began screaming at the woman. She screamed back and I walked out, leaving the ticket agent with a roomful of angry passengers who now knew that he was a liar and a cheat.

My money recovered, I hopped on the bus and nestled into the top level, where I watched the highway unfold before me—the first paved highway I'd seen in nearly a week, painted with lines and divided into four separate lanes. The rounded hills swirled with pink and beige sandstone, layered in pretty pastel stripes. White llamas grazed beneath the cloudless sky and giant green cacti grew taller than me, spindly and weird. Once again I was in the desert, but already northernmost Argentina felt so different from the country I'd just left behind. The yards were swept and the brick houses had water tanks to collect rain on their roofs. There were schools and painted curbs and Rotary Clubs, and a single-file line of concrete telephone poles running between one remote town and the next. Bolivia had felt so poor and the people so kind while Argentina seemed so rich, and yet the only person to scam me on this trip was an Argentine.

The first sign in Argentina read "Ushuaia 5,281 km." That meant 3,281 miles left to go, the same as driving from Miami to Seattle. Argentina was the Texas of South America—impossibly big and proud of it. The numbers made me panic: I had traveled some seven thousand miles by bus, but now I had another three thousand to go. The *MV National Geographic Explorer* sailed from Ushuaia in eight days' time, and if South America had taught me anything, it was this: expect delays.

I used my four-hour layover in San Salvador de Jujuy to clean up and repack. For twelve dollars, I split a day room with George and Jody, a Canadian couple who had traded the Yukon winter for the hot streets of summery Argentina. There was no hot water in the hotel, so I stood under the icy stream in the coffin-size shower, grateful for soap and shampoo and then glad for the sun that dried my bare skin through the open window. I napped shirtless on the bunk bed, then wandered over to a café with my new Canadian friends, where we sat under slow ceiling fans and sipped cold drinks before saying good-bye forever. They left for Buenos Aires, and I left for Córdoba on the nicest-smelling bus I had ever known.

The black leather seats reclined all the way back. A waiter with a black bowtie served dinner: focaccia and fresh salad followed by tenderloin kebabs and chilled tiramisu. Then I slept six blissful hours—the longest uninterrupted sleep I had known on my journey.

After so many muddy days in Bolivia, the luxury of Flecha Bus was shocking. There were no chickens squawking underfeet, no popped tires, no children vomiting—and no gun-toting guards or midnight breakdowns. There was only the song of tires on asphalt, a soft humming like a smooth airplane engine soaring across Argentina. Summer lightning flashed yellow, followed by a scatter of water droplets that turned into sheets of rain. In the morning, thick mist filled the road, a gray backdrop to the windbreaks of watercolor trees.

I had lunch in Córdoba at a big café that served hefty *lomitos*—steak sandwiches too big to fit in my mouth. Sitting next to me was Francisco, a police officer obsessed with Unión—the soccer team from Santa Fe that right then was winning on TV.

"You like *fútbol*?" he asked me.

"*Sí*," I lied, craning my neck around the lunch crowds and pretending to follow each new kick of the scrambled game in play.

"You play?" asked the policeman. He bit into his sandwich and dripped a spot of wet mayonnaise on his uniform.

"*Sí*," I lied again. I *had* played soccer—back when I was nine years old. When I wasn't catching the ball with my face, I was staring down at the trodden turf, imagining the soccer field was a huge world map and that each grassy patch was an island or continent of its own. After our team won the city championship, my dad pulled me aside and told me that I didn't have to play soccer anymore.

"You should only play if it's something you want to do," he explained.

"Well, I don't want to play soccer," I confessed, still gripping the golden trophy in my hands. The hollow metal figurine had been poorly cast so that the androgynous soccer player was kicking the ball with an awkwardly bent left foot.

"That's simple!" said my dad. "Don't play soccer—try something else instead. Just keep trying until you find what you like."

Twenty-odd years later, I still did not want to play soccer, nor did I enjoy watching team Santa Fe running up and down the field over and over for an hour. I preferred watching the people in the café—moms with their jumpy kids, dusty construction workers in hard hats, office secretaries, salesmen, and chauffeurs—and all of us stuffing the exact same sandwich into our mouths.

I found a hotel and rested. I washed my clothes. I discarded half the load in my pack—all the things I no longer needed. Then I found a gym in the city and worked out. A month on the bus had turned me soft—my body was lighter than when I started, and I was down to the last hole on my belt. Lifting weights in a Córdoba gym seemed a waste of time, but like those astronauts who have to pedal for hours on a bike to prevent atrophy in space, I knew I had to exercise and keep my strength up for the long haul ahead. After traveling so many thousands of miles of open landscape, it felt silly to run in place indoors, staring at a brick wall.

A new wave of loneliness came over me in Argentina—the empty miles of land coupled with long silence made me hungry for human contact. In Córdoba I threw myself at every stranger I met—I was eager for conversation, if only with the baker at the pizzeria. Back at the bus station, the first human to speak to me was an Arab man in a gray dishdasha.

"*As-salamu alaykum!*" he greeted me in Arabic, nodding to me and then shaking my hand as if we belonged to the same secret brotherhood. The man stroked his beard as he passed me with a hard glance. My own beard was blond and ambitious—nearly as long as his. He thought I was a Muslim—that I belonged to his tribe.

"Peace upon you," I replied in Arabic. *Alaykum-salaam*. He smiled and kept walking across the giant polished floor of the station. The Córdoba bus station felt like a newly opened airport, with over fifty buses loading or unloading at any given time. Long passenger lines snaked out from each gate and a dozen different bus companies all competed for business, calling out to passing travelers. In the midst of the terminal, a Peruvian band played "Wind Beneath My Wings" on wooden panpipes while dancing in the gigantic eagle-feather headdresses of the North American Sioux.

I stocked up on *alfajores* and bought a bus ticket to Trelew—first class. The plush black leather seat reclined all the way back, and a small side shelf contained chilled bottled water and extra snacks. I had my very own full-size flat-screen TV and a library of DVDs—including *Terminator 4*! The bus was even more luxurious than the previous night—and so cheap: just over seventy dollars to cross a thousand miles of flat, green nothing.

I knew about La Pampa from *National Geographic*, and from my Argentine roommate at BYU who grew up in Santa Rosa. Now that I was here, I found the place mostly unremarkable and alarmingly similar to my own native Ohio. Wide open cornfields stretched out on either side of the road—just like home. Roadside vegetable stands sold orange and yellow squash and striped melons—just like home. And on farmhouse porches, potted petunias grew out of cement geese planters—just like Ohio, eight thousand miles to the north.

The green summer corn continued for hours—a sea of grain separating scattered islands of barns and shiny steel silos. Each distant farm bore the family names of Italian settlers: Mastrangelo, Bertini, Ambroggio, Cestassi, Fiatorri, Tonelli. After Realicó, the road never diverged—the bus followed a straight line for two hundred miles. The driver could have tied the steering wheel in place and gone to sleep for hours, and the only danger might have been hitting a cornstalk. I saw my own childhood in the landscape—I imagined the awkward school dances, the ticking hours in church pews, and the family expectations to grow up and be as vacant and fertile as the land, framed only by evenly knotted barbed wire fences.

February was hot in La Pampa—like a windless August in Ohio. Twilight came and the humans emerged—a team of gauchos galloped at the edge of the road with their leather chaps flapping. This time, though, it wasn't a book. I wasn't flipping through the pages of *National Geographic*—this time I was here, in La Pampa, where the gauchos belonged. Now it was nothing at all like Ohio. It was summer in February and there were no fireflies, but there were fruit-sniffing dogs at checkpoints and police who stood lazily by the roadside sharing a bowl of maté.

A ghoulish copper half moon glowed in the sky as we ate dinner on the bus. Mónica had been riding next to me from the start, but now that she was awake, we talked. She was kind and motherly—a large woman with bobbed black hair and friendly eyes. Her daughter was at the university in Córdoba, she explained, and every other week, she took the bus to visit.

"It's a long trip, but I can do it overnight on the bus," she said. "Normally I stay up there for two or three days, and then I go back to Trelew."

"How many times have you taken this bus?" I asked.

"Oh," she laughed, "so many times. Maybe twenty? Thirty?"

Forty or fifty thousand miles by bus, back and forth across La Pampa and the great cornfield that separated Mónica from her daughter. I thought of an equivalent distance in the United States—a mother driving from Missouri to Manhattan round-trip every two weeks.

"It's not so bad," said Mónica. "It's not expensive and this way, we get to spend more time together."

"Do you have children?" she wondered.

"No," I said. "Not yet."

Mónica called her daughter to wish her good night over the phone. Then she called her other children down in Trelew to let them know she would be there in the morning. Then she wished me a good night.

"Sleep well, Andrew," she said, and we both lowered our seats back and wrapped ourselves under the individual blankets handed to us by the bus attendant.

I slept very well, and the next morning, the sun rose like the Argentine flag—a smiling ball of yellow beneath a stripe of soft blue. La Pampa was gone and the land was brown. From my window I caught the silver stripe of the Atlantic Ocean on the left. Cheerful billboards featured happy penguins with their little wings pointing toward nearby attractions. A cluster of abandoned carnival rides sat rusty and silent behind a loose brick wall spray-painted "*Tanya, te amo.*"

Mónica hugged me good-bye in Trelew and handed me her e-mail address on a torn piece of paper.

"Travel safe and let me know when you reach Antarctica," she said. "I'll be following your journey."

"OK," I agreed, as if my own mother was asking me to stay in touch. Then Mónica walked away, and I walked around town, looking for a new bus to carry me across Patagonia.

32 MARCHING AS TO WAR

The park was filled with crumpled dead leaves and the occasional Hollywood celebrity, as thousands of marchers poured from the Metro station flapping their flimsy cardboard signs: "Hate Is Not A Family Value" and "Equality Now." Others posed important questions—"If Liza Can Marry 2 Gay Men, Why Can't I Marry One?" "Legalize Gay" was the message on T-shirts, while eager volunteers painted protestors' faces with "NOH8," a holdover reference to California's Proposition 8.

The ballot measure had passed the year before, amending the state constitution to read, "Only marriage between a man and a woman is valid or recognized in California." Brian and I had followed the campaign closely. It started when marriage equality had passed in California. We hoped that someday we might be free to marry. Gay couples were getting married in San Francisco and Los Angeles, kissing passionately on the front pages of newspapers, blubbering on the news and showing off their wedding bands. We watched on TV as elderly lesbian couples shielded their eyes from the flash of the cameras and outside, psychotic evangelicals screamed, "Sodomites! Faggots!"

But the real threat came from my own church, the Church of Jesus Christ of Latter-day Saints. The Mormons had spearheaded the anti-gay campaign in California and ensured Proposition 8 was on the ballot. Then, the First Presidency of the church issued a call to arms in the form of a letter, read aloud from the pulpit in every Mormon chapel:

We ask that you do all you can to support the proposed constitutional amendment by donating of your means and time and to assure that marriage in California is legally defined as being between a man and a woman.

241

The result was tens of thousands of LDS volunteers knocking on doors, preaching the gospel of heterosexuality and exclusion. The result was $22 million donated in record time, a tidal wave of money that drowned out the opposition. The result was that Proposition 8 passed, same-sex marriages halted overnight, and massive protests formed around LDS temples and chapels in California.

It was Brian who showed me the list online—name by name, every individual who had given money to outlaw gay marriage. I found them quickly—first my brother and then his wife. A thousand dollars was a lot of money for a struggling family with five children, yet this is what the church had instructed them to do, and they believed they were following God's living commandment.

It was the same unwavering obedience that my family had followed for seven generations. My ancestors had given up their homes and lives in Scotland and Wales and sailed the Atlantic, then pulled handcarts thousands of miles to Utah to build Zion. In 1878, after the U.S. Supreme Court ruled against the Mormons' right to polygamy, my own great-great-grandfather was arrested and thrown into a federal penitentiary. Better than anybody else in America, Mormons can understand the inherent dangers of blending church and state, yet now they had become the face of antigay discrimination and political manipulation. The blatant hypocrisy upset me.

When Proposition 8 passed, I became sullen and depressed. "A religion can't claim the rights promised by the constitution while denying the rights of others in the same breath," I whined out loud to Brian. "Mormons can't have their separation of church and state and eat it, too!"

Brian had a different attitude: "Honey, this is probably the best thing in the world for us. By passing Prop 8, the church just hit the fast-forward button on nationwide recognition of same-sex marriage. Prop 8 is unconstitutional, it *will* be overturned in federal courts, and it will end with the Supreme Court having to rule on a heap of lawsuits."

But deep down I still believed the church had God on its side, just like that time, a week after I visited my very first gay bar, a freak tornado ripped through Salt Lake City and demolished the building in seconds.

"It's the only way," said Brian. "The church has just made gay marriage a national conversation. They've advanced the movement by ten years at least. I should really send the prophet a thank you card that says, 'Dear President Monson, thank you for forcing the Supreme Court to legalize my relationship and letting me marry my husband.'"

It was wishful thinking, and now nearly a year after Proposition 8 had passed, Brian and I were walking hand in hand past the White House along with hundreds of thousands of protestors for equality. The marchers had come from all across America—from Alaska to Florida, Puerto Rico to Maine. We had only come from ten blocks away, but we all wanted the same thing—equality. We wanted the right to marry, the right to live in the same country as our spouse, the right to serve in the military, the right to go to school without getting bullied or beaten. This nonsense had gone on too long; we had been too patient, too meek. Too many lives had been ruined, and even after the explosion of empathy and acceptance in the media, there was still too much suffering.

My family and church had the right to fight for their beliefs, but I had the right to fight for mine. Let the Mormons knock on doors in California—I was marching to the Capitol with the man I loved. We had been together nine years now, side by side through life, and yet the law still counted us strangers—mere roommates with different names and different passports.

From the beginning, the world had told me that I did not belong. Every day at school, somebody was there to remind me with a slur or a punch. At church, they told me that I did not belong, then they put me before a court and formally kicked me out of their fold. My own family had categorically excluded me from their lives. Now I felt half the country was shouting at me, claiming my kind did not belong in America. Only this time I was shouting back, no longer timid or afraid. I was simply fed up, adding my own voice to the roar on the National Mall.

The power of the crowd was like nothing I ever felt before. People were happy and hopeful—we believed the world would change. We believed that someday—someday soon—we would be able to marry. I believed that someday, I would have my family back. Already, things had changed.

Years had passed since my father had asked me never to come home again—then came a different e-mail, completely out of the blue. He was abnormally brief—no mention of the weather down in Texas or his attempts to trap the elusive armadillo in the backyard.

"I'm sorry" was all he wrote to me. He was sorry for what happened and how it happened. He never mentioned my excommunication, but he did invite me back home. "Come visit us sometime. We would like that," he said. So I flew down to Houston and spent three days dancing around the hole in our relationship. He took me to a baseball game and together we watched the Astros lose. He took me to Six Flags and NASA, and I took him to the Museum of Fine Arts.

Perhaps we wore different uniforms in the culture war that seemed to be splitting America in two, but he was still my father and I was his son. No matter all the hurt that had come between us, I still loved him and everything that he was. And he still loved me—so very unmistakably gay, but on the inside so Mormon, even now.

Standing among hundreds of thousands of homosexuals on the Capitol steps, I felt proud to be me—a big, gay, Mormon nerd who still knew all the capitals and countries of the world, who cried easily in touching movies or when hearing some old hymn, who still prayed to God like a kid begging Santa Claus for presents, and who was about to take a bus all the way to Antarctica.

Reaching the bottom of the world had always seemed so elusive, as did getting married. Both were faraway dreams that I had chased for a lifetime. Would I ever get there? I couldn't say, but I had come to a point in my life when I could actually try. After so much trying and failing, all I could do was march ahead.

33 THE END OF THE WORLD

Day 37

It cost two pesos to go to the bathroom in Patagonia. After snapping the bill from my hand, the old man at the door offered me toilet paper, which I used to clean my glasses. He paid no mind as I stripped down to my boxers and bathed in the sink, splashing icy water onto my face and chest. I brushed my teeth and changed into clean clothes, then paced the station for two hours waiting for my bus to Río Gallegos.

Down here the earth was dry and olive green, as if the entire country were dressed for battle. The land rolled down from the faraway crest of the western mountains, spreading out to the coast, disappearing into the silver stream of the open ocean. Over and over, the wind shoved at our bus, while outside, scrubby clumps of dead grass clung to the sandy soil.

"How will you get back?" asked my seatmate, two minutes after meeting me. Marcello was cheerful and rather obese so that his body pressed into mine. He had long and stringy black hair on his head, was unshaven, and sort of resembled a prison mechanic.

"I will probably fly home," I told him, knowing that I, also, was a hairy hobo. It was the first time I considered my life after Antarctica. My only plan was getting there.

"You can always come back with me," he offered. Marcello smuggled cars into Argentina, buying new vehicles at the tax-free ports of Tierra del Fuego, then driving back to Córdoba, where he sold them for considerable profit.

"How long does that take?" I asked.

"Four days exactly," said Marcello.

"And you make money?" I wondered out loud, adding the cost of gas and hotel and the bus to get down there.

"Thousands of dollars on each one," Marcello said proudly.

"What kind of cars do you . . ." I searched for the right word. "Import?"

"Mostly Peugeots and Chevrolets," he answered, then handed me his card. "Here's my e-mail. If you need a ride back to Córdoba, just tell me and we'll get you back there, no problem. No cost." It was a kind offer, though backtracking for a week across the flattest bit of Argentina seemed a far less romantic journey than racing south through Patagonia.

We had a short break in Comodoro Rivadavia, a city of concrete blocks and slow-moving oil pumps that seemed spread out like mold on dirt. I sent some tweets from the bus station, then used my phone to slowly translate the graffiti in the bathroom stall: *¡Todos los del norte son putazos!*—"Everybody from the north is a fag."

That word again. I had spent a lifetime running away from the call of "faggot" only to have it echo back at me at the opposite end of the world. I stared at my tired face in the mirror as water trickled into the sink. *Putazo.* I said the word out loud, listening to the way it sounded in Spanish. The graffiti was just some stupid adolescent scribble, but I wanted to track down the idiotic oil town bigot and rebut his claim with hard facts: less than 2 percent of the human population is homosexual, and I am one of them, but by "everybody from the north," was the artist referring to the north of Argentina, or the entire northern hemisphere? Either way, that's a hefty generalization, since 88 percent of humanity lives north of the equator—and in Argentina, only 5 percent of the population lives in Patagonia, inferring that 95 percent of all Argentineans are faggots. If that were true, Argentina would need to change their flag *pronto.*

No, I could not let this one go. I entered the bathroom stall once more, then opened my backpack and took out my trusted black sharpie pen. I popped off the cap and inhaled the sharp alcohol scent; then I went to work, blacking out the untruth on the wall with artsy curlicues and doodles. Editing the Patagonian bathroom stall felt like justice to me.

The forever road curved along the coast—afternoon sunbursts hit the window every time we rounded a new hill. Clouds of yellow dust hovered in the air like blowing gusts and the long empty beaches went on for miles, washed by a steel-blue sea and scattered with white seagulls that lifted with every gust before floating softly back down to the surf. Down here, the wind shaped everything, shaking the single-file line of telephone poles that held hands from one remote town to the next. Yet there was no phone signal—no way to communicate all the beauty— and so I settled down with my headphones and Puccini and the great brown nothing of Patagonia.

"There's only one bus a day from Río Gallegos," Marcello explained to me hours later, when I awoke. "The bus to Ushuaia is always full— *muchos turistas* right now—but you'll be fine if you have a reservation."

"I don't," I answered. The only reservation I had was a berth aboard the *National Geographic Explorer*, departing in four days' time.

"My cousin works for the bus company in Río Gallegos," said Marcello. "I will talk to him."

"*Gracias.*" No matter how far I'd traveled, I could not shake the feeling that somehow I was doomed—that something would happen that would keep me from reaching my goal.

"You are going to love Antarctica. It is such a beautiful place," said Marcello.

"You've been?"

"Yes—a few times," he said. "I was in the Argentine military. We delivered supplies to the bases." Marcello made it sound like no big deal—for him, going to Antarctica was just a short flight from Ushuaia— the same distance as me flying to Florida from Washington, DC.

"What's it like?" I asked, in awe.

"*Muy frío.*" He laughed. "And very white. It's beautiful—penguins everywhere. I was always on the base, but flying over the ice you see everything. Antarctica is big and white. But why did you take the bus the whole way?" he asked. "Because it's cheaper, right?"

"Yes, it's cheaper." It was an easy explanation. "Also, I wanted to take the bus. I don't just want to *see* Antarctica—I wanted to know everything in between, from my home to the bottom of the world."

"But is it the bottom?" Marcello winked at me. "What if Antarctica is actually at the top of the world?" He flipped an invisible globe in the air. "Then Argentina would be the northernmost country. The southern hemisphere only exists because the northern hemisphere drew the first map. What if the whole universe were the other way around and we're always drawing it upside down? What if right now you're actually headed toward the North Pole?"

The Río Gallegos bus station looked like a makeshift morgue, the floor covered in slow-breathing bodies stuffed into the kind of high-tech sleeping bags sold in European camping stores. This was the bottleneck of backpackers Marcello warned me about and all of them were waiting for a spot on the lone bus to Ushuaia. I was so tired but waited with the sleeping masses until the ticket office opened at 3:00 a.m.

"There's no use waiting," said one French backpacker. "All the tickets to Ushuaia are sold out."

"How long have you been waiting?"

"Three days—and I'm still waiting," he said, discouraged. "Río Gallegos stinks—it's the most boring place in the world. Don't get stuck here," he warned, but I had to stop. I had been riding the bus nonstop for thirty-six hours. I needed to sleep, and I had four more days to get to Ushuaia.

"Take me to a good hotel," I mumbled to the taxi driver, flopping my head on the backseat. He steered through the blue streets, dim with the approaching sunrise.

"You speak English?" He chatted to me over his right shoulder. "Do you know my favorite band, Crash Test Dummies?"

"Uh-huh," I murmured back.

"Oh good—you can help! Will you translate my favorite song for me, into Spanish?"

"*No hablo*," I replied. My eyes were shut and my brain asleep.

"But you're speaking it now!" he countered. "Tell me what this song means." He hit play and the singer began to moan, "*Mmm mmm mmm mmm.*" It was the way I felt at that moment and, incidentally, the title of the song.

"Tell me! What is he saying? What does it mean?" the driver demanded, and I chuckled back like a drunk man.

"There's *uno chico*. He can't go to school. He has white hair, *entonces* it is black. *Mmm mmm mmm mmm.*"

"*¿Qué significa eso: Mmm mmm mmm?*" he asked.

"*Nada*. It means nothing at all," I said.

"Then why do they say it so much?" he asked, but I had already moved on to the second verse.

"Now there's a girl. She does not like school," I said.

"Why not?"

"Because the other girls are not friendly," I answered.

"Oh," he said.

"Last verse," I said. "There is this boy. His parents are *muy estricto*. They go to church a lot."

"Then what happens?" he asked, parking next to the small bed-and-breakfast.

"Nothing—that's the end of the song," I said and handed him some money. I closed the door and thanked him, but he looked stunned—I had just rendered his beloved mysterious poem into bland gibberish. Sometimes it's better not to understand.

I slept like a dead man until afternoon. Not a single human soul walked the perfect square blocks of Río Gallegos—it was cold and the wind blew in gusts of sixty miles an hour, animating every dead object: street signs shook violently, rippling plastic bags snagged on the barbed wire, and all the trees grew sideways, as if running. In place of public trash cans, locked metal cages were anchored to every corner, as the garbage tumbled around inside.

A woman stared at me from her front door, pushing wisps of gray hair beneath her red kerchief. She was the first person I had seen in two hours, and she was calling to me, motioning me closer with her hand, so I opened her garden gate and approached.

"What's your sign?" she asked me as I approached. Her eyes were silver with cataracts and a pink wart sat on her left cheek like a fleshy jewel.

"My sign?" I asked. "I'm a Leo."

"Ah! Of course you are." She smiled, searching my face with her spotted vision. "All my lovers are Leos. What are you doing in Río Gallegos? Nobody ever comes to Río Gallegos."

"I'm going to Antarctica."

"You must be a scientist," she said. "Only scientists go to Antarctica."

"No," I said. "I'm not a scientist. I'm just traveling."

"Well. I am sorry that you are here. There is nothing to do here. I moved here when I was twenty years old and I still hate it," she said. "I *really* hate it!"

"Then why don't you leave?" I asked plainly.

"My husband," Elena said. "He's a Libra—his job is here, so we are still here. But I hate it. Every day I hate Río Gallegos a little more. See right now?" She nodded to the dishwater sky. "This is summer—the best time of year, and I cannot see the sun."

I never shared her hate for Río Gallegos (or *río ga-shay-go* as they say it in Argentina), but it took me three days to leave. In the end, Marcello's cousin came through for me, snatching up a single seat from a last-minute cancellation. My final bus ticket was just a square scrap of newsprint—*Río Gallegos a Ushuaia, 220 pesos*—and I was the last man to board the bus, swerving my hips and shuffling along the narrow aisle to the farthest seat in the back, number 40. Unlike my other buses in Argentina, this one was filled almost exclusively with foreign tourists—most of them young Israeli backpackers jabbering excitedly in Hebrew. It almost felt like a school field trip; I was even sitting next to a teacher.

"I'm Giorgio!" said my new seatmate, shaking my hand. Giorgio taught geography in Italy and his one great dream was to see Tierra del Fuego.

"I'm Andrew," I said as I smiled back at him, "and I'm going to Antarctica."

"Lucky man," he said. "I would love to see *Antartide*! All these years I have been teaching South America to high school students and yet I've never seen it. Now I am here and it is so . . . *glorioso*!" I envied Giorgio's energy and enthusiasm. He reminded me of how I normally behaved when traveling—thrilled beyond words—but now I felt more subdued, concentrating like a doctor preparing for surgery, thinking through every problem before it might happen.

"How long will it take us to get to Ushuaia?" I asked the bus driver when we parked at the Chilean border.

"Eight to twelve hours," he grumbled robotically, disappearing into the customs office to drink maté with the border patrol. The rest of us filed out and waited in line for two hours in order to get our exit stamps out of Argentina. Then we climbed back on the bus, drove exactly one hundred meters south, parked, exited, lined up once more, and waited an hour to get our entry stamps for Chile.

I had grown comfortable with the slowness of everything in South America. The bungled mechanics of movement no longer bothered me—with patience, you could go anywhere in the world. When we arrived at the water's edge, the Strait of Magellan looked long and blue— like a finish line drawn across the earth, or a long banner that read "You're almost there." But the sea was too rough to cross, explained our driver as he parked us back on the road. "We will wait here until the wind goes away," he said.

Four hours later, we had not moved and the wind had picked up, turning the water white and frothy and spitting salt into the air. Restless passengers came and went, gathering on the roadside with other travelers, huddling from the cold and studying the sea. Several hundred cars and trucks had lined up behind us, trailing back for miles.

"Are you the guy going to Antarctica?" asked an Israeli girl, tugging at my jacket.

"Yeah," I said. Apparently, Giorgio had spread the word.

"There's somebody who wants to talk to you," she said, leading me off the bus. All the Israeli kids were hanging out in the only building around—an abandoned café without any tables or chairs. They sat on the floor, laughing and playing cards.

"We all did military service together," she explained, then walked me over to the far corner to a short man in a heavy oversize black coat. A black yarmulke sat on his head and his wispy red beard framed his pale face. The girl spoke to us in Hebrew and introduced us.

"You speak any Hebrew?" she asked, as if I should.

"No, I do not." I shook my head in apology. "Sorry."

"Well, I don't know how you're going to talk then—he doesn't know any English, but he really wants to go to Antarctica. Can you just tell him how to get there?" The young Hasidic man spoke to her and she translated.

"He wants to know if you speak Yiddish," she said, interrupting herself to tell him no, that I was a goy and did not speak Yiddish. Beyond *oy*, *schmuck*, and *nebbish*, I knew nothing. Except *schlong*—that was Yiddish, right? It's the same word in Russian.

"I speak Russian," I offered.

"*Russky?*" he jumped in.

"*Da, da,*" I answered, and our conversation took off—in Russian.

"And I'm out," said the Israeli backpacker as she walked back to her friends.

"My name is Nathan," he introduced himself quietly.

"And I'm Andrew." I shook his hand.

"Are you Russian?" he asked.

"No—but I used to live in Ukraine."

"Really?" he asked, surprised. "Me too—what were you doing over there?"

"I was a missionary for my church. You?"

"We have a Hasidic community in Uman and I have worked there for many years."

"Are you Breslov?" I asked him directly. Nathan's face turned up into a smile.

"Yes. How do you know this?" He seemed genuinely surprised, if not suspicious.

"I have been to Uman," I said. "I have seen Rabbi Nachmaan's grave—and that of the Baal Shem Tov, in Medzhybizh."

"You have?" Nathan's eyes got bigger. "How? Why?"

"I wanted to see those places—I was writing a book about Ukraine," I explained. Nathan had been traveling south from Buenos Aires— alone, without any knowledge of Spanish or English. I was incredulous.

"How did you make it this far?"

"I hitchhiked here from Río Gallegos," said Nathan. "I want to go to Antarctica—I've always wanted to go there." He was twenty-seven years old and oddly unmarried. "My father keeps telling me that I must get married, but I said no—because I wanted to travel and see Antarctica first. So I have come to South America—and I told him that I am trying to get there. He says that when I go home to Israel, I will have to get married." I understood Nathan too well. My own father had wanted the same for me. The constant expectation of marriage seemed like an end to all my hopes of exploring the world.

"Do you have to get married when you go back?" Nathan asked, but I wasn't sure how to answer him. We had so much in common; we shared this unbeatable desire to reach the cold, white end of the planet—even to hitchhike if necessary. We spoke Russian, we had both worked as missionaries in Ukraine, and now we both had beards. I too had once dressed in all black, like he was now, with dress shoes that suffered from the elements. I too had once worn the sacred white under-garments of the faithful, like Nathan with the knotted fringe of his tzitzit hanging from his waist. We both came from large families with traditions that we loved, and we both had desires and dreams that contradicted those same traditions. What if Nathan really was like me—a *faygel*—an impossible plight. What did gay Hasids do? Where did they go?

"I must set foot on Antarctica," he said, looking up at me, determined. He was just like me, I thought. Just a map nerd in love with the atlas and the world it represented. He was a traveler without a ticket or a plan—just a man with a dream and a big black coat.

"If you get to Ushuaia before me, you will tell them that I am coming?" he asked me. "Maybe find a ship that has space?"

"I will try," I said, promising myself to look around. Nathan had no e-mail address and no phone, nor did he have any of the necessary gear for walking around the coldest place on Earth. He showed me his bag—a small black knapsack for his clothes and toothbrush, nothing more. He had no boots or gloves, only his big black winter coat from Ukraine.

"How cold will it be?" he asked me, as if I knew.

"Cold," I said, "but not as cold as Ukraine in winter." Nathan smirked—he knew the same cold that I knew.

"Take these. So you don't get too cold!" I handed Nathan my only pair of gloves. He thanked me and pulled them on over his bony red hands.

"Thank you," he said to me. "I hope to see you again—maybe in Antarctica!"

"Maybe," I said. We shook hands and then bent over into a short and awkward hug.

"Travel safely," he said.

"You too," I replied before climbing back onto the bus and waiting for the ferry to sail into the darkness.

34 PIONERO

Day 40

The darkness of the storm left me blind.

All day long, waiting to cross, I had watched from shore as the constant whitecaps leapt at the steel-colored sky. Then, like someone unplugging the TV, night came and disappeared the view.

Rain hit the windows like fistfuls of gravel, and as we rocked from side to side, I pressed my face against the cold glass to try to look back to shore. It was only black—forever black—though a vague and passing beam lit up the scene for a brief moment. For half a second, I saw the mottled span of midnight clouds—then down we swung, hovering over the black ink spill of the ocean below.

Waves crashed against the quivering glass, leaking seawater through the window seams. I touched my finger to my lips and tasted the salt, felt the rush of unbearable cold from outside against the overbearing warmth inside the bus, where the air was stuffy and dead. With each breath, I smelled the stink of unwashed travelers hanging on for their lives, clinging to their fuzzy polyester seats and wishing for seatbelts.

No one spoke—not a whisper. The storm screamed against our silence, tossing us up and down like a cheap carnival ride. With every wave that hit, our bus tilted opposite the rolling ferry. The laws of physics played out in my falling stomach—we were unattached to any surface, poorly parked on the slick deck of a bucking flatbed ferry, deadweight in a balancing act of fatal proportions.

I had been riding the bus for forty days and this was my fortieth night. It was also my fortieth bus, and by some mystical coincidence, I was stuck in seat 40—the last open seat on the last bus of the week to the end of the longest road in the world. We had barely crossed into Chile before we hit the Strait of Magellan, where, after ten hours waiting for calmer seas, the ferry decided to cross.

Now the tremendous waves crashed onto our double-decker bus, the water slapping against my window on the upper level. This was meant to be a quick crossing—less than three miles from shore to shore—but after ten minutes of turmoil, the ferry gunned the engines and began to turn us around. We were heading back from whence we came—we had too much weight, the ferry sat too low in the water, and the seas were too rough. The pilot had changed his mind and was taking us back to safety.

If we turned back, the bus would bring us back to Río Gallegos. Even if the weather calmed and I caught another bus the very next morning, I would still miss the boat in Ushuaia. I would be left behind, and I would never make it to Antarctica. Alas, a failed dream is better than a failed life, and I gazed silently into the black nothingness, accepting the fate that is bad weather.

Wham! A wall of water slammed us from behind, spinning the ferry like a bath toy. The current was too strong, pushing us swiftly downstream and away from the nearest shore. The glimmering lighthouse beam was smaller, and I could feel us getting pushed farther and farther from the docks on either shore. I sensed the pilot's indecision—either he turned back to the original course and made the crossing, or else we got carried way out into the ocean, or capsized, or smashed against some rocky beach. There was no choice but to go forward. The ferry wobbled around once more and the engines bellowed below. How many times had I read in the news about some ferry tipping over somewhere in the world? I could already type out the AP version in my head:

A car ferry in southern Chile capsized and sank around 8:30 p.m. last night. The Pionero *was carrying a bus in a routine crossing of the Strait of Magellan when it was blown off course and struck by high waves. All passengers are missing and presumed dead.*

It happened all the time—bad weather and poor judgment in a country with relaxed safety laws—but now the cards had been dealt, and my hand spelled death by exposure and drowning. I would die at the final edge of the world, alone in the dark—except for the thousands of readers who were waiting and watching on Twitter. The battery on my phone had dropped to 10 percent and the reception showed no bars, but the 3G symbol was still there.

I tapped out a simple and desperate tweet: *Feeling a fear I've never known before—the fear of drowning on a bus. No joke.*

I clicked SEND and spent more than a minute of precious battery life watching the spinning circle on the screen, waiting and waiting until the words appeared: *Message Sent.* There was nothing I could tweet that would bring us any prompt rescue, but at least the world would know what happened to me.

Drowning by bus seemed so stupid and banal. It was not "natural causes." It was not adventurous—it was simply asinine. Ferdinand Magellan got shot with a poison arrow, but he died fighting on a beach in the Philippines, an explorer who failed to finish his journey—just like me.

At least you tried. That's what my parents would have said to me, and what would I say to them? What could I say? I picked up my phone once more—this was my last chance. There was no signal for a text message, but I thought I might be able to tweet them directly. I struggled to type with my thumbs, lost for words.

If you could only speak 140 characters before dying, what would you say? Twitter was my only chance to send my Last Will and Testament, though I had no assets to leave anyone. I had spent all my money on bus tickets. My laptop and cameras would sink with me. I only had a few boxes of books back home—Brian would discard the Mormon ones, and my parents would throw away the gay ones. Thus my life had been lived and now all I had to show for it was a fleeting text.

Whatever I wrote would be seen by the whole world. The final message to my family would be in the public domain. Time was running out, and so was my battery, so I turned off my phone and waited, humming an old Scottish folksong:

The water is wide, I cannot cross o'er. And neither have I got wings to fly. Build me a boat that can carry two . . .

The Israeli backpackers began shouting and pointing out the window. I got up from my seat and saw the arched splashes springing up from the waves outside. *Dolphins!* I counted a dozen of them, leaping in rows behind the ferry. Their slick bodies gleamed, even in the pitch black of the storm, and I was glad for this fantastical escort across the River Styx. Was it a sign? I had never been chased by dolphins before, especially on a bus, but there they were, this platoon of gentle mammals, unbothered by the cold and splashing around us like old friends. It was a glad sight, and I felt less lonely. Maybe we had a chance after all. I listened to the passengers pray in Hebrew, English, and Spanish. I was ready for the moment—ready for the cold water.

It was time. I zipped up my coat and pulled a wool cap over my head. Then I pulled out my phone and tapped my final message:

I love you Mom & Dad. I'm sorry. I love you Brian. Thank you.

35 THE DRAKE

Day 40

My intended eight-hour drive to Ushuaia had become a twenty-four-hour ordeal that peaked with our collective near-death experience on the Strait of Magellan. Yet we made it, I never sent that deathbed tweet, and once we had rolled safely off the ferry and onto the road in Tierra del Fuego, the bus erupted into a manic explosion of joy and emotion. Strangers hugged strangers, some bus passengers cried, others laughed. The Catholics crossed themselves and the rest of us made peace with our gods.

Blowing snow made for a fuzzy view—I could barely read the sign welcoming us to the bottom of the world. "Welcome to Argentine Antarctica!" it said, a wishful claim that the pie slice of Antarctica between 74° and 25° W is in fact part of Argentina. We had only reached Tierra del Fuego, but Argentina had already welcomed me to a land that lay six hundred miles beyond its shores.

The other backpackers on the bus had traveled all this way because, as they explained to me, "it was just like going to Antarctica." There were snowy mountains wrapped in dense fog, leftover bits of glacier, and, if you knew where to go, designated colonies of tiny, smelly penguins. But hosteling in Ushuaia did not equal my own grand plans—no more than standing on a beach in Key West equals visiting Cuba. Unlike the twenty-something tourists and gap-year kids, I could never be content with "almost there," and I realized that this made me a terrific snob. Like them, I had spent my twenties traveling to the places I could get to with the money I had—but now I wanted the real thing. Now that I was standing at the dock that would lead me there, it felt so real.

The last bus stop in the world stands in a parking lot at the edge of a sad, gray harbor. Falling rain left open puddles on the cement, shining with the same color as the sea—it seemed as if our sagging bus could just keep driving into the Beagle Channel and beyond to Antarctica. Walled in by the circle of stone mountains, the blank sky pressed down on me and the wind blew a long sigh. I felt the weight of finality—I had traveled forty days and forty nights on nearly forty buses, if I counted the taxis and that milk truck in Nicaragua.

"Exhausted, ecstatic, jubilant. I made it!" I tweeted to the world, but it was still too early back in Washington, DC, so I heard no online applause. I wanted the world to cheer for me and my great success, but the fact is that I was standing alone in a parking lot in the pouring rain. And what had I actually achieved? I had sat my butt on a bus for forty days—nothing more. I felt as gray as Ushuaia, a city still patched with snow, cheated of summer and sunshine, with every window facing south toward the end of the world. I walked a mile in the rain only to discover that every hotel room in town was full.

"This is high season," said Mercedes, the all-night receptionist who took pity on me, soaked and dripping in her lobby. She handed me a towel and a mug of maté then called every hotel and bed-and-breakfast in town.

"I found a room for you—way up on the mountain, but it's a nice guest house that's warm and dry," said Mercedes, drawing out the directions on a map. "It's called La Posada del Fin del Mundo," she said. On my way to the Inn at the End of the World, I passed the telltale structure of a Mormon church, complete with the branded sign: "Church of Jesus Christ of Latter-day Saints." No matter where I wandered, the church was there. This had to be the southernmost chapel in the world.

Ushuaia reminded me of some swishy ski town, like Aspen or Park City, with steep chalet-style roofs and a main street of outdoor clothing stores, a serious camera shop, and an Irish pub for all the sailors. The

Ushuaia post office was a good two miles away, but the rain had stopped and I walked the distance, prodded by the stimulus of civilization after so many empty days in the wilderness of Patagonia. At a little window with metal bars, I gave my name and showed my passport—a minute later, my suitcase appeared, mummified in brown packaging tape, my return address scrawled in Brian's handwriting: Sixteenth Street, where I boarded my first bus. Postage paid: $111.10. That's how much it costs to mail a suitcase to the bottom of the world.

Nothing was missing inside. It was all there, just as I had packed it more than a month before—my waterproof pants and heavy sweaters, extra pairs of long underwear and wooly socks, knit caps, scarves, and heavy mittens for subzero temperatures. I smelled the clothes and remembered home.

The *National Geographic Explorer* sailed into the harbor that night, and I watched from my room on the hill, enthralled by the massive blue hull and tall, white bridge lit up in port, complete with the smart golden rectangle of National Geographic. It was distinguished and scientific, sleek and seaworthy—just as I had imagined it from the travel brochures. For the next month, that ship would be my home.

The next day, I walked up the gangway with great purpose, counting every step as a step closer to Antarctica, relishing the gradual approach and the final excitement of crossing the threshold. On the floor of the entryway, set with stained inlaid wood, was the seal of the National Geographic Society, identical to the one at headquarters in Washington, DC, complete with its map of the western hemisphere. I stared down and retraced my own route on the wooden map, from our office back home, down through the Deep South, across Texas, through Mexico and Central America, over to Colombia, through Ecuador and the long coast of Peru, then over the Andes, through Bolivia and then the full length of Argentina. It was only a couple of feet on that map, but in real life it was ten thousand miles by bus.

"Most of us didn't think you'd get here in time," said Henrik, flashing the customer service smile of the ship's hospitality manager before sending me off to cabin 350, where my name was printed on the door. The room was spacious and spotless, smelling of freshly laundered linen. Like a little kid in his very first hotel, I ran the length of the cabin and back again, flinging open the closets and drawers, yanking the blinds open to my extralarge picture window. This was my very own room and this was my glass desk, complete with a full-size, unabridged *National Geographic Atlas*, cracked open to page 96 with its beautiful map of Antarctica! This was my childhood dream come true.

My bed rocked gently with the ship—back and forth, up and down. Here was the open sea and the infamous Drake Passage, synonymous with spontaneous storms, gigantic waves, and scary winds that can blow a ship off course, but that was not my experience at all. By morning, the sea had turned calm, like a sphere of cold, blue glass reaching to every horizon. They call it the "Drake Lake," and I took it as a good omen. The *National Geographic Explorer* sliced through the water like a line on the map, farther and farther south until we hit land. I hung out on the bow of the ship, watching the forever calm of the sea and sky. Gulls and petrels dropped down and then flitted back up in the sky, and over several hours, I saw three different wandering albatross—still my favorite bird in the world. The giant albatross is a lifelong traveler and they mate for life. Watching them hover so lightly behind our ship made me miss Brian a little more.

I had gone from traveling solo to traveling with one hundred fifty other guests—guests who had paid a significant price to sail on such an elite expedition aboard a ship that was custom-built for polar exploration. The expedition leader had already introduced me as a writer on assignment for National Geographic, causing a wave of surprise and laughter when he mentioned that I had traveled overland by bus. Couples stopped me in the halls to chat, mostly asking, "Why would you travel by bus?" Most of them were elderly and retired, and while they were friendly and kind, I still felt overwhelmed to be part of a group tour.

Sisse and Cotton saved me, grabbing me away from the rush of curious people for our first lunch.

"We've been assigned to shoot you," said Cotton, followed with a short burst of laughter. "We just found out today." Now that I had actually made it to the ship, the magazine was taking my story serious enough to assign photographers. So Keith had hedged his bets on my success, but I was glad to have these photographers with me. As wife and husband, Sisse Brimberg and Cotton Coulson were veteran photographers with long and established careers shooting some of the most iconic pictures for *National Geographic*.

"I know this picture," I said, pointing to the image that Sisse had shown me. I recognized it right away—the darkened chamber and pre-historic paintings in the Caves of Lascaux in southern France. "I used to have that stuck to my bedroom wall."

"Well, I shot that," said Sisse. It was truly a beautiful picture, and the more they showed me, the more I felt star-struck, amazed that I was no longer the little kid flipping through the ink-scented pages of the magazine but traveling through the pages myself and even dining with the photographers. I had stepped inside the world of *National Geographic*.

That afternoon I attended their photo workshop and pretended that I already knew all the important fundamentals of photography they were patiently teaching: Never place your subject in the dead center of the frame. Change your camera angle. Get close. Seek out contrasting light. Always be watching and waiting. Be patient—I had been patient. I had waited through years of school, waited a child's lifetime, and then waited all those weeks on the bus. Now I had to wait two more days. The captain wanted to take advantage of the quiet seas and sail us as far south as he could get. We hoped to make landfall well below the Antarctic Circle.

I loved being at sea—I loved the constant gentle rocking of the great calm and the way the glasses clinked in the bar. Sometimes the deck would shudder and I would stumble forward, catching the rail with both hands and staring headlong into the rippled water as we moved with purpose across the vast blue map of the world. To be at sea is total freedom, with never-ending waves that whisper the truth—that they can take you anywhere.

I wanted the world to know how far I'd come, and I updated them regularly on Twitter—how I had just crossed 60° S, which put me safely inside Antarctica waters where small chunks of blue ice hinted at the ice to come; how after lunch, a pod of orca whales had swum so closely to our ship that I saw their gleaming black eyes and heard the sputtering sigh from their blowholes. Later came the humpback whales and then a small family of fin whales—the second largest animal in the world. I wanted everyone in the world to be as amazed as I felt, and I wanted them to congratulate me for being there to witness the beautiful truth of the earth in action.

My giddiness grew by the hour until the culminating moment of day 2 at sea, when a slab of chalk-white ice the size of a city parking garage floated past us. It moved as freely as a truck floats down the freeway, and I chased after it, sprinting to the bow of the ship and leaning out over the prow in just a T-shirt and jeans. The tabular iceberg was square and chiseled, with a dotted line of black specks on top. *Penguins!* I focused my binoculars. *Chinstrap penguins!* I counted them . . . *16, 17, 18!*

The iceberg seemed close enough to touch and I inhaled the freezing blast of air that blew over from its cold surface. No matter that I was shivering—I could not leave deck as long as I could see those little penguins on the ice. They had always been down here in their world—unobserved, untouched, and undocumented—living their little penguin lives until I showed up to gawk. The black-and-white birds did not appreciate the intrusive attention and eventually they moved on, waddling up and over the crest of the ice to the other side of their floating island.

After the penguins, I could not calm down, nor could I sleep. I rotated through the ship, from the chart room with its maps, to the library with its wealth of books about Antarctica, and to the bridge to check our ever-changing location. We crossed the Antarctic Circle around 1:00 a.m. and I was there on the bridge, watching the glowing green numbers flicker on the GPS, resting for two seconds at 66 33.333 S, 69 13.731 W.

Sunset overlapped with sunrise, and the sky was airbrushed yellow and pink against the deep indigo dawn. The air was strikingly cold but every hour I went out on deck to check, wearing only my pajamas beneath my big, blue parka.

At 6:00 a.m. I saw it—the faint outline of my lifelong dream on the horizon. Three pointed mountains rose up from the sea—a stony shadow above the ocean and a new memory tattooed on my brain forever. It was real—the place on the map was real. There was something actually down here at the bottom of the world, a place that so few knew despite it always being there, even before humans showed up on the planet.

Nice to meet you, I thought. The wind blew into my eyes, and I blinked away a few joyful tears.

36 ANTARCTICA

Day 45

For seven seconds, the world disappeared from view, the cold wrapped around us, and my face turned wet with icy mist. Opaque, flintlike icebergs floated around us, as big as suburban houses. The zodiac sliced across the milky blue bay; our humming motor echoed back from the great wall of ice before us, filling up the silence.

Sisse shot at me like a firing squad. With every click, the shutter snapped three times—*click, click, click.* Meanwhile, Cotton held his enormous video camera on his right shoulder and told me to smile, but not too much.

"Do you want me with or without glasses?" I asked, pulling the lenses from my face. Without them, Antarctica looked even whiter and fuzzier than before, but this way, in the decades to come, I would never run the risk of someone laughing at my out-of-fashion glasses. I imagined my portrait on the cover of the magazine—the toothiest nerd on the planet. I tried staring boldly at the horizon but ended up squinting at the shore I couldn't see. I was missing Antarctica.

"Just wear your glasses," said Sisse, pausing the machine-gun fire of her camera. "That is who you are."

And who was I? A thirty-four-year-old boy finally getting his way while all the world was watching—if not on Twitter, then on TV and radio interviews and podcasts I'd been doing over the ship's satellite. These were the friends I never had, but I knew they were out there now, watching me play dress-up: my beard was bushy and too long; I wore a royal-blue National Geographic parka; my ears were tucked beneath a wooly, gray National Geographic cap; and a pair of National Geographic pocket binoculars hung around my neck. I was branded to the hilt—I was nothing more than a walking advertisement for the great and historic National Geographic Society.

To call me an explorer was ludicrous. I was not rediscovering Machu Picchu or stepping onto the moon or dropping to the bottom of the sea in a ball of steel. A luxury travel company was taking me ashore the seventh continent, and beneath all my layers of clothing, I was wearing my lucky boxer shorts dotted with happy little penguins.

I was only one of the 21,622 tourists who would land in Antarctica that season, but when the zodiac finally hit the stony shore, I felt like the first human ever to grace that frozen spot. I wanted to press pause and move through those seconds frame by frame. I wanted to savor standing up in the zodiac, moving to the bow, and then leaping in slow motion from the black rubber craft, suspended in the zero degree air until the tip of my boot touched down on the shattered granite, or to paraphrase Lao Tzu, *the journey of ten thousand miles ends with a single step.* Alas, that is not what happened.

The Lindblad crew did not indulge my theatrical notions. They cared only about unloading the boat safely before the next wave hit the shore and flooded or capsized us or dragged our ill-suited mammal bodies into the deadly cold water. There was urgent shouting and a strong pair of gloved hands that gripped my shoulders and heaved me onto the beach.

Now I was standing in Antarctica. Now I was taking off my bright orange life jacket. Now there were miniature black penguins, blinking at the human invaders on shore. Now I was walking uphill, scrambling up a polished granite boulder and staring into the stadium of mountains and ice.

"Right here, Andrew," said Cotton, pointing his video camera at me. I blinked back at him, fighting back tears and inhaling the polar air through my nostrils. *Click, click, click.* Sisse's camera shutter measured out the passing seconds.

"I'm here," I spoke to the camera. "I made it to Antarctica!" I spread my arms out in a victory pose; then I got down on my knees and kissed the cold stone, waiting for the camera to capture my moment. From my backpack I took the green, blue, and brown-striped National Geographic flag that I had carried all the way from Washington, DC, unfurling it in triumph. No, I was not one of the great explorers, but I had followed their tradition the best I could and carried their flag to the bottom of the Earth. I had tried and I had invented a spectacle for the world to see. Best of all, I had made it—Andrew the weird gay kid from Ohio was standing in Antarctica, a dream fulfilled. I had crossed the globe—*by bus*; I had accomplished exactly what I set out to do, and it felt magnificent.

"How do you feel?" asked Cotton, eager for a few more spontaneous sound bites.

"I feel like crying," I replied honestly. Standing atop that gray boulder on Marguerite Bay, I felt the heavy swell in my chest, the gulp in my throat, and the weighted bundle of my whole life untying itself and dissolving in the fog.

"Then cry, dammit!" shouted Cotton, letting out an exasperated laugh and kneeling in closer to film any glistening tears that may tumble from my eyes. But I did not cry—not for the camera. Already, that emotion was gone, and now I just wanted everything to stop. I wanted the world to freeze like the textbook glacier in front of us. I wanted time to stop and with it, the pictures and the rolling camera. I did not want this to be recorded. I did not want the other passengers approaching me to shake my hand or pat my back and offer a heartfelt "congratulations." I just wanted to be alone with my triumph.

"No. No more," I said, stepping off the rock and walking away like a spoiled actor. Cotton lowered his camera and let me go. Like a kid exploring in his own backyard, I scrambled over more rocks, hiking my way up to a small bluff that was filled with penguins. That is where I wanted to be—in Antarctica, away from the other people, surrounded only by great nature and the beady-eyed locals who had begun to close in on me.

Adélie penguins are not big at all—only around two feet tall—but they are so beautiful, hooded in glossy black feathers, with bright white chests that inspired the original idea of penguins as quintessential English gentlemen in white ties and dinner jackets. Perfect white rings circled their black eyes that blinked and blinked at me, as if trying to refocus their vision and determine if I was a friend, foe, or just another speckled piece of rock.

I sat down on the ground and watched and counted the dozens— and then hundreds—of Adélie penguins that hopped about, goose-stepping over the rocks into huddled-up groups, fluffing out their feathers for warmth. Their necks seemed rubberlike as their heads rotated around before lowering beak to breast. Ever so slowly they closed their little bird eyelids—like me, they were too tired to stay awake too long.

I felt my own exhaustion take over, felt the dreamlike moment of quiet ecstasy slip away into my cold, hard reality. My fifteen minutes of fame had passed. I had wanted to come to Antarctica, I had come, and now it was done. Already, the other passengers were making their way back to the ship, where a hot and hearty lunch was being pulled from the galley ovens and laid out in the dining room.

I stayed put though, ignoring the numbness of my backside and my freezing seat among the smelly penguins. I almost wished the ship would leave me behind me, forgotten and abandoned on the coast of Marguerite Bay. I belonged here—alone. I felt like Antarctica was my country—my place on Earth.

"Come on, Andrew!" shouted one of the crew. "Time to head back." My first full hour in Antarctica had passed and I had spent most of it on a rock, gaping at all the penguins, in awe of the ice shield encircling us. The fog grew thicker, erasing the view beyond the rocky beach where a few molting penguins trotted around, pecking away their dead gray feathers. I lingered until the last zodiac, not wanting to admit that the moment was over and that I had crossed that fine line of always wanting to go to Antarctica to having been to Antarctica.

Stepping back into the warmth of the ship, my face flushed red, and I hurried up to the reception area to connect to the ship's satellite. I texted Brian the news: "I made it! I'm in Antarctica!" I wanted him to know first.

"Congratulations, honey!" came back the reply, and then, "Happy Anniversary!"

It was February 14—nine years had passed since our first date on that cold Valentine's night in England, huddled over a table in a dank English pub. Nine years I had lived with this man and right now, more than anything in the world, I wanted to be with him.

A big bowl of candy hearts lay on the reception desk, and I quickly fished through them, inhaling the powdery sugar scent while sifting through the "Cutie Pie" and "Be Mine" hearts for just the right message. I snapped a close-up phone pic of the orange candy heart with its romantic imperative etched in Red Dye #3: "Marry Me." I sent Brian the text and waited two whole minutes for his reply from twelve thousand miles away.

"Yes, let's get married," he typed, as if adding the task to a list on the fridge: Buy Milk, Rent Check, Call Mom, Get Married. "Maybe this spring?" he added in a second text message.

Maybe this spring—if the new law was not stayed or overturned or repealed, or if Congress did not hold up the measure in a knotted tangle of legal hurdles. We had seen what happened in California and how quickly all the hope and excitement came crashing down after the passing of Proposition 8. The same could happen in Washington, DC, and when it did, we would be just as powerless as the tens of thousands of California couples who now faced the uncertainty of their own marriages becoming invalid. If and when the law went into effect, we had to act swiftly. In a single morning, I had reached my impossible dream of arriving in Antarctica, and just like that, my heart longed for my next impossible dream— to get married. If I could overcome deserts, swamps, mountains, and waves to reach the bottom of the world, surely there was a way for me to say "I do."

I adapted quickly to the routine of the ship—jumping up with the wake-up call, dining with all the other exuberant guests, and then getting suited up in layers and layers of cold-weather clothing. I hopped into the zodiacs with a peppy nonchalance, as if gliding alongside fur seals and curious gentoo penguins was something I did every day. The mythological backdrop of sweeping volcanic valleys and frosted stone peaks now seemed almost normal. Sailing through the brash ice made a wonderful sloshing sound against the side of the ship, and though the wind grew colder at times—biting into my face like a bee sting—I stayed out on deck, observing our measured movements up the coast of the Antarctic Peninsula. At times the ice-cold water looked as black as polished onyx, and sometimes, in the late evening, the unnamed mountains seemed to be coated with a fine dusting of light-blue powdered sugar.

Between our various outings on land and sea, I sat at my laptop and transmitted a steady stream of tweets and photos, bombarding my readers with the glory of what they were missing. I established my office at the front of the ship, in the chart room, equipped with Wi-Fi, jugs of hot cocoa, and an endless supply of Danish butter cookies. Sometimes it took up to ten minutes just to post a single tweet, but the tidal wave of responses was encouraging.

"More penguins!" tweeted a follower from Alabama. "Lots more penguins."

How did I tell them that there were literally millions of penguins along these shores, that after just a few days, they seemed as common as the sparrows back home? Yes, they were beautiful and quizzical creatures with terrific facial expressions and a comical gait, but real penguins were far from cute and cartoonish.

During an afternoon hike along a lonely frozen beach, I latched onto Peter Carey, a visiting zoologist who was working on the ship. As one of the world's key experts on penguins, Peter told me things I would never learn from the Internet. "Penguins are colonial but not cooperative," he said, pointing toward a rookery of gentoos, messy with guano and the blowing gray feathers of the lazy chicks. "In principle, they like being together, but they always nest within a beak's length of one another."

"Just like people," I joked, remembering my time in the Deep South and how people sat on the bus, apart from the others, stashing their backpacks in the empty seats like a protective buffer zone.

"Yep, just like you always have that strip of grass between you and your neighbor's house. That's what penguins do," said Peter.

"And the pink snow?" I asked, pointing to the rosy swath of snow that stretched halfway up the mountain from the seashore.

"Penguin poop," said Peter. "Poop is pink when they're feeding on krill—when they're out at sea. Krill are those tiny shrimplike crustaceans that make up this huge biomass in the Southern Ocean. Penguins eat loads of this krill, and all those carotenoid pigments concentrate in their digestive tract—that's what turns their waste pink." This was nature's pink—the same pink as the blushing veins in a flower, the pink of wild flamingos in the Camargue and the fleshy salmon of Alaska.

"Once the penguins lay their eggs and start incubating, they stop eating altogether," continued Peter as he led me over a pile of black boulders. The other guests were busy taking pictures of one another on the beach and I had become his audience of one.

"Just like that, they're done." He sliced his hand through the air with finality. "They sit on their eggs for over a month without eating— they lose a good deal of weight—and all the green poop you're seeing everywhere?" Peter pointed to the ground in front of us, splotched with a slimy green mess. "That's bile—so that's poop from penguins that aren't feeding on krill."

"Pink and green?" I asked.

"Yep. And that's how you can tell what stage of breeding season we're in right now. This colony is pretty far along in the process, so you've got the green stuff coming from the parents that are still feeding their chicks, and then all the pink poop from the others who have gone back to eating krill."

We had entered the densest part of the rookery now, skirting the edges so as not to disturb the birds and their chaotic crying young, hungry in their nests. As I turned my back to the wind, the pungent smell of penguin poop hit me like a fishy slap in the face. I gulped back my own bile and started breathing through my mouth, exhaling little frozen clouds that hung in the cold air and then disappeared into the great white nothing.

Baby gentoo chicks, eager and plump, waddled quickly from one adult to the next, crying out for food. "Feed me, feed me!" they seemed to cry with a chatter of peeps and squeaks. Most had already lost their fluffy baby down, replaced by the subadult plumage of white bellies and charcoal-gray wings and back. These were the awkward teenage penguins, fat from their parents' constant feeding, warmed by their parents' own body heat, and now wanting more than their parents could ever provide.

"These chicks are about ninety days old. The parents have stopped feeding them and left, so they're pretty hungry. See how they're chasing any adult penguin they see? When they peck at their faces like that, normally that's the signal for the parent to regurgitate a meal for them, but the free meals are finished." Peter paused his matter-of-fact explanation.

"So what happens next?" I asked.

"The penguin chicks get really hungry and really aggressive. They will run after any other adult penguin trying to get fed. All that running around and hunger will finally bring them down to the water, where they get wet and realize that they can swim much better than they walk. And by swimming, they'll learn how to catch their own food. That's how they become successful adults."

I watched the adolescent gentoos chasing after the few adults in the colony, screaming and flapping their sleek wings in pursuit of a potential meal. The mature penguins acted as if they were being mugged, out-running the babies and disappearing into the water, leaving the young ones to contemplate the clear waves that lapped at their tiny webbed feet. Hundreds of young and spoiled penguins confronted the harsh decision—stay on land and starve to death or venture into the cold, black unknown. I witnessed the few brave penguin souls that dipped themselves into the water, shaking off a shower of droplets and then diving in again. I loved watching them discover water—how this was the place they belonged, how their bodies were made for the sea.

"Penguins have a hard life," said Peter. "They don't show this stuff on TV, but it's a fight just to survive. See all these penguin chicks still running around up there?" He pointed up the hill at the penguins trying to bum a meal on land. "Winter is coming soon, and in a few weeks, about a third of those birds will starve and freeze to death. Another third will barely make it into the water before they get snatched up by a skua, a leopard seal, or an orca. Best-case scenario, the remaining third might make it through their first year of life. It fluctuates from year to year, but that is nature's math."

So, after all the hard work of incubating, hatching, and feeding their babies, the most successful penguin parents are the ones that abandon their chicks. That's their only chance for surviving a place like Antarctica. At first they get a heated nest and room service, but in a flash that all disappears and they are left to fend for themselves and figure out life.

I sat down on the ground amid the guano and stones, overwhelmed by the stark truth—how two out of every three of these cute, rambunctious penguins would never make it past their first birthday. The little birds brayed louder and approached me, curious and hungry. Antarctic protocol is that you never touch a penguin—but a penguin can touch you. So I sat still and waited until two baby gentoos hopped right into my lap, pecking at the zippers on my coat pockets in hopes that I might regurgitate a fishy meal for them.

"I got nothing," I apologized to the baby penguins. The birds shifted in my lap, blinking their wrinkled eyelids at big, blue, strange me. One of them let out a piercing peep and the other one echoed back. They had both hatched from eggs, born into a world of snow and unfortunate odds. They did not know the meaning of winter yet, but they would find out soon enough. I wanted them to live—how I wished I could make them my pets and coddle them with hugs and nicknames and fishy treats—but that is not how you rescue a penguin. Instead, I shooed them off my lap and I walked away, back to the zodiac and our waiting ship, anchored in the bay and surrounded by a thousand swimming penguins.

37 THE BLACK PENGUIN

Day 56

I leaned into the roaring wind and dug my toes into the sand, posing on the beach like an awkward sprinter awaiting the crack of a gun. Ice crystals stung my skin and I felt the broken volcanic shards press into the aches of my bare feet. Behind us sat a ring of black mountains, marbled with patches of snow beneath a white sky.

"Go!" yelled a few of my fellow travelers, most of them wrapped in their parkas, huddled together in the cold.

Go, I told myself before running, leaping over the first line of waves, leaping and leaping until I was hovering waist-deep in the frozen ocean, feeling the ancient tide pulling at my paralyzed legs. My knees began to fail and the only thing to do was dive forward, embracing gravity and its grave consequence. The black water enveloped me, slapping my whole body and squeezing my forehead like an angry fist. For a second, I opened my eyes to the inky black hole, then blinked and erupted back on the surface.

I tried to breathe but failed. My lungs stayed empty, and I felt the weight of the entire ocean press against my naked white chest. I panicked a little and tried to breathe once more, then plunged myself back into the Antarctic waters. Only then did I hear my own gracious gasp. Beautiful, soft salty air.

The dark sea around Deception Island was not merely cold—it was an ice bath of white caps and sloshing white icebergs. I stayed in the sea less than a minute, and when I emerged, I was grinning and warm.

Bizarrely, the wind felt warm on my bare skin and I felt the rush of new blood shooting through my body. I felt clean and new.

"Get dressed. Quickly!" The ship's doctor shouted at me, slapping my bare back. Along with a row of ready staff, she was there to hand out hot chocolate or, if needed, to administer CPR. I disobeyed the doctor and stood shirtless on the beach, blushing from the seeming warmth of the wind and basking in the triumphant sun. I gulped down the brown cocoa that was handed to me and then rubbed my arms and legs with a beach towel. The others were leaving already, headed back to the ship with its bubbling engines and heated cabins, but I lingered on the black volcanic sand, exuberant and wistful.

The end of my adventure was nigh and my own future was as blank as the blocks of white ice we sailed past on our way to South Georgia. I had no job and no money and it was unlikely that I would ever get to return to this, the rarest corner of the globe. That was the difference between me and all the other travelers on our ship.

We came from different worlds and generations, but we shared a burning passion to explore—to investigate all the new places in the world and to get back to the old places we still loved. Together we explored the incredible shores of South Georgia, and together we rejoiced in the blanket of penguins on the beaches, all of them braying like an off-key chorus of heavenly angels. Together we laughed at the snoring, farting elephant seals; we cooed over the baby seal pups that played just like puppies in the waves; and together we soaked up the silence of the barren mountains that cut the sky like an axe blade.

I wished my own parents could have seen this. My mom and dad always made a point of showing us kids the best our own country had to offer—things like the Grand Canyon, Old Faithful, and the Mississippi River. Whenever we encountered a place, an idea, or a word that we did not know, my mother looked it up in the encyclopedia or dictionary and read us an explanation at the dinner table. Before every family vacation, each of us kids was assigned a topic—a state, a bird, a moment in history—for which we had to write and present a report to the rest of the family. My parents fostered a curiosity in me that had led me to this faraway island where the wind whistled night and day. I wanted them standing next to me on deck, feeling the roll of the waves and catching glimpses of blue whales.

Every day in South Georgia felt bigger and more spectacular than the day before, and yet every day it all seemed a little more normal. By now I was used to the smell and sights of the vast king penguin colonies—I had stopped trying to photograph every bird.

On that particular morning, I was fixated on the red-brown kelp that swirled like fettuccine in the bubbling tide along the bouldered beach. Scattered iron stone stood like red lumps above the gray-black pebbles flecked with stripes of white quartzite. Hiking next to Cotton, I barely paid any mind to the jaywalking penguins who crossed in front of me. In such a short while, I had accepted this new world where penguins outnumbered humans about a million to one.

"You wanna see a melanistic penguin?" shouted David, a lanky Lindblad naturalist with long hippy hair and a goofy hat. I liked David because he seemed as awkward as me, and now here he was, leading me to the most unusual penguin on the beach. The adult king penguin stood tall and aloof with his neck reached high and his beak pointed upward—almost defiantly. He took two steps forward, then waited. Then he turned around and showed us his front.

The penguin was black—completely black. His feet, legs, back, wings, and belly all shone a deep midnight black. Only the sleek marking on the side of his beak was orange. I walked closer to make sure I had seen it correctly—with so many penguins on the beach the birds can blend into each other. But not this one—he was in fact all black, front and back. Indeed, his black belly was darker than the lighter grayish fading around his shoulders. The bird was so unusual and beautiful—and fast. He did not appreciate the extra attention from the gawking tourists and with careful steps, his leathery black feet moved away from us.

I snapped a few pictures and checked my LCD screen, shaking my head in disbelief.

The other guests and staff got bored and walked away, but I hung back and waited, crouching down about a hundred yards from the black penguin. What a remarkable bird—what a curious difference! Out of all the millions of king penguins on South Georgia, this bird was unique—dressed in black from head to toe. I sat and watched him for a few minutes longer. He seemed to behave like all the other penguins— he had a mate, it seemed, with normal color patterns and the two of them strolled down toward the water, wings touching.

I watched him waddle down to the water, and like the other penguins, flop forward in the waves, diving his head down and moving through the sea, fluidlike, batting his wings like oars on a racing shell. Like that, he was gone with his mate, off to fish and to be left alone in this part of the sea that he called home. Did the black penguin know he was different? Could such an animal ever be cognizant of his own unique self and that he was not just one of the millions, but one *in a* million?

We had another hour designated for exploring, but I took the first zodiac back to the ship and rapidly shot out four tweets, each with a unique photo of the black penguin attached. Then I carried on with my work and the rest of my journey. I wrote dozens more blog posts and published photos and videos. We spent many more days at sea, wrapping up our expedition in the Falkland Islands. A violent earthquake shook Chile, closing down major airports across South America and leaving us stranded on the dock of Ushuaia. In the end, Lindblad Expeditions chartered a jet and flew all of us back to Miami—a twenty-hour flight that leapfrogged over my entire bus trip.

Sixty-five days had passed since I had left on a bus from National Geographic headquarters, and now here I was again, speeding past the office in a taxi, a mile up the road to my building, where I rode the elevator to the seventh floor and knocked on my own door.

Brian's face met mine through the widening crack in the door and I dropped my bags to the floor. We hugged, then kissed, and my friends erupted with cheers from the living room. "Welcome home!" they shouted in unison before closing in on me with heavy hugs, congratulating me on my accomplished journey. They had followed me every single day and now they had crammed inside our tiny studio to celebrate my return—some drank champagne and there were homemade cupcakes with tiny National Geographic flags on toothpicks and a quickly drawn sign that read "Welcome Home."

This was my home, and now I was home with Brian, surrounded by wonderful friends. I felt blessed and spent, exhausted and weak, but overflowing with the peace and calm of having finished something I had started long before. Spring had filled the city, melting away the snow of winter and streaming sunlight into the apartment. I saw the passing time in my own eyes and felt it on my face as I shaved away my unkempt beard of the last two months. In minutes, I wiped away the façade of a weather-beaten monk and appeared youthful and pink, with cheeks chapped from the fierce southern wind.

"Honey, come see this." Brian called me to the computer and began clicking through a long line of search results. In one short week, the Internet had exploded with stories of my special black penguin. My photos had gone viral—hundreds of thousands had viewed and shared the images of the rare bird. I read about my "discovery" in British and Chinese newspapers, on websites from Australia and Mexico. "National Geographic Photographer Discovers Rare Black Penguin" read one exaggerated headline.

"Except I'm not a photographer, nor did I discover the penguin," I corrected the newspapers aloud from my kitchen. My editor Janelle called that afternoon—to welcome me home and to fact-check the story.

"Andrew, it's unbelievable—I mean, this is the highest-hitting post we have ever published."

Janelle had already interviewed a leading ornithologist—Dr. Allan Baker at the University of Toronto, head of natural history at the Royal Ontario Museum. His initial response was disbelief: "Wow. That looks so bizarre I can't even believe it."

"He made me swear on a stack of *National Geographic* magazines that the photo was real," said Janelle.

"Well, it is real," I said. "I just saw it with my own eyes, as did forty-some other people who were down there with me."

"I know, I know—I believe you, of course, but there is so much interest from around the globe. The professor says it's a 'one in a zillion' kind of genetic mutation—that the animal has lost control of its pigmentation patterns."

"It's called *melanism*," I said to Janelle, as if correcting the ornithologist myself. "Just like the black squirrels here in DC. Other scientists have observed similar phenomena in South Georgia and other sub-Antarctic islands." I had done my own research aboard the *Explorer* and found two separate scientific papers documenting color aberrations in king penguins. In 1995 a juvenile penguin on Crozet Island was described as totally black due to "total melanism." More recently, scientists had documented a "more common" case of partial melanism in South Georgia's king penguins—as common as one in every 250,000 birds.

"I know—Dr. Baker explained that even melanistic birds have white spots where the melanin fails to color the feathers, but it's extremely rare for the melanin to occur where they're not usually located—like on the penguin's belly."

"Exactly," I agreed. "This one is totally melanistic. You can ask any of the other travelers that saw it with me—or the Lindblad naturalists."

"I would, but all these news outlets are asking for proof—please, please tell me that you shot some video. Anything at all?"

"Nope. Sorry. I already checked. I don't have any video—only the pictures I posted." I had already removed the photos from my Facebook and Twitter feed—National Geographic had licensed the images and was only releasing them to paying customers. Meanwhile, the greater public was calling me a liar.

"That thing is photoshopped. I can tell," said one commenter.

"Fake, fake, fake," said another. For every reader who was amazed and intrigued by the penguin, there was another denying its existence.

For the first time in my life, I felt the onslaught of the great peanut gallery that is the Internet. Some claimed that I had simply spray-painted the penguin black and then photographed it on the beach. Others explained that this was obviously a type of animatronic manipulation. Then came the personal attacks—that I was penniless and desperate for fame and how pitiful of me to concoct such a poorly executed hoax. Then came the racist trolls, exposing their own hate against an animal that happened to be black.

I found the clip a week later as I was duplicating my hard drives from the trip. Thirteen seconds—that was all that I had shot on my tiny flip camera. Thirteen seconds of that beautiful black penguin waddling away from me on the beach, shy and different but so real.

"Hallelujah," said Janelle. "Fantastic," said my agent. The next morning, the video played in a loop on CBS. "All Black Penguin Is One-in-a-Zillion" read the headline. Then came ABC and NBC and a host of other TV channels and radio interviews and a second eruption of online coverage. For a few hours, "black penguin" was the twenty-fifth most popular search on Google, and then it faded away like everything online. And yet today, it is still the thing I am asked about most. My answer is always the same: No, I did not discover one of the rarest birds in the world. All I did was follow my guide down a far-flung beach, then post the pictures on Twitter. All I did was share the most magnificent thing I had seen.

No, I am not one of the great explorers—I am only a traveler who ventured far from home and tried to show the world something new and different. In that very small way, I followed the tradition of the National Geographic Society, and in the end, I added my story and a few humble shots into the illustrious canon of *National Geographic*. After all I have lived, this was my one small contribution—a black bird on a black beach at the bottom of the world—yet that was enough, worth all the days and nights on the bus, worth all the bumps in the road, to cross the entire Earth and know the astonishing beauty of one in a zillion.

"Beautiful Bird. 100% melanistic. Extraordinary." @Bus2Antarctica, South Georgia, February 25, 2010

EPILOGUE

Exactly one week before the Washington, DC, city council's Religious Freedom and Civil Marriage Equality Act went into effect, Senator Bob Bennett and Congressman Jason Chaffetz (both Mormons from Utah), along with Congressman Jim Jordan (representing the very corner of Ohio where I grew up), introduced a bill to force a ballot measure that "only marriage between a man and a woman is valid or recognized in the District of Columbia." Despite their fervent efforts, the city of Washington, DC, began issuing marriage licenses to all couples on March 3, 2010. Soon after returning home from Antarctica, Brian and I joined the lines at the courthouse and were granted permission to wed. We married that June on the rooftop deck of the tallest building in Washington, DC. My parents and seven of my siblings chose not to attend our wedding—though my youngest brother was there.

We honeymooned in Bermuda, because it was warm and close—just a short ninety-minute flight from home. Also, the buses in Bermuda are pink. Five years after our own marriage in Washington, DC, the U.S. Supreme Court declared marriage equality in all fifty states. As promised, Brian sent a big bouquet of pink roses to the prophet of the LDS Church, along with a personal card thanking him for inadvertently advancing our full rights and protection of the law under the U.S. Constitution.

To reach Antarctica from my office at National Geographic, I had traveled more than ten thousand miles on forty different buses. The total cost of my ground transportation from Washington, DC, to Ushuaia was $1,122.93. My feature story "Bus2Antarctica" was published in the September 2010 issue of *National Geographic Traveler*. For the next four years, I traveled the world as National Geographic's Digital Nomad, completing thirty assignments that spanned all seven continents. Following the global interest in the black penguin, National Geographic licensed my thirteen-second video of the rare bird, which is how I paid for our wedding.

In time I received a letter from a British TV company asking for help. They were making a wildlife documentary and traveling to South Georgia in hopes of filming penguins, and could I please send them the coordinates for the rare black penguin? Maybe they could get some footage, too.

I wrote back saying no, I could not reveal the bird's location, though with a bit of research, anybody could pinpoint the location. Alas, there are too many folks out there with the wrong intentions—bird collectors and trophy hunters, wildlife bullies, taxidermists, and ill-intentioned museums with polished glass cases waiting to be filled.

"No, I'm sorry. I can't tell you," I replied.

Subsequent expeditions of the *National Geographic Explorer* claim to have seen the all-black penguin, still happy and healthy, standing out so boldly from the crowd. I can only hope that it's true. I have since returned a few times to the remote island of South Georgia, and I have walked that same beach where I first saw the black penguin, but I have not seen him again.

In a way, I hope that nobody ever finds him again. I know what it's like to never blend in with the crowd—to stand out too much—and I believe that more than anything, the black penguin wants to be left alone, to walk freely on the beach, unbothered, next to the bird he loves most.

Acknowledgments

I owe this entire story to the marvelous Marilyn Terrell, who landed my outlandish idea on the right desk at the right time and has always been a true friend. I must also include a very special thanks to my magazine editor Janelle Nanos, who followed me tirelessly on my bus journey and worked many long desk hours to make the story a success. I am grateful for the support of the whole team at *National Geographic Traveler*, including Dan Westergren, Krista Rossow, Jeannette Swain, Gio Palatucci, Amy Alipio, Norie Quintos, Jayne Wise, and George Stone. I am particularly indebted to Keith Bellows for believing in me and for simply saying yes. We miss you, Keith.

I'd also like to give a tremendous thank you to Sven-Olof Lindblad and Lindblad Expeditions for providing me passage to Antarctica, and to Lynn Cutter, Scott Kish, and National Geographic Expeditions for supporting me in this adventure and so many others. I owe a huge thank you to the marvelous staff and crew of the *MV National Geographic Explorer*, with special thanks to Peter Carey, Eric Guth, Jim Kelley, Jason Kelley, Lisa Kelley, Stephanie Martin, Jim Napoli, Tom Ritchie, and David Stevens, who added so much to my maiden voyage; and to the inspiring Sisse Brimberg and unforgettable Cotton Coulson, who photographed the story for the magazine. I am glad to have shared such an important moment of my life with you.

I wish I could name everyone who helped me on my bus trip. To those included in the pages of this book, I thank you for joining me on my journey. For those whose names I never knew, thank you for your conversation and companionship along the way.

Thanks to my amazing parents, John and Mary Ann Evans, who have patiently endured my wanderlust over a lifetime—*I love you*; to my many wonderful brothers and sisters; and to my awesome cousins, who encouraged me through the long haul of writing. I am blessed to have many friends who have cheered me along the way: Paul Cadario, Daniel Gordon, and Dave Burton, who sent me off at the bus stop on that January day; and Todd Williams, Joe Puzzo, Mike Tringale, Debbie and Todd Weaver, and Leonardo Martinez. Thanks to my friends Sally Painter and Karen Tramontano, who provided me with a quiet place to write in Maine; and to Rob Bannister, for use of his home in Florida; and a very special shout-out to Pam Mandel, who sustained me almost daily through the writing process via text, chat, and Skype.

Thank you to Eliza Reid, Erica Green, and the Iceland Writers Retreat; and to David Farley, Susan Orlean, Simon Winchester, and Wade Davis for their kindness and generosity to me as a writer. Thank you to Nicole Gharda, Elizabeth Brandon, and Cynthina Cannell, who provided critical feedback on early drafts of the manuscript; and to Peter Winkler, for his keen eye and valuable insights on the final drafts.

I owe much gratitude to Raphael Kadushin, Sheila McMahon, Michelle Wing, Adam Mehring, Amber Rose, Andrea Christofferson, Sheila Leary, and Bibiana Snyder, along with the entire team at the University of Wisconsin Press who so carefully brought this book to life. Thank you for wanting to tell my story.

I would be remiss not to include my two dogs, Wasabi and Binga, who sat with me through much of the writing process, and most of all, I am grateful to my husband, Brian Gratwicke, who asked that I not mention him in this book. Sorry, honey. Thanks for being the rare bird in my life.

Transportation
from Washington, DC,
to Antarctica

Date	Transport	Destination	Cost
January 1		Depart National Geographic Society, Washington, DC	
January 1	S2 Metrobus	16th & M to 11th & G NW, Washington, DC	$1.35
January 1	Washington Metro	Metro Center to Union Station	$1.35
January 1	Greyhound bus	Washington, DC, to Atlanta, GA	
January 2	Greyhound bus	Atlanta to Mobile, AL	
January 2	Greyhound bus	Mobile to Houston, TX	$152.00
January 4	Americanos bus	Houston to Reynosa, Mexico	
January 4	ADO bus	Reynosa to Coatzacoalcos	$129.00
January 5	ADO bus	Coatzacoalcos to Tuxtla Gutiérrez	$23.25
January 5	OCC bus	Tuxtla Gutiérrez to San Cristóbal de las Casas	$2.00
January 6	OCC bus	San Cristóbal de las Casas to Ciudad Cuauhtémoc	$6.82
January 6	chicken bus	Guatemala border to Huehuetenango	$3.00
January 6	chicken bus	Huehuetenango to Quatro Caminos	$3.00
January 6	chicken bus	Quatro Caminos to Guatemala City	$4.30
January 7	Tica Bus	Guatemala City to San Salvador, El Salvador	$15.00
January 8	Tica Bus	San Salvador to Managua, Nicaragua	$30.00
January 8	taxi	Managua to Costa Rica border	$100.00
January 8	milk truck	Costa Rica border to Esparza	
January 9	hitchhiking	Esparza to San José airport	
January 9	Lindblad bus	San José airport to Herradura	
January 9	Lindblad ship	Herradura to Colón, Panama	
January 16	car	Colón to Portobelo and Panama City	
January 18	Copa Airlines flight	Panama City to Cartagena, Colombia	$370.00
January 19	Brasilia bus	Cartagena to Bogotá	$60.00
January 22	Bolivariano bus	Bogotá to Ipiales	$50.00
January 23	colectivo van	Ipiales to Ecuador border	$0.65
January 23	colectivo van	Ecuador border to Tulcan	$0.65
January 23	chicken bus	Tulcan to Quito	$4.00
January 25	Panamericana bus	Quito to Guayaquil	$9.25
January 26	Oromeño bus	Guayaquil to Tumbes, Peru	$30.00
January 27	Flores bus	Tumbes to Lima	$35.00
January 29	Oromeño bus	Lima to La Paz, Bolivia	$90.00
February 1	Bolivian bus	La Paz to Uyuni	$12.00
February 2	Bolivian bus	Uyuni to Villazón/Argentine border	$11.32
February 3	Balut bus	La Quaica to San Salvador de Jujuy	$63.35
February 4	Flecha Bus	San Salvador de Jujuy to Córdoba	$85.00

(Continued on next page)

Date	Transport	Destination	Cost
February 6	Andesmar bus	Córdoba to Trelew	$71.88
February 7	Andesmar bus	Trelew to Río Gallegos	$71.88
February 10	Marta bus	Río Gallegos to Ushuaia	$56.88
February 11	Lindblad ship	Depart Ushuaia	
February 14		Arrive at Marguerite Bay, Antarctica	

Total ground fare		$1,122.93
Total cost with airfare		$1,492.93

LIVING OUT

Gay and Lesbian Autobiographies

David Bergman, Joan Larkin, and Raphael Kadushin
FOUNDING EDITORS

CPSIA information can be obtained
at www.ICGtesting.com
Printed in the USA
LVHW011438080119

603165LV00017B/596/P

9 780299 311445